Pat is magic with his family, with his community, with his team. *Go For the Magic* is terrific. A great read.
—Pat Riley
Head Coach, Miami Heat

Pat Williams is truly one of the most creative and innovative people in sports today. He is also a shining example for us all in what he has done for his family and friends. This is a must-read book!
—Fran Tarkenton
Former NFL Quarterback

The real story of how one man put the magic in Orlando and how you can put magic in your life.
—Regis Philbin
TV Show Host

Pat Williams weaves an inspirational message in this book which is as magic as the work he has done with the Orlando Magic!
—Al Neuharth
Founder, *USA Today*

Pat Williams has written a truly inspiring book. He sheds light on the truth about dreams—they don't mean anything unless you're committed to making them a reality. Sure, it means hard work and the possibility of failure, but when you make your dreams come true—that's true success! It should be recommended reading for everyone who has dreams.
—Dave Thomas
Founder, Wendy's Old Fashioned Hamburgers Restaurants

A fascinating story which also contains as much good advice on how to achieve success and happiness as any book I have read in the past thirty years.
—Og Mandino
Author/Speaker

I have never learned anything by speaking . . . only by reading and listening. Consequently, I try to study the techniques, attitudes, and philosophies of the people that are very successful. Anybody that has ever followed the work of sports knows the tremendous accomplishments of Pat Williams and the Orlando Magic. This book gives you an insight as to why Pat has enjoyed success and will enable you to adopt many of his philosophies.

—Lou Holtz
Head Football Coach, University of Notre Dame, 1986–1996

I have known Pat Williams for over thirty years. His new book, *Go For the Magic*, is everything I thought it would be and more. It will change your life.

—Sparky Anderson
Former Major League Baseball Manager

The story of the Orlando Magic is one of the greatest modern-day stories in U.S. sports. Pat Williams tells it in a fascinating way. *Go For the Magic* is a good read.

—Mark McCormack
Chairman and CEO, International Management Group

Pat Williams is an NBA visionary. This book even opened my eyes. Pat is a witty, charming, caring man, and this book certainly doesn't disappoint.

—Roy Firestone
ESPN Sportscaster

Our friend Pat Williams has made the sometimes hazy road to the American dream a lot clearer with *Go For the Magic*. He takes some time honored principles for meeting one's personal potential and adds a whole new spiritual dimension with his perspective and experience. *Go For the Magic* is really a handbook for life's great pursuit of everyone's God-given potential.

—Jack Kemp
Co-Director of Empower America, Former Secretary of HUD

GO FOR THE MAGIC

GO FOR THE MAGIC

Pat Williams

with Jim Denney

A
JANET
THOMA
BOOK

THOMAS NELSON PUBLISHERS

Nashville

Published in Nashville, Tennessee, by Thomas Nelson, Inc.

The Bible version used in this publication is THE NEW KING JAMES VERSION. Copyright © 1979, 1980, 1982, 1990, Thomas Nelson, Inc., Publishers.

Library of Congress Cataloging-in-Publication Data

Williams, Pat, 1940–
    Go for the magic! / Pat Williams; with Jim Denney.
      p. cm.
    Includes bibliographical references.
    ISBN 0-8407-7436-2 (Hardcover)
    ISBN 0-7852-7094-9 (Paperback)
    1. Williams, Pat, 1940– . 2. Basketball coaches—United States—Biography. 3. Christian life. 4. Success—United States. 5. Orlando Magic (Basketball team) I. Denney, James D. II. Title.
GV884.W55A3 1995
796.323'07'7092—dc20
[B]   95-17951
                                                                                          CIP

Printed in the United States of America.
3 4 5 6 — 00 99 98

I dedicate this book to two remarkable Americans who have greatly influenced my life: Rich DeVos and the late Walt Disney.

CONTENTS

FOREWORD

When I was a little girl, I believed in magic. It wasn't any particular trick that caught my attention; it was the magician: one person having the power and the skills to make people believe in what they really didn't see. Magic was fascinating to me because I had always dreamed of doing something great or becoming someone whose accomplishments would be hard to believe—even though the eyes had seen it. So when I crossed the finish line of the 100-meter race at the 1988 Olympic Trials and the clock read 10.49, my magical dreams had come true! I had surpassed the numbers I dreamed about running, and that's what's so magical about the power of the mind!

Pat Williams has written a significant book that will continue to inspire the lives of those who have already experienced magic, and those who have not. His book motivates and encourages us to believe in ourselves, and then tells us how. I used to believe that only rich people's dreams came true, but I later learned that anyone can make their dreams come true, as Pat's book says, if they only believe.

If anyone is looking for advice, direction, guidance, and suggestions, they need look no further than *Go For the Magic*; it has all of the magic that one needs to live out one's dreams! Next to the Bible, *Go For the Magic* says it all, and needs to be read by everyone. Not only will I read it over and over, but I will also share it with my family and friends so they can share it with others. Just reading a few lines in the morning motivates me to have a great day, and before bed it inspires me to give thanks for another beautiful day.

Florence Griffith Joyner
Five-time Olympic Medalist

ACKNOWLEDGMENTS

This book would never have been published without the guidance, direction, and writing/editing skills of Jim Denney and Janet Thoma.

CHAPTER 1

Hammering Dreams into Reality

○ *Whatever you can do, or dream you can do, begin it.*
Goethe

○ *You look at any giant corporation, and I mean the biggies, and they all started with a guy with an idea, doing it well.*
Irvine Robbins, cofounder of Baskin-Robbins Ice Cream

○ *Dreams become reality when we keep our commitment to them.*
Judy Wardell Halliday, weight control expert

Just a drive to the airport? That's what I thought— but I was wrong. It was a *big* turning point in my life!

Looking back, I credit the very existence of the Orlando Magic basketball team to the fact that I happened to drive to the airport with Jimmy Hewitt that Sunday morning in September 1985. It was clearly the launching pad for what would take place over the next few years. I was general manager of the Philadelphia 76ers basketball team at the time.

I was sitting in the front passenger seat. Sitting in the back seat was a buddy of mine, John Tolson, who was on the pastoral staff of First Presbyterian Church in Orlando. Our "chauffeur" was Jim Hewitt, one of Orlando's leading businessmen and an acquaintance I had met some years earlier in San Antonio, Texas. Jimmy was a very involved layman at First Presbyterian, and I had sat next to him in the front pew during the service. He was kind enough, along with John, to give me a lift back to Orlando Airport for a flight back to Philly.

"You know," I said offhandedly, "the NBA is thinking of expanding—and Florida could get one of the teams."

"A pro basketball team in Florida?" said Jimmy, taking both hands off the wheel to gesture excitedly. "Yeah, oh, yeah! Now, Bubba, that's an idea whose time has come!"

Jimmy is a character: exuberant, enthusiastic, transparently honest and open, and as warm and charming as anyone you've ever met. He's a short, stocky guy with a big grin. He calls everybody "Bubba." In business, he's a heavy hitter with a velvet touch—the kind of guy who plays with business ventures like other kids play with electric trains. You've just gotta love ol' Jimmy Hewitt. He's passionate about everything he's involved in—his faith, his family, his businesses, and his sports, and especially Florida State football.

But Jimmy isn't the only one who got excited when I mentioned the possibility of bringing professional hoops to the state of Florida. "Long overdue!" added John from the back seat. "I mean, it's hard to believe that in a state this size, with pro football teams in Miami and Tampa Bay, we don't have either a pro baseball or basketball team!" You should have heard the enthusiasm in his voice! Sometimes I think John is a basketball fan first, a preacher second.

"If you guys were in charge," I continued, "where would you put the team—Miami or Tampa?"

Instantly, both men shouted in chorus, "No, no, no!"

Surprised, I turned and looked at Jimmy, then John. "Huh?" I asked.

"Not Miami!" said Jimmy, screwing up his face in a grimace.

"And certainly not Tampa!" said John.

"Well, where—?"

Jimmy took his hands off the wheel again and spread his arms out wide. "Just look around you, Bubba!"

"Orlando?"

"Did you ever see a cleaner, more beautiful city?" asked John. "With Walt Disney World right on the edge of town, Orlando's already the entertainment capital of the world. Pro basketball would fit this city like a glove!"

"Orlando!" I said, a dream already taking shape in my mind. I looked out the window at the passing scenery and tried to picture it. Orlando was a nice, growing little community—but an NBA franchise city? I didn't think so! You have to understand that this was in 1985, after Walt Disney World, but before Universal Studios, the Barnett Bank Building, and the SunBank Center. I mean, the city didn't even have a skyline!

But the more I thought about it, the easier it became to picture a shining new sports arena rising in the center of this growing central Florida city. I began to imagine a youthful, dynamic NBA championship team charging onto the court of this new arena, shaking up the sports world. And I pictured myself managing this new team, striding the concourse in a jacket with the team logo on the back, the Orlando—

The Orlando what? The Orlando Oranges? The Orlando Herons? The Orlando Seminoles? Hey, it didn't matter what you called them. What mattered was that Orlando just might be the perfect place to build a brand-new powerhouse organization from the ground up. Here, in the shadow of the Magic Kingdom, you could build a team that would work magic with a ball and a backboard.

"Gentlemen," I announced, "you have captured my imagination."

A few minutes later, my friends deposited me at the Delta terminal. I shook hands with them and said, "Well, guys, I'm getting on that plane and heading back to Philly. There are a lot of great ideas that never get beyond the stage where we are right now. We can drop the ball right here and now—or maybe, just maybe, we can make it happen. If you guys are serious about this thing, then now's the time to begin exploring while the NBA is at least listening to expansion plans."

"Well, where do we begin?" asked Jimmy.

"With the NBA commissioner, David Stern," I said. I pulled out my address book and scribbled the phone number down and handed it to Jimmy.

"Bubba," said Jimmy, "I'll check it out and let you know."

End of conversation. I boarded my plane and headed back to Philadelphia to prepare for the 1985–86 season. There is a lot of high-flying talk in this business about dreams that never quite get off the ground. Frankly, I didn't really expect to hear from Jim Hewitt again.

Boy, was I wrong!

PUTTING SHOE LEATHER TO THE DREAM

As I returned to work, starting my twelfth year as general manager of the 76ers, my thoughts kept straying southward, toward sunny central Florida. I continually asked myself, *Pat, what are you thinking of? You love managing the 76ers! You like the people, the players, and the fans. You've been racking up a string of winning seasons. Everything's going great! Why would you want to start from scratch in a brand-new city with an unknown team in an untested venture that just might fall flat on its face?*

But I couldn't help myself. I couldn't stop thinking about it. The dream had taken hold of me, and it wouldn't let go. What I didn't know at the time was that this same dream had also taken hold of Jim Hewitt.

Jimmy went right to work. He got hold of NBA commissioner David Stern in New York and made an appointment. Then he flew up for a meeting and pumped Stern with questions: "How do you put an ownership group together? How much does it cost to build a new team? How do you recruit quality players? What league regulations do we need to be aware of? How do we get a basketball arena built?" Then Jimmy called me up and said, "Pat, this thing is rolling down the tracks and picking up speed. You'd better hop on quick."

By December, it was snowing in Philadelphia, and that Orlando sunshine started looking better and better. I had another speaking engagement in central Florida, so I jetted back to that magical place I had come to picture as my future hometown. While in Orlando, I again met with John and Jimmy and some other guys who were interested in this dream of ours. I asked a lot of questions about Orlando. They asked a lot of questions about running a pro basketball team. It was clear by the time I left Orlando that this idea was picking up a lot of momentum.

Arriving home in Philadelphia, I picked up my phone messages and found one from Bill Gaither, an old friend and a big-time gospel music mogul, the songwriter behind songs like "Something Beautiful," "There's Something about That Name," and "The King Is Coming." I mean, Bill is the Babe Ruth of gospel music. He's also a colossal basketball fan. So I called him back and we got to talking, and right out of the blue Bill said to me, "Pat, when I give up this music business, what I really want to do is get into your business."

"My business?"

"Yeah. I want to get into the basketball business."

"Really?" I said. "Bill, what do you want to do in the basketball business?"

"Well, I'd really like to own a piece of a team someday."

"No kidding," I said. "You know any teams that have an interest for sale?"

"No, not an existing team. None of the existing teams are located in the right place. It would have to be a new team. An expansion team. And it would have to be in the right city."

"Oh? What city is that?"

"Only one city," he said. "Orlando, Florida."

I was stunned. Speechless. I hadn't said word one to Bill about the dreams I had been dreaming or the talks I had been having about starting a team in Orlando. I hadn't even mentioned to him that I had just flown in from Orlando. I stammered and sputtered and finally said, "Bill, that's unbelievable! Why did you say Orlando?"

"Well," he said, "of all the places we travel to on our concert tours, one place really stands out above the rest, and that's Orlando, Florida. There's just something about that whole area—the atmosphere, the spirit of the community, the attitude and style of the people there. It's just an incredibly special place. I keep thinking that would be a nice place to retire to, and if I could be an owner or part-owner of an NBA team in Orlando, that would just complete the dream."

As things turned out, Bill Gaither never did buy a piece of the team. But he tossed his dream out there where I could see it, and it gave added impetus to my own dream. The timing of his comment was so astounding it seemed to go beyond mere coincidence. I had to see where this dream was leading us.

A lot of people were dreaming this dream at the same time, and as we dreamed together, we started hammering that dream into a solid reality. All through that winter, Jim Hewitt assembled an ownership group and set in motion all the preliminary steps for bringing NBA basketball to central Florida. During that time, I talked to Jimmy by phone almost daily.

Finally, in June 1986, I left the 76ers and moved to Orlando to begin putting shoe leather to this dream. From the moment I arrived in Florida and on into the following year, every day was a high-intensity adventure of rallying the community, revving up the machinery of building a sports arena, convincing the NBA to expand, and selling the NBA on Orlando as the best site. In late April 1987, the NBA board of governors voted to add four new teams, including a team in Orlando, to start play in the fall of 1989.

What should we call this team? Somehow, that little detail just clicked into place: *Magic!* Just about anywhere you go in Orlando, you catch a sense of wide-open optimism and wonder; it seems to float into town on the breeze from the Magic Kingdom. All of us in this new venture were infused and inspired by it—so what else could we call this team but the Orlando Magic!

On the court, however, we found that basketball magic doesn't just happen with the wave of a wand. The Magic's first season,

1989–90, was spectacularly unspectacular. We won 18 games and lost 64, ending up second from the bottom in the NBA.

But after that first tough season, the Orlando Magic began to show a glimmer of improvement. Our 1990–91 season ended with 31 wins, 51 losses. We were advancing into the middle of the rankings. The next season, 1991–92, we slipped a bit, ending the season with a 21–61 record, but soon our fortunes began to change as we won back-to-back draft lotteries. (What are the odds of winning the number one pick two years in a row? Is that honest-to-gosh *magic* or what?) The first winning lottery, in May 1992, produced an amazing young center from Louisiana State University. His name: Shaquille Rashaun O'Neal. The next lottery, in May 1993, yielded an outstanding point guard from the University of Memphis, Anfernee "Penny" Hardaway. From then on, O-town's magical roundball team has been on a roll. The Magic ended the 1994–95 regular season with a 57–25 record, and a 39–2 mark at home, the second best home record in NBA history.

It all started with an idea, a dream, a conversation in a car on the way to the airport. When you *go for the magic,* you never know how far it can take you!

FIVE MAGICAL SECRETS

My first couple of years in Orlando were—dare I say it?— *magical* years. If I could think of a better word, I'd use it. But *magical* is the only word that fits. There was the magic of watching our team and our staff grow together into a winning organization—not just winning games but winning the minds and capturing the hearts of fans. There was the magical response and support we received from the community. And there was more, another kind of magic, something that was all around us and in the air, something tangible yet indefinable, something I could almost taste but couldn't put my finger on. I kept thinking, "Bill Gaither was right. There *is* something special about this town, an indefinable *something* that is different from any other place I've been."

But what that special *something* was, I couldn't say.

Then, one day, I happened to pick up an issue of *Reader's Digest.* I was flipping through it and came upon an article that absolutely jumped off the page and grabbed me. That article was "Walt Disney's Five Secrets of Success," written by John Culhane. The article was a five-stage formulation of something I had already seen with my own eyes but hadn't really understood.

During my first few years in Orlando, I had numerous encounters with Disney execs and had come to know a few of them fairly well. The Disney organization had been very helpful to us in building the Orlando Magic and enabling us to establish productive ties with the local government and the business community. As a result, I had spent many enjoyable, inspiring hours with men like Bob Matheison, Dick Nunis, and the late Bob Allen, and I was privileged to hear them relate many firsthand tales of Walt Disney's life. Many of these Disney execs broke into the business under Walt's personal tutelage and spent their early careers at his side, learning his philosophy of business and of life.

Without realizing it, I had seen "Walt Disney's Five Secrets of Success" in action, operating through these Disney executives and through the Disney organization. I had been living in the towering shadow of Walt's big-eared mouse for several years, but I hadn't understood *why* that mouse casts such a long shadow. Once I read John Culhane's article, I instantly understood why Orlando is such a special place: This is where the amazing creator of that mouse lives on! Walt Disney is alive and well in Orlando, Florida! His five secrets of success are like an aura that has infused Walt Disney World and the entire Orlando area with its magic.

As I read the Culhane article, my excitement grew—the excitement of discovery, of epiphany, of "Eureka! I've found it!" The words of Bill Gaither came back to me: "There's just something about that whole area—the atmosphere, the spirit of the community, the attitude and style of the people there. It's just an incredibly special place!" And I thought, *Yes! And now I know where that specialness comes from! It's the imprint of Walt Disney's unique personality on the central Florida area. Walt Disney World is so special and sets such a high standard that everything and everyone in this area is challenged and inspired to reach for that same standard. That's why Orlando has the most beautiful airport in the world! That's why Orlando has the friendliest, warmest people in the world! That's why Orlando is one of the cleanest, most beautiful cities in the world! It's all right here in Walt Disney's five secrets of success!*

According to Culhane, those five secrets that enabled Walt Disney to make his own dreams come true, and that have become so much a part of the Walt Disney World style and the Orlando culture, are:

1. Think "Tomorrow."
   Make today's efforts pay off tomorrow!
2. Free the Imagination.
   You are capable of more than you can imagine—so imagine the ultimate!
3. Strive for Lasting Quality.
   "Good enough" never is!
4. Have "Stick-to-it-ivity."
   Never, never, *never* give up!
5. Have Fun.
   You're never truly a success until you *enjoy* what you are doing!

As I read those five principles, I realized that they could be applied to *anyone's* daily life. In the years since I gained this insight, I have practically made a second career of researching these five secrets, collecting stories and quotations that support these five secrets, speaking on these five secrets, and building them into my life.

SOARING WITH WALT

I've often wondered what it would have been like to have been with Walt Disney, to have worked and built and dreamed alongside him in those formative days of the Disney entertainment empire. The tales of Disney's early struggles are the stuff of legends. In the depths of the Great Depression, Walt poured $1.5 million of his own and investors' money into the first-ever feature-length animated cartoon. This was three times the original budget and an astounding sum of money to spend on any motion picture in the 1930s, live-action or animated. Industry pundits predicted doom. Audiences conditioned to seven-minute Mickey Mouse cartoons would *never* sit still for a movie-length fairy tale called *Snow White and the Seven Dwarfs.* If the film had failed, as conventional wisdom predicted it would, Walt Disney would have been financially ruined, personally and corporately. But Walt's five secrets of success prevailed over conventional wisdom. *Snow White* was *the* must-see movie of 1937—and continues to be a big moneymaker for Disney more than fifty years later!

In the early 1950s, Walt took on an even greater challenge: turning a tract of southern California orange groves into a totally new kind of amusement park. He didn't want to build another dirty, dangerous, foul-smelling collection of rickety roller-coasters, grubby carny barkers, and surly Ferris wheel operators. He dreamed of a sparkling wonderland of smiles and fun, all based on themes from classic Disney movies. The dream grew from the 1952 "Kiddieland" concept (to be built on a corner of the Burbank studio property for about $10,000) to the twenty-two-attraction, seventeen-million-dollar entertainment city that opened on July 17, 1955.

"I could never convince the financiers," he later recalled, "that Disneyland was feasible, because dreams offer too little collateral."[1] Disney mortgaged his own future and that of his production company to provide some of the capital. He cut deals with corporate sponsors and sold his Disneyland TV series and a one-third interest in the park to ABC in exchange for cash and loan guarantees. The very existence of Disneyland is a tribute to one man's dogged persistence in pursuit of a dream.

The last great challenge of Walt Disney's life was the realization of his dream of bringing Disney magic to the East Coast. I would have loved to have been on that private airplane flight in the early 1960s, when Walt first soared over the groves and swamplands of central Florida, a magical dream in his eye. I can picture that plane banking low over an orchard of citrus trees and this man looking out the window, his features gentle and grandfatherly, but his eyes afire with visionary ambition.

"You know," he might have said to his business associates in the plane, "down where those orange, tangerine, and grapefruit trees are growing, I can picture a giant castle coming up out of the ground, where millions of children from all over the world can come and have the entertainment experience of a lifetime."

The plane may have turned over a lake, where an alligator lay sunning on the bank, and where a blue heron stood on one leg. "Around a lake like that one," Disney might have said, "I can picture the people of the world building monuments and pavilions to their countries and their cultures—a permanent World's Fair where people can come and travel the world in a day. A thing like that could really bring this old world together, and help create international understanding—and it would be so much *fun!*"

As the plane settled in low over a marshy bog, the man in the plane might have said, "And look there! We could drain that swamp and put in acres of studio buildings and back lots! There's no smog here, and plenty of sunlight. What a great place to make motion pictures!"

Walt Disney died on December 15, 1966, long before Walt Disney World became a reality. But he would be pleased—and I think, amazed—to know what has become of his dream. Today, all of central Florida bears the imprint of this man's personality, his vision, and the organization he created.

Yes, it would have been an exciting and memorable experience to have been at Walt Disney's side as he flew over central Florida and foretold the incredible future of those orchards and swamplands. And yet, I think it is even more exciting to think about the future, the limitless possibilities that are within our reach as we discover and then implement these five magical principles.

AN E-TICKET RIDE TO SUCCESS

What do you want out of life? Are you looking for success in business? Do you place a high premium on being a successful parent, raising healthy, happy, well-adjusted kids? Is there some artistic achievement you've been wanting to complete—a novel, a screenplay, a painting—yet you are afraid to attempt it because you might fail? Do you just feel that your life is disordered and frayed at the edges, and you need to find your focus? Whatever the word *success* means to you, these five magical secrets will put the keys to success in the palm of your hand.

I live these secrets in my own life. I teach them to my kids. I implement them in my family. I have seen them being built into the fabric of the Orlando Magic organization. They are the success formula behind a magical kingdom, a magical basketball team, and a magical, miraculous way of life.

In this book, I'll take you on a guided tour of these five magical secrets. I'll show you how they have been the key to success not only in Walt Disney's life, but in the lives of people like Shaquille O'Neal, Henry Ford, Bill Veeck, George Allen, Rich DeVos, Penny Hardaway, Larry King, Danny Kaye, Florence Griffith Joyner, Brian Shaw, Ted Williams, Bill Russell, Muhammad Ali, Donald Royal, and many, many more. I'll show you some of the amazing wonders that have come about because people dared to dream their dreams—and then had the courage, ingenuity, and perseverance to hammer those dreams into reality!

After all, what is a dream? What is an idea? A vision? It's something completely intangible, an electrochemical trace along the tiniest fibers of your brain cells, less substantial by far than the invisible air you breathe. But come down to central Florida, step into Walt Disney World, gaze at its sights, touch the buildings, ride the attractions, taste the food, listen to the music. It's a fantasy world that is also tangible and real. Consider this: All of that incredible, tangible reality called Walt Disney World was once nothing more than a dream in one man's mind!

Now, perhaps, you begin to glimpse something of the power that can be unleashed by a dream. Would you like to make your dreams come true? Would you like to know how to hammer your dreams into reality?

Then come along. Strap yourself in for an E-ticket ride!

Destination: Success!

MAGICAL SECRET

NUMBER 1

Think "Tomorrow"

CHAPTER 2

Yesterday, or, The Past Is a Canceled Check

○ *One nice thing about living in the past—it's cheaper.*
Ken Hussar, American humorist

○ *If what you did yesterday seems big, you haven't done anything today.*
Lou Holtz, former Notre Dame football coach

○ *You can't think clearly about your future if you're obsessed with the past.*
Mark McCormack, sports representative and author

I vern Ball said, "The past should be a springboard, not a hammock." Now, I haven't a clue who in the world Ivern Ball is. Maybe his (or her) only claim to fame was having uttered this one piece of advice. If so, then I say, "Way to go, Ivern Ball!" Because that is one *fantastic* piece of advice!

I learned this lesson a number of years ago when I was managing the Philadelphia 76ers. Our 1983 team was an incredible squad of great players. The roster included outstanding players like Moses Malone, Julius Erving, Bobby Jones, Andrew Toney, and Maurice Cheeks. It was an absolutely wonderful team. That year, we roared through the play-offs, we swept the Lakers in four straight, and we took the NBA championship. We had a pep rally at Vet Stadium before about fifty thousand people, and the city of Philadelphia gave us a parade down Broad Street, with a couple million people whooping and celebrating like crazy. At the end of it all, we kicked back and basked in the glow of a really pleasant summer. We designed the championship rings and reflected on the wonderful year we had just had as an NBA championship team.

Then, all too quickly, the 1983–84 season began. Opening night in Philadelphia was a real celebration. NBA Commissioner Larry O'Brien came to Philly for the ceremonies and presented us all with our championship rings. We put them on our fingers, the crowd roared, and the new season was under way.

But then I noticed a very strange thing happening to me. I found my eyes being drawn to that ring, again and again and again. Whenever I had a few minutes of slack time, I'd sit and gaze at that ring. Time passed, the new season was several weeks old, and it suddenly hit me that I hadn't even focused on the new season! I wasn't really paying that much attention to *today* because I was having too much fun focusing on that ring and recalling memories of *yesterday.* They were good memories, exciting memories—but that's all they were: memories.

I realized that ring was causing me a lot of problems. Memories weren't going to fill any arenas or win any games. I needed to bear down on *today,* tackle *today's* challenges, and make *today* pay off. I saw that I was going to be weighed down and pulled off course by that ring unless I did something radical. So I took the ring off my finger, put it back in its little box, and tucked it away in a safe place. That was more than twelve years ago, and I haven't worn it since. I haven't even looked at it. I made a decision not to let that ring anchor my mind in yesterday.

THREE BLOCKS OF TIME

The first magical secret of success behind a magical kingdom, a magical basketball team, and a magical, miraculous way of life is: *Think "tomorrow."* Make today's efforts pay off tomorrow. Don't get mired in the failures of the past. Don't wallow in the glories of the past. Live in today, and focus your efforts on tomorrow. That is how you make your dreams come true. Throughout history, that is how all the truly great makers and shakers have hammered their dreams into reality.

Who is your role model for success? A sports figure like Shaquille O'Neal or Joe Montana? An entrepreneur like Walt Disney or Bill Gates? A great military leader like Norman Schwarzkopf? A top corporate executive like Lee Iacocca or Michael Eisner? A great political figure like Franklin Roosevelt or Ronald Reagan? A leading entertainer like Tom Cruise or Mariah Carey? A prolific, best-selling author like Tom Clancy or Tom Peters? A great religious leader like Billy Graham or Charles Swindoll? How did each of these individuals become so successful? I would submit that one of the most important keys to their success is the way they have chosen to use the irreplaceable gift of their *time.*

We all have three blocks of time in our lives: *yesterday, today,* and *tomorrow.* Those three blocks of time are there for all of us to take and use as we see fit. You have the same amount of time in your day that the Shaq or Stormin' Norman or any other successful person has. Everyone gets sixty seconds per minute, sixty minutes per hour, twenty-four hours per day, no more, no less. I am convinced that the secret that allows certain people to rise above the pack is *the way they choose to deal with those three blocks of time.*

First, we should take a realistic look at *yesterday.* Yesterday is a canceled check. We can never get it back. As the great humorist Will Rogers said, "Don't let yesterday take up too much of today." We don't want to forget the past, because that is where we find lessons for today. But neither do we want to get stuck in the past, because no one becomes successful in the past. We make our dreams come true by the things we do *right now.*

As a boy growing up in Philadelphia, one of my boyhood idols was a fellow named Cornelius Alexander McGillicuddy—more popularly known as Connie Mack, the "grand old man of major-league baseball." Mack was a catcher with various teams from 1886 to 1896. (He shortened his name so it would fit in the box score.) When his playing career ended, he began a new career in 1901 as owner and manager of the Philadelphia Athletics. In fact, he was still managing the A's at the very first baseball game I ever saw in 1947. He was well into his eighties at that point, but he was still at it, and would stay at it until retiring in 1950 at age 88. Under his leadership, the A's won nine American League championships and five World Series.

Connie Mack had a secret of good management: He didn't get mired in the past. "I discovered," he once explained, "that worry was threatening to wreck my career as a baseball manager. I saw how foolish it was and I forced myself to get so busy preparing to win games that I had no time left to worry over the games that were already lost. You can't grind grain with water that has already gone down the creek." The great Connie Mack has long been a role model of mine, and in recent years I've tried to build his philosophy into my own life and management style. There was a time, however, when I tried to grind my grain with water that was long gone.

I've spent more than thirty years in the sports world—a world that lends itself so easily to paralyzing retrospection. Coaches and managers are in the world's leading second-guessed business. There are always fans, sportswriters, sportscasters, players, owners, and other coaches and managers looking over our shoulders, asking, "Why didn't you do this? Why did you do that? Why did you draft this player when you could have had that player? What ever possessed you to make that trade?"

I've made plenty of bad draft choices, absolutely horrible mistakes, where I ended up stuck for years with a player who just didn't do anything for our team. I've known the experience of looking back, year after year, on a decision and saying, "What an idiot I was! How could I foul up so completely?"

Case in point: The year was 1970, and I was general manager of the Chicago Bulls. We were getting ready for the college draft—the first I had ever been involved with and a very important moment for the team. Our college scout was Jerry Krause, who's now general manager of the Bulls. He had zeroed in on a promising guard named Jimmy Collins, who was playing for New Mexico State. We had spent a great deal of time watching, studying, and talking to Collins, and we had a very good feeling about him. In late March, as the draft was about to take place, our coach, Dick Motta, came back from an NCAA regional game in which Texas El Paso had played. Motta was all excited, waving his hands and raving, "You oughta see this little guard playing for El Paso! The guy is brilliant, absolutely brilliant! I want that guy playing for the Bulls!"

"What's his name?" I asked.

"Nate Archibald," said Motta.

"Okay," I said, "let's talk to Archibald and see if he looks like a good fit for the Bulls."

So we got in touch with Nate Archibald the day of the draft, and we told him to wait in his college dorm room for a call. We were interested in him, and we would be in touch with him. Then Dick, Jerry, and I had a meeting and planned our strategy for the college draft: We would take Jimmy Collins on the first round, and if Nate Archibald was still there when our second-round pick came up, we would take him too. Coach Motta wasn't comfortable with this decision—he *really* wanted Nate Archibald on his team—but he went along. At the end of our meeting, I said to him, "Dick, tell me this: What happens if Nate Archibald is not there on the second round?"

He looked at me and said something that haunted me for years to come: "Then we'll play against him."

The draft began, and we picked Jimmy Collins. The first round ended and the second round began. We waited anxiously for our turn. Then, just a few picks ahead of us, Nate Archibald was taken, snatched up by Cincinnati. Dick Motta shook his head grimly.

The wrap-up of the story is this: Jimmy Collins never turned out to be the brilliant NBA guard we envisioned when we saw him on the college courts. Two years after we grabbed him as a first-round draft pick, he was gone, out of the game for good. Nate Archibald, however, went on to have a brilliant fourteen-year career in the NBA. Just a few years ago, he was voted into the Hall of Fame. Every day for fifteen years, I looked back and slapped my head like the people in those V-8 commercials and said, "Man! I coulda had Nate Archibald!" What did we see in this other player that turned out not to be there? What successes and triumphs did we miss in later seasons because of a fateful decision we made about our first-round draft pick?

The truth is, I have a career filled with those stories. It's the flip side of the championship ring story. Both your past successes and your past failures can paralyze you—if you let them. I know. It has happened to me. For many years, I beat myself up so badly with regrets and self-recrimination that it really threatened to ruin my career. Whether yesterday is grim or glorious, you just can't park there. You've got to get your head out of yesterday and get it back into today. You've got to face today's challenges and solve today's problems.

On one of his PBS specials, author Leo Buscaglia talked about his appreciation for culinary personality Julia Child. "I just love her attitude," he explained. "She says, 'Tonight we're going to make a soufflé!' And she beats this and whisks that, and she drops things on the floor. She wipes her face with her napkin and does all these wonderful human things. Then she takes the soufflé and throws it in the oven and talks to you for a while. Finally, she says, 'Now it's ready!' But when she opens the oven, the soufflé just falls flat as a pancake! But does she panic or burst into tears? No! She smiles and says, 'Well, you can't win 'em all. Bon appétit!'"

And so it should be with us. Each of us is whipping up some kind of soufflé—a business venture, a new career move, an investment, a first novel, a new church program. It may be the best and highest rising soufflé anyone ever tasted, or it may fall flat. But do we make our future any brighter by flogging ourselves over the next ten years because of that flat soufflé? No way!

Someone once said, "The most tiring exercise in the world is carrying yesterday on your back." It's true. None of us is perfect, so let's enjoy our humanity. Let's laugh at our mistakes and go on. If you flopped the soufflé, then open a can of beans and get on with your dinner—and your life!

One of America's most beloved presidents—plain-talking, pragmatic Harry S. Truman—had a healthy perspective on yesterday. "Whenever it comes to making a decision," he said, "I make it and forget about it, and go to work on something else. When important issues came before me as the president of the United States, I made a decision on them, and went on to the next thing. You never have time to stop. You've got to keep going because there's always a decision just ahead of you that you've got to make, and you don't want to look back. If you make a mistake in one of these decisions, correct it by another decision, and go ahead."

It's all a matter of monitoring our self-talk, that inner conversation we have with ourselves. Many of us talk to ourselves in negative, self-condemning ways. We have a habitual, self-defeating vocabulary that we use again and again and again: "If only . . ." "I always blow it . . ." "I'm so stupid . . ." "Why does this always happen to me . . . ?" We say these things to ourselves, and we defeat ourselves. We say these things aloud in our homes, and we defeat our spouses and children. We say these things in the workplace, and we bring our whole organization down.

Backward-looking, hopeless, gloomy words produce failure. Such words look in the wrong direction, backward, toward a past that can't be changed. Everybody fails; the trick is to "fail forward," to keep your life pointed toward tomorrow, not yesterday. Everybody has problems, pain, and disappointment; the trick is to accept what can't be changed—a lousy childhood, a mate who committed adultery, a divorce, an illness, the loss of a job, a bankruptcy, a betrayal—and to say, "That was then; I'm going to live now and keep my eyes on a brighter tomorrow." Everybody sins; the Bible says that if we confess our sins, God forgives us, cleanses us, and puts us back in business again.[1] So take your eyes off your past failures, your past problems, your old pain, and the sins of the past that have already been forgiven. Face forward and change your self-talk. Instead of saying, "If only . . ." or "Why me?" or "I blew it again . . ." say, "I'm ready for the next adventure!"

LEARNING FROM THE PAST

You've probably figured out by now that I love quotations— the wisdom of the ages condensed into a powerful sentence or two. I'm a compulsive collector of the pithy, and my files overflow with quotes, poems, sayings, and anecdotes. For a while, I kept a box full of magazine clippings and scribbly envelopes. Eventually, I got my quote collection retyped onto cards and organized in a computer file. Admittedly, this habit of mine has driven my editors crazy, because editors love footnotes and orderliness, and how do you footnote a box full of clippings? So you'll just have to trust me that the people I'm quoting actually said these things at one time or another.

Richard M. Nixon was a man who achieved a lot—and a man who made a lot of mistakes. In the last years of his life, he was at least partially able to recover from the disgrace of the Watergate scandal, and he was often consulted by Presidents Reagan, Bush, and Clinton for help and advice in matters of foreign affairs. His recovery was perhaps due to the attitude he expressed when he said, "I don't like yesterday except as a learning tool for tomorrow." Even the shame of Watergate had its lessons, and it was clear that Nixon tried to learn those lessons without reliving its pain.

What was Richard Nixon saying? That the past has a positive value—not as something to live in or dwell on, but as something to learn from. Walt Disney felt the same way. He said, "I think it's important to have a good hard failure when you're young. I learned a lot out of that. Because it makes you kind of aware of what can happen to you. Because of it I've never had any fear in my whole life when we've been near collapse and all of that. I've never been afraid. I've never had the feeling I couldn't walk out and get a job doing something."

Yesterday shapes who we are today, just as what we do today shapes who we will be tomorrow. Look at it this way: Life is like driving a car. It's wise to check the rearview mirror now and then, but the rearview mirror is only there for us to *glance* at, not to *stare* at. Staring at where you've been will only land you in a ditch.

In 1993, General Colin Powell, former chairman of the Joint

Chiefs of Staff, addressed the students of Lawson State Community College in Birmingham, Alabama. Perhaps the most important piece of advice he had for those students was this: "The only thing you do with yesterday is learn from it. What did I do wrong? . . . How could I improve on what I did yesterday and how well can I use that today? So live for today, every minute of it, every hour of it. Save part of today to prepare for tomorrow, but dream about next week."

So you fouled up yesterday. So what? That was yesterday. All the money in the world can't buy yesterday back, so why agonize over it? This is today. Give yourself a clean blackboard and start writing the story of the rest of your life.

Alvin Dark, the former manager of the Kansas City Athletics and other major-league teams, used to say, "There's no such thing as taking a pitcher out. There's only bringing another pitcher in." This is a key not only to effective sports management but to effective *life* management. In other words, don't look back at the bad pitches, the walked runners, the mistakes and the errors of the past. Focus on the next pitch and how to get it past the batter. Until the last out of the final inning, the only thing that matters is that next pitch. When you take the old pitcher out, you don't do it to get even with him. You do it to get the next guy out. You do it to win. You do it to achieve success.

So think of your past as a tired pitcher. He's done his best for six or seven innings, but he's lost his stuff. He needs a relief man. So put in a new pitcher. Try a new approach. Set some new priorities and goals. Learn from your mistakes—but don't beat yourself down over them. Focus on the next pitch, the next challenge, the next problem that has to be solved.

FORGIVING THE PAST

Right now, you may be thinking, "That's fine, Pat. It's easy for you to say, 'Don't dwell on the past,' and 'Live in today.' But Pat, you have no idea what I've been through! You don't know the disaster my life has been! How can I forget what So-and-so did to me? Or how can I forget the terrible mess I made of my life?"

You've got a point there. Life is hard, and it's frequently unjust.

To paraphrase a popular bumper sticker, "Stuff happens." It happens to you, to me, to all of us. And some of it we do to ourselves. But we have to find a way to put it behind us if we are ever to make our dreams come true.

Elbert Hubbard wrote, "A retentive memory may be a good thing, but the ability to forget is the true token of greatness. Successful people forget. They know the past is irrevocable. They're running a race. They can't afford to look behind. Their eye is on the finish line. Magnanimous people forget. They're too big to let little things disturb them. They forget easily. If anyone does them wrong, they consider the source and keep cool. It's only the small people who cherish revenge. Be a good forgetter. Business dictates it, and success demands it."

If life has kicked you around and roughed you up a bit, if you've ever felt betrayed, unjustly treated, imprisoned by circumstances, or down in the pits, then allow me to introduce you to someone who knows exactly how you feel—someone who was able to triumph, to succeed beyond all imagining, and to literally make his dreams come true. His name is Joseph, and you meet him in the Old Testament book of Genesis, chapters 37 through 50.

As a young man, Joseph was an out-and-out dreamer, a true visionary. He went to sleep at night, had dreams about the future; then the next morning he went around and shot his mouth off about his dreams. A couple of his dreams depicted Joseph lording it over the rest of his family—and this didn't set well with his brothers. Joseph came from what we now call "a dysfunctional family." His father, Jacob, stirred up trouble in the family by favoring Joseph over the other brothers. So when Joseph told his dreams of one day ruling over those eleven brothers, they decided enough was enough. They grabbed Joseph, tossed him in a pit, and sold him into slavery.

As a slave, Joseph went to work for an Egyptian businessman who happened to be married to a lusty, seductive wife. Day after day, she came on to Joseph, practically forcing herself on him, and day after day he steadfastly refused to cheat on his employer or disobey his God. Finally, the boss's wife got tired of this game and to get even with him, she actually accused Joseph of attempted rape! The boss believed her, and so did the judge, so Joseph was tossed into jail. The irony of the situation was that he received this unfair treatment not only *despite* his innocence but precisely *because* he was innocent, because he refused this woman's sexual advances.

While in prison, young Joseph had plenty of time to gripe and moan about how unfair his life had been. He was sold into slavery by his brothers, then put in jail for trying to do the right thing. His misery was compounded when one of his fellow inmates was released and promptly went back on a promise to help Joseph obtain a pardon. If anybody had reason to have bitter feelings about his yesterdays, it was Joseph.

But Joseph refused to be consumed by bitterness. He refused to stare backward at the injustices of the past. Instead, he chose to entrust his future to God. And later—to make a long story short—Joseph was released from prison and elevated to a position of influence as an adviser to the king of Egypt. His wisdom and God-given ability as a planner and policymaker were so impressive that the king promoted Joseph to a position that was second in power only to his own.

There, at the pinnacle of his success, many years after being sold into slavery, Joseph was again brought face to face with his brothers. They had come to Egypt during a time of famine, seeking food from the Egyptian government, and as they came into Joseph's presence, it was clear to Joseph that they didn't even recognize him! What an opportunity to get even for all the misery and injustice they had put him through! His power as the Number Two Man in all of Egypt was practically limitless: "Revenge? Hey, not a problem! I can have these guys sliced, diced, fried, boiled, broiled, and we'd just be getting started!"

But that was not the way Joseph approached life. He first tested them to see if the years had changed them and made them repentant over the evil they had done to him. Then he revealed himself to them, forgave them, embraced them, and reinstated them as his brothers. The key to Joseph's positive, forward-looking attitude in the face of all he had suffered is found in Genesis 50:20—"You meant evil against me," he told his brothers, "but God meant it for good." We can always find some good, some lesson, some benefit, some increased wisdom in the painful experiences of the past.

Someone once defined *forgiveness* as "the fragrance a flower gives off when somebody steps on it." When you and I get stepped on—and it happens to everybody, sooner or later—we can give off a positive and forward-looking attitude. We can demonstrate a special kind of character to the people around us that says, "I'm bigger than the petty, hurtful things people can do to me. I refuse to give in to bitterness. I refuse to let other people control the way I feel by their stupid or destructive behavior. I choose to get on with my life and keep moving on toward a beautiful, exciting future."

After Joseph's rise to power, he married an Egyptian woman who bore him two sons. The firstborn was named Manasseh, which literally means, "remembering no more," and the second-born was named Ephraim, which means "fruitfulness" or "success." Through these two sons, Joseph commemorated the fact that God had taken all the sting out of his memories and had made him a success in the land where he had once been a slave and a prisoner. Joseph didn't forget his past, but he also didn't stare at it and brood over it. He learned the lessons of yesterday, applied them to today, and looked forward to tomorrow's success.

If you're holding on to grudges and bitterness over the things that have happened to you in the past, then you are stuck in yesterday. You are allowing the people who hurt you in the past to keep on hurting you in the present. If you are brooding or resentful over yesterday, then you are allowing someone from the past to occupy a place of importance in your present-day thoughts. And that's going to weigh you down and hold you back in your efforts to make your dreams come true.

You need to forgive the past. This doesn't mean you necessarily have to go to a person who hurt you and say, "I forgive you. Let's be friends." If there have been hurtful, destructive people in your life—an abusive parent, a friend who betrayed you, an overbearing and too-demanding boss—you may be much better off just consigning that person to the "yesterday" block of your life. But you *can* forgive people without reconciling with them. You can release them from your anger and judgment, even if you never speak to them again. The important thing is to clear your own mind of poisonous emotions, such as bitterness and resentment.

The 1995 NBA All-Star Game was held in Phoenix and marked the fourteenth consecutive year that a chapel service was held before the game. Norm Sonju, general manager of the Dallas Mavericks, lined up a great program featuring the music of Glen Campbell and an inspiring talk by the former National League pitcher, Dave Dravecky.

But the part of the program that most impacted me was the opening prayer by the Phoenix Suns' guard, Elliott Perry. Right in the middle of his prayer, he said, "Lord, thank You for our enemies and bless them as well." What a powerful concept!

Forgiveness is a *decision*. It takes place in the mind and the will. The problem is that the bitterness we often feel takes place in the *emotions,* not the mind or the will. So you and I may think, "Sure, I know I should release the past and get on with my life, but emotionally I just can't do it." Bringing our emotions in line with what our mind wants and what our will chooses can be a mighty tall order sometimes.

Radio personality Bruce Williams, host of NBC Westwood One's "Talknet" advice show, tells a story about how he dealt with an unhappy yesterday in his life:

> I was a sophomore in my mid-twenties, married, two kids, making eighty dollars a week running the school snack bar. My boss was Professor So-and-so, who once ran a snack bar in a drive-in theater. One day I said, "Professor, it's pretty tough going through school and feeding a wife and two kids on eighty bucks a week. I need a raise."
>
> "Williams," he replied, "you have grandiose ideas. You'll never be worth a hundred dollars a week."
>
> Years later, I was invited to sit on the school's Board of Trustees. By this time, I owned a few businesses, had been elected mayor of my community for a couple of terms, and was hosting this thing I do on radio. I declined the invitation, but while I was on campus to meet the Board, I saw a door with Professor So-and-so's name on it. I raised my hand to knock—then I changed my mind and kept walking.
>
> I had been prepared to go in and say, "Well, Professor, here I am

with my grandiose ideas. I've got a feeling I make more in two weeks than you make in a year." But I thought, *What would that accomplish? Here I am, ready to pick on an elderly man who never really had much success in his life beyond getting out of the drive-in and getting his Ph.D.*

Then I realized I really owed him a debt, because whenever things got tough, I'd hear those words spurring me on, "Williams, you have grandiose ideas." In a perverse way, Professor So-and-so was my inspiration to succeed. Someday, I may go back and pay the professor a visit. But if I do, it'll be to *thank* him for telling me I had grandiose ideas.

In his own way, Bruce Williams is saying the same thing Joseph said in Genesis 50:20—"Professor So-and-so, you intended that remark for evil, but it worked out for good in my life. That insult of yours was a spur to my backside, driving me on to success."

I hope you have found some added insight and perspective in this chapter to enable you to let go of yesterday and keep moving on toward tomorrow. But if you find it impossible to forgive and get on with your life, then get some counseling from a pastor, psychologist, or therapist—someone with whom you can talk it through and get specific insights into your own feelings. One way or another, you've got to find some way to get beyond the past and get on with the present. Otherwise, you'll always be spinning your wheels.

The American Red Cross was founded by a sweetheart of a woman named Clara Barton, who was widely reputed never to hold a grudge. Once, a friend reminded her of some hurtful act done to her years before. When Barton seemed to draw a blank on that event, the friend persisted, "Don't you remember how much that person hurt you?"

"No," Clara Barton cheerfully responded, "I distinctly remember forgetting that."

That's what you and I have to do with our yesterdays. As we aggressively forgive the past and turn our faces toward the future, we will begin to move steadily in the direction of our dreams. Always remember the words of Dr. Martin Luther King, Jr.: "Forgiveness is not an occasional act; it is a permanent attitude."

IF YOU WANT TO PLAY IN THE BIG LEAGUES . . .

One thing I've learned in all my years of association with the sports world is that the lessons and principles that produce greatness in sports are also the ones that produce greatness in life. The greatest sport of all is the game of life. You're playing it, I'm playing it, we're all on this great big team together. So as we come to the end of this chapter on the subject of yesterday, I want to bring in a few of your "teammates" in the game of life. I'll let them share with you the lessons they've learned from the sports world—lessons on how to look at yesterday:

- "I try not to look back," says baseball Hall of Famer Steve Carlton. "It brings up the past. It's nowhere. [The past] doesn't exist anymore. If you keep it current, then it becomes current and you have double problems—current and past."
- "I've played with a lot of really mentally strong players who are able to take advantage of every opportunity," recalls Billy Beane, former major-league outfielder. "The good ones forget about yesterday, just look at tomorrow and don't look too far in advance. I came up [to the major leagues] with Lenny Dykstra, and he had a great mental attitude. He could forget about yesterday and look ahead to tomorrow. . . ."
- In 1980, Red Auerbach, president of the Boston Celtics, said, "I think I'm the same person I've always been—a little older, a little mellower. But I don't live in the past."

If you want to play in the big leagues—and who of us doesn't?—that's how you have to deal with that block of time we call "yesterday." The past, with all its glories and all its pain, is a canceled check. Learn from it. Savor the good memories now and then. Glance at it—but don't stare. Winners learn from the past and let go of it. Losers yearn for the past and get stuck with it. Winners realize that past victories aren't enough to carry you through the rest of your life. As we're about to discover in Chapter 3, the only day that really counts is *today*.

CHAPTER 3

Today, or, What to Do Until Tomorrow Gets Here

○ *The only way to live is to accept each minute as an unrepeatable miracle. . . . Work at your work. Play at your play. Shed your tears. Enjoy your laughter. Now is the time of your life.*
Margaret Storm Jameson, physician and administrator

○ *Life is easier if you dread only one day at a time.*
Charles M. Schulz, creator of Peanuts

○ *Children have neither past nor future. They enjoy the present, which very few of us do.*
La Bruyère

I'm absolutely fascinated with the life of the Magic's former star center Shaquille O'Neal. The Shaq was criticized rather severely in his first three years as a pro because of all the things he did apart from basketball—an enormous number of things. Here is a kid who has been Rookie of the Year, is one of the league's top scorers; was the starting center for the East in three consecutive All-Star Games, has had a remarkable start to a career—all by the age of twenty-two! He has also recorded two rap albums, starred in the movie *Blue Chips,* and has made a ton of money from product endorsements. He has done everything a man with his talent and goals could possibly want to do. A lot of people are critical of that. Frankly, I think a lot of people are just flat-out, green-eyed *jealous* of that. When Shaq was still with Orlando sometimes people would say, "Pat, don't you think the Magic oughta rein the guy in?" In other words, they wanted us to lock Shaq up in a gym and have him do nothing but shoot free throws all day.

My answer to that is "Shaq knows what life is about. He knows the importance of making an absolute feast out of *today.* Don't try to hold him down. Learn from him! He is living *today* to the absolute maximum. He leaves nothing on the table, nothing untried. That's why he's such a draw and a crowd-pleaser. People come to the games just to see the Shaq Attaq! They come to see a man play basketball with a supreme and ferocious *joy!*"

In his early career, Shaquille gained a lot of notoriety—and even criticism—for the way he attacked the basket. During one game in his phenomenal career in high school, Shaq caught the ball close to the basket, leaped, grabbed the hoop with one hand while driving the ball through the hoop with the other—and bent the rim of the basket! The game had to be stopped until a new basket could be installed. Even as a youngster, Shaq was that powerful and aggressive.

During his rookie year with the Magic, Shaq went on to top other "shattering" performances when his famed "Shaq Attaq" collapsed the support standards of the backboard, bringing it crashing to the floor! And he did this not once, but twice, once in Phoenix and once in New Jersey. Fortunately, both of those arenas kept spare standards on hand, so each of those games was delayed for about forty-five minutes while the new standards were installed, and the games continued. As a result of such memorable "attaqs," the Shaq quickly gained a reputation as someone who didn't just shoot baskets—he *destroyed* them!

The point is not to glorify destruction. In fact, Shaquille is not a destructive guy, nor was he trying to destroy those goals. He was just scoring points and winning games, and he was doing it with every ounce of energy, prowess, speed, and enthusiasm he possessed. He held nothing back. That's the secret to his success, both on and off the court. Shaquille O'Neal attacks life the same way he attacks a backboard. I admire and respect him for it. He can teach us all a lesson about living today to the fullest.

FEAST ON TODAY

In this chapter, we look at the second block of time we all must deal with in order to make our dreams come true: *today*. Yesterday is history, tomorrow is our goal, but *today* is what gets us from one to the other. The only time we truly have is *now,* and that is the time we must take advantage of in order to hammer our dreams into reality. This sounds so simple and self-evident—yet I'm continually amazed at how many people hinder their own success and growth by focusing on either the past or the future and failing to grasp the revolutionary importance of that wise Latin slogan, *Carpe diem!*—"Seize the day!"

If there is one lesson I have learned over the years, it is this: To have a happy, positive, joy-filled life, you have to feast on today, you have to pig out on today, you have to absolutely suck the marrow from the bones of today.

I see this "suck-the-marrow-out-of-the-bones" philosophy every time we serve chicken to our children. Our sons from the Philippines and South Korea (we've adopted a few children as you'll learn later) have the unique ability to clean a drumstick to the bone, but at that point they've only just begun. They then split the bones and eat the marrow inside the leg. It's an amazing sight to behold. So if you want to get the most out of every day of your life, just think of the Williams boys eating their drumsticks.

This is your moment. Live in this moment. Use it. Love it. Devour it. Exploit all the riches of today in order to reach tomorrow's goals. I know from personal experience that seizing the moment is not easy to do.

I was invited to play in Charles Barkley's Celebrity Golf Tournament in July 1993. It was held at one of the courses on the Disney hotel property in Orlando. I have to tell you, I'm the world's biggest duffer. I have a wonderful short game. Unfortunately, it's off the tee.

Also in this tournament was basketball great Michael Jordan. If you know much about Air Jordan, you know he's a great golf enthusiast. He is also a great competitor, a great needler, and an opinionated guy who'll shower you with his opinions like a grenade showers you with shrapnel. And wouldn't you know it? His foursome was right behind mine! The entire media corps was with Michael, following him everywhere. As we were moving along, I looked back and saw Michael and all these cameras and reporters just one hole behind us—and gaining on us. Everything slowed down around the thirteenth hole, a par three, up on a hill, shooting downward over some water. We had to wait for the foursome ahead of us to move on, and by the time I got to the tee, Michael's foursome—and his media entourage—had descended upon us.

Let me tell you, I had not hit a ball solidly all day. Now, there I was at the tee, surrounded by all these TV cameras and watchful eyes, and I had to produce a shot under all this scrutiny! It was horrible—but that wasn't all. There was Jordan, smirking and needling, giving me the business the whole time I was warming up and trying to muster my concentration. I mean, you talk about sweaty palms and prayer! *Lord,* I said, *if I can just hit one ball well, I'll be satisfied!*

I settled down, planted my feet, visualized a long, straight, sailing drive—then I took my shot. It was amazing. It climbed into the sky, high, straight, and true. There was total silence all around me as everyone watched the magnificent flight of that ball. . . . even Michael was at a loss for words! The ball headed for the green like a radar-guided Tomahawk missile and landed a nice little putt from the hole. As the rest of my foursome and I took off down the hill toward the green, I could hear Michael's voice: "Hey, Pat! It's easy to see that you don't spend much time at the office!"

That last little jab from Michael Jordan was the finest compliment my modest golfing skills had ever received!

Well, I got down to the green and—far from the glare of the TV cameras and Michael Jordan's frightening grin—I totally blew the putt! But I couldn't have cared less at that point. I had made the one shot I really wanted to make. I had focused on my one brief moment of time, I had fully inhabited that moment, and I had produced an impressive shot.

That's the thing about golf. It is a game that is compressed into a single moment of time. A golf swing is such a simple little maneuver, yet everything depends on the precise moment of that swing. All your concentration must be brought to bear on the *now*. Your last slice or dubbed shot must be forgotten. You don't dare worry about the next tee. The great golfers have learned to do consistently what I was able to do just once in that tournament: For a few brief instants of time, your entire universe must be compressed down to a ball, a club, and a fairway. You must fully inhabit the immediate reality in order to achieve your goal.

In this sense, the game of golf is a concentrated, distilled form of the game of life. In life as in golf, you must fight the battle of the moment, undistracted by the burden of yesterday or the burden of tomorrow. The remorse of yesterday and the dread of tomorrow will drag you down. "Yesterday" is not a day of the week; neither is "someday." Only when you keep your feet firmly planted on the fairway of today can you truly soar!

Former child star and U.S. diplomat Shirley Temple Black learned this truth about living for today. When someone asked her the key to a successful marriage, she told a story about her husband, Charles, and his mother. When Charles was a boy, he approached his mother and asked her, "What was the happiest moment of your life?" His mother surprised him by answering, "This moment, right now." Charles blinked, then asked, "But what about all the other happy moments in your life? What about when you were married?" She laughed and said, "My happiest moment then was then. My happiest moment now is now. You can only really live in the moment you're in. So to me that's always the happiest moment."

Reflecting on this story from her husband's childhood, Mrs.

Black said, "That's the way Charles and I try to live, sharing this moment, right now. There are many nice things to look back on, many to look forward to, but right now is the moment we share together."

Joe Restic, former Harvard football coach, understood this principle and used it to build a winning football team. "I have no agenda," he once said. "I don't believe in five-year, ten-year plans. That's why communism failed. I believe in living for the day. That is what I always have told my players. Enjoy today. Enjoy this practice. Enjoy being with your friends. So many people go through college worried about their future, worried about everything. They miss the moment." Joe Restic knows: Never put off living for some other day. "This is the day the LORD has made," wrote the psalmist. "We will rejoice and be glad in it."[1]

As a baseball-crazy kid growing up in the 1940s and 1950s, I always idolized Stan "The Man" Musial of the St. Louis Cardinals. It was a real thrill when I met him at the Ted Williams Hall of Fame and Museum in February 1995.

Even though Stan's career ended more than thirty years ago, he is really focused on today. I saw him sign dozens of autographs (including one for me), and he personalized every one. Mine read, "To Pat—a great fan—Stan Musial."

On our way to the ceremony in which Stan was voted into the Hitter's Hall of Fame, I walked behind him through a crowd of fans. Suddenly Stan stopped, turned toward the crowd, reached into his coat pocket, pulled out a harmonica, and played "Take Me Out to the Ballgame." You talk about some excited fans.

Then when Stan was introduced to the crowd at the ceremony, he stooped, went into his famous "peek-a-boo" stance, and took a swing at an imaginary ball. He sure was making the most of the moment.

As I watched Stan giving an example of living life to the fullest today, I thought of the story St. Louis sportswriter Bob Broeg told about Stan when he was still an active player.

Broeg said, "A player came into the clubhouse and started to bubble and said to Stan, 'I feel great. My home life is happy. I'm in a groove. I feel like I'm going to get two hits today. Ever feel like that, Stan?' Musial just looked at him and said, 'Every day!'"

Dr. William Osler, whose book *The Principles and Practice of Medicine* (1892) completely transformed the teaching of medicine, once gave a talk to a class of medical students. The subject of the talk: How to succeed in the demanding role of healer. "Banish the future," he said. "Live only for the hour and its allotted work. Think not of the amount to be accomplished, the difficulties to be overcome, or the end to be attained, but set earnestly at the little task at your elbow, letting that be sufficient for the day; for surely our plain duty is, as Carlyle says, 'Not to see what lies dimly at a distance, but to do what lies clearly at hand.'"

That is the same point Jesus made when He said, "Therefore do not worry about tomorrow, for tomorrow will worry about its own things. Sufficient for the day is its own trouble."[2] He wasn't saying (as some people say these days), "Let's just live it up today, live only in the moment, throw caution to the wind and forget about tomorrow." Tomorrow *is* important, but our focus must be on today, not on worries about some other day's troubles. Our goal should be to live fully in the present, focusing on today's tasks, *so that life will be better tomorrow.* To make our dreams of the future come true, we must start *right now,* designing *right now,* hammering and sawing *right now,* sanding and polishing *right now.* Not "someday." Not "when I get around to it." Not "when things settle down a bit." Not "when I get more time." *Now!*

You will never get more time than you have this very day—so *feast* on today!

TIME EQUALS LIFE

"You don't really pay for things with money," says author Charles Spezzano in *What to Do Between Birth and Death*. "You pay for them with time. 'In five years, I'll have put enough away to buy that vacation house we want. Then I'll slow down.' That means the house will cost you five years—one-twelfth of your adult life. Translate the dollar value of the house, car, or anything else into time, and then see if it's still worth it. Sometimes you can't do what you want and have what you want at once because each requires a different expenditure of time. The phrase 'spending your time' is not a metaphor. It's how life works."

Each of us only has a finite number of heartbeats, a finite number of seconds, a finite number of minutes, a finite number of years. When they run out, they're gone. When your time runs out, your life is up. Why, then, are we so nonchalant about "killing time"? When we waste time, we waste life. When we kill time, we kill our own lives. If life is precious, then so is time—and we dare not waste a moment of it.

Someone once made this analogy: Suppose your bank made you a special offer. It will put $86,400 in your account every single morning, and it's all yours to use exactly as you see fit on anything you wish. There's only one catch. Whatever you fail to spend by the end of the day, the bank will take back. The next day, same deal: $86,400 in your account to use as you want—but the bank keeps the unspent surplus. What would you do with that bank account? You *know* what you'd do! You'd go to that bank, first thing every morning, and draw every nickel from that account.

Well, the amazing truth is that this deal has already been made to you. There's an account with your name on it, only instead of dollars, it's filled with seconds—86,400 seconds. At the start of every morning, you have 86,400 seconds to spend any way you choose; at midnight, they're all gone. The next morning, you start all over again, same deal, 86,400 seconds. You can spend those seconds any way you want to. Accomplishing your goals. Exercising your body. Flying paper airplanes. Sleeping. Writing your novel. Calling on clients. Taking a night class. Twiddling your thumbs. Working extra jobs to pay off the bills. Watching TV. Going out on a date. Working out in the gym. Spending time with your kids. Reading a book. Going to a Bible study. Kicking back with friends. Shooting baskets with your kids. Ladling soup at a homeless shelter. Staring into space. Thinking.

I'm not passing judgment one way or the other on any of those activities. Maybe you need a little extra sleep or some "downtime" to recharge your batteries; only you can decide what is a productive use of your time and what isn't. The point is, it's your life and your choice. If you *fail* to make wise use of today's deposit of precious, irreplaceable seconds, then the loss is yours as well.

People who have developed a sense of the preciousness of time are a valuable resource. They are the go-getting, entrepreneurial spirits of our society. They are the trustworthy, reliable, promotable employees. They are the businesspeople, craftspeople, politicians, doctors, researchers, scientists, entertainers, writers, and tradespeople you can count on to get the job done. They are the people who make the world a better place. Leaders, managers, and employers who respect the value of time also respect others who value time. They know that a respect for the preciousness of time is a key ingredient to success—and they always select such people for advancement, praise, and promotion.

I can tell you from my own experience that the great sports leaders of our time have understood this principle too. In our game, basketball, time is everything. You have four twelve-minute quarters to do the job you came to do—forty-eight minutes to score more points than the other guy. Time is everything, even on individual plays. As soon as the ball is inbounded, the shot clock starts ticking: twenty-four, twenty-three, twenty-two . . . They can't just stall and hem and haw and pass the ball around. They have just twenty-four seconds to shoot, or else the ball turns over to the other team. Time is precious in basketball, in football, in hockey, in soccer—in practically every sport but baseball!

And life is like that: Every moment counts as we keep struggling to move closer to our goals. Meanwhile the shot clock is ticking. In basketball and in life, we rarely find ourselves open, with plenty of time to take a nice, leisurely shot. Usually, we find ourselves double-teamed, with nothing to do but force the shot any way we can, all the while conscious of that shot clock, tick-tick-ticking down to zero. The big difference between basketball and life is that the rules of the game allow you to call a time-out. The rules of life don't afford you that luxury. In life, you have to take your best shot while the clock is ticking, under the pressure and stress of the moment. Sometimes your shot will bounce off the rim, sometimes it'll miss the backboard altogether—but sometimes you'll make that pressure shot, and it'll slip through the hoop like water through a sieve, nothing but net. (And, of course, you can always hope for a three-pointer!)

There's no finer feeling in the world, my friend—in the sports world *or* the real world—than coming through with the pressure shot.

TWO "ENEMIES OF NOW"

We have to live in the now, act in the now, achieve and accomplish in the now in order to experience the fruit of that action tomorrow. There are several great "enemies of the now" that we are all prone to and that will defeat us if we let them. Two of these "enemies of the now" include procrastination and waiting for "just the right moment."

Procrastination

We all too easily defer our dreams, postpone our projects, and miss our opportunities. "I'll do it tomorrow," we say. "I'll start it tomorrow. I'll finish it tomorrow." But what is this thing called "tomorrow"? *It's a day that never comes!* The problem with "tomorrows" is that if you pile up enough of them—procrastinated tomorrows, daydreamed tomorrows, "someday" tomorrows—you eventually discover that you're left with nothing but a life filled with empty yesterdays.

"The tragedy of life," said Richard L. Evans, "is not that it ends so soon, but that we wait so long to begin it." So do it today. Do it now. Wring every drop of benefit you can from the present moment.

"But I can't do it today!" you may say. "I've got too many other priorities, emergencies, crises, and interruptions in my life right now! I want to do it today, but there aren't enough hours in a day!" Wrong. You've got just as many hours in your day as the next person. And everybody has priorities, emergencies, crises, and interruptions. But some people rise above those hindrances and still accomplish their goals and make their dreams come true. How do they do it? It's not a question of how many hours a person has, but how much desire a person has. If you really want it bad enough, you'll get it done. If your dream is really all that important to you, you'll make it a priority, you'll treat it as an emergency, you'll wade through every other crisis and interruption in your life in order to make that dream come true.

If something bristled inside you as you read the previous paragraph, if you felt like screaming, "No! My situation is different!" and if you felt like throwing this book against the wall, then I would suggest that perhaps you are in some sort of denial state. When it makes us mad to hear the truth about ourselves, that's denial. Let go of your defenses, my friend. Recognize that *you* are responsible for all the hindrances you allow to get between you and your dreams. Make a decision to make your dreams your top priority. Don't procrastinate and don't wait for just the right moment.

Waiting for "just the right moment"

Philip Brewer, executive director of Emmaus Christian Leadership Assistance Program in southern California, recalls a trip he took to Europe in 1977. "I went to England and interviewed John Stott," he recently told me, "and I went to Switzerland and interviewed Francis Schaeffer and Paul Tournier, the great Swiss psychiatrist. These were some of the great Christian leaders of our time, and I wanted to learn from them all I could about their thinking. I came away from each of these meetings profoundly impressed and changed by all that I heard. But there is one statement that Dr. Tournier made which has particularly impacted my life ever since.

"He said to me in his wonderful French-accented, broken English, 'People are always looking for the right time and the perfect place to write, to paint, to accomplish some goal. They say, "I have to be in the mountains, I have to be on the coast, everything must be just so." But if you look at all the great achievements of history, you will see that they have largely been done in cold, cramped, unpicturesque conditions. The birth of Christ was like that; it took place in a smelly stable. Look where all the great people and all the great achievements have come from, and you see that they always seem to come from deprived, uncomfortable, unromantic situations.'

"That hit me right between the eyes. It took me years to fully absorb the truth that Dr. Tournier had given to me. I'm still absorbing it. I think he saw in me that perfectionist streak that so often keeps me from starting a project until 'just the right moment.' I want a cup of coffee, but I want to drink it on the beach in Maui. The point is this: If you're going to write the Great American Novel, then write it. Don't put it off until everything's just so. If you don't have a computer to write with, get a college-ruled notebook and a fountain pen. Can't afford that? Then use the back of your cut-off notice from the gas company and one of those stubby little pencils from the library. Just *do it*. And do it *now*."

You can avoid both of these "enemies of the now" by adopting the Grab 15 Principle.

THE GRAB 15 PRINCIPLE

Few of us are truly aware of how much priceless, irreplaceable time slips right through our fingers, as if it were nothing more than sand. In her book *Stress That Motivates*, time-management expert Dru Scott shares a secret that is literally worth *millions*! That secret is called "The Grab 15 Principle," and it is the key to "procrastination-proofing" your life.

The idea is simple: First, select an important task that you have been wanting to get accomplished, one of your dreams, the kind of task about which you keep saying, "Someday, when I get the time . . ." It might be the book you want to write, the garage you want to clean, the garden you want to grow, the exercise program you want to begin, the room you want to remodel, the business you want to start, the new computer skill you want to learn, the new language you want to master.

Next, make a commitment to yourself that you will "Grab 15" every day without fail—that is, that you will devote just fifteen minutes of every day to your cherished dream, no matter what, come rain or come shine. There are several reasons that this technique is so powerful. First, all those little fifteen-minute chunks of time add up—fast! As Dru Scott points out, even if you take Sundays off from your "Grab 15" commitment, those fifteen minutes a day times six days equals ninety minutes a week—*or a whopping seventy-eight hours in a year!* What you are doing is taking time that might otherwise just fall through the cracks and using it to add the equivalent of *almost two forty-hour workweeks* to your life! Think what you could accomplish if someone gave you an extra two weeks out of the year to work on it!

Another reason this technique is so powerful is that it boosts your creativity. It keeps you constantly thinking about your project, day by day by day, because you are working on it on a continual, daily basis. Instead of having to start over from scratch every six months and say to yourself, "Now, where was I on this project?" you have *momentum* built up. Ideas and insights will come to you in the shower, on your commute, and over breakfast, because your project is continually on your mind! You'll be more productive and creative in each of those fifteen-minute blocks of time.

Another reason this technique is so powerful is that you'll find it hard to stop at fifteen minutes! "Some days," says Dru Scott, "after you finish your fifteen-minute commitment, you will be on a roll. You will feel like continuing. And you will. That bonus effort will bring you that much closer to your goal."[3]

WHAT IF YOUR "NOW" SEEMS HOPELESS?

At this moment, your dream of success may seem as far away as the far side of the moon. You may be wishing for financial security, college money for your kids, a big house with a three-car garage—yet at this moment you may be out to the max on six different credit cards with no way in sight of ever paying it off. Or you may be wanting to go back for that college degree you let slip through your fingers when you were "just a kid"—but you don't see how you can find the time for school while working two dead-end, low-wage jobs back-to-back. Or you may be wanting to remodel your house, but your busy schedule doesn't offer any hope of a letup between now and the next millennium. It's hopeless. You're sunk. Ain't no way, right?

Wrong!

You just need a clearer perspective on your problems and your goals. You need to break down your goals into a series of "doable" mini-goals, then knock down each of those mini-goals one by one until you reach your destination. Can't be done? It *has* been done. People can and do beat the odds and attain their long-shot, "hopeless" goals—and they do it by determination and by taking on their big goals, one little task at a time.

Red Auerbach, the former head coach of the Boston Celtics, gives us another one of those sports lessons that all of us can apply to our everyday lives. He recalls two thrilling, unbelievable championship play-offs the Celts played after he quit coaching, one in 1968, the other in 1981. Both of these seven-game series were against the Philadelphia 76ers—and I vividly remember the '81 series because I was the general manager of the 76ers at that time! In both of those series, Boston found itself at the end of game four with only one win and three losses. Just one more loss and that was it for the entire play-off, over, the end, period, finis. Hopeless situations, right?

"Guess again," said Auerbach. In both play-offs, '68 and '81, Boston came back to win the next three games straight! Incredible? You bet! Impossible? Of course not—though it must have seemed so at the end of game four. So how did they do it?

"Simple," explained Auerbach. "You don't try to win three straight games. You don't even think of that. Game seven is not important at that point. Neither is game six. And for that matter, you're not even concentrating on winning game five. Here's what you tell yourself: 'They haven't won a thing yet. They still have to beat us one more time, and that's not going to be easy.'" That's the first step: Don't look too far down the road. Don't focus on the future. Don't worry about games you're not even playing yet. Focus on what you have to do right now.

"You break it down like this," Auerbach continues. "You say to yourself, 'Let's win the first quarter of game five. That's all we're concerned with now, the first quarter. Then we'll just play them even in the second and we'll have the lead at the half. That'll give them something to worry about. Second half, same thing. Win the third quarter and increase our lead. Then stay with them in the fourth. If we can do that, the game's ours.'"

That's the trick: Break the goal down into "doable" tasks. Don't think, "Oh, wow, we've got to win three games straight." That's too big, too forbidding, too intimidating. Just say to yourself, "My job right now is to win this quarter, this little twelve-minute segment of the game. Hey, I can do that!"

Auerbach compares this approach to the "one day at a time" philosophy of Alcoholics Anonymous. "Don't tell a man he can never have a drink for the rest of his life," he explains. "That's too long, too much to deal with. No one can discipline himself forever. But today? Yeah. I can get through today all right. Great! Then let's not worry about tomorrow right now. Let's just get through today. We'll worry about tomorrow when it comes."

(Okay, I've let Auerbach have his say—and he makes a great point about staying focused on the present moment and the present task. But keep this story in mind, because in Chapter 10, I'll come back and give you *my* perspective on that 1981 series between the Sixers and the Celts—because there's a point *I* want to make from the flip side of that same story!)

So how do you translate Auerbach's basketball story into a workable strategy for everyday life? You start by looking carefully at your big goals, and then you break those big goals down into small tasks. Need to pay off six credit cards? Don't look at all those credit cards and the job of paying off all that money. Instead, start with one credit card, the one with the highest interest rate. Get a part-time job and apply every cent to that one card. Discipline yourself to live within your means. Chip away at your debt week by week and month by month. When you get one card paid off, move on to the next. In time, you'll clear up all of that debt—and then you'll start building net worth. The only way to get out of a financial hole (apart from winning the lottery) is the same way you got in: a little bit at a time.

You can take this same approach with any goal. That college degree. That novel you've been dreaming of writing. That home remodeling project. Reading the Bible through in a year. A weight-loss program. Just break your goal down into bite-size pieces and chew slowly. Practice the Grab 15 Principle. Stay disciplined and determined. Be true to your commitment. Work hard. Persevere. You'll come out on top and be a champion—just like those down-and-out Celtics. "When you're down three to one to Philly," Auerbach concludes, "you fight your way back, one step at a time, one quarter at a time, one game at a time. It works. We've got the flags to prove it."

YOU HAVE ALL THE TIME IN THE WORLD

"Life is too short!" "There aren't enough hours in a day!" "If I just had more time!" You've heard those complaints—and probably even voiced them a time or two. "Those who make the worst use of their time," observed Jean de La Bruyère in a stinging rebuke, "are the first to complain of its brevity."

This world is full of people who are standing around, "marking time," "killing time," wondering when someone is going to tap them on the shoulder and point them to their purpose and goal in life. It isn't gonna happen. You were put on this planet for a reason and you'd better hurry up and figure out what that reason is because you're not going to be on this planet forever. I can't think of a greater tragedy in life than coming to the end of it and having to say, "I wonder what I was supposed to do with my life. I never really had a chance to live. I never did anything meaningful with my life. I never knew what my purpose was."

How about you? Do you know what your purpose in life is?

And are you using your time—the precious, irreplaceable raw material of your life—to move yourself closer to your goals?

Most people just daydream about their goals. The successful people are those who have learned how to hammer their daydreams into hard reality. Like Mariah Carey, they dream of a musical career, then they go out and work and sacrifice on a daily basis—and they make it happen. Like Shaquille O'Neal or Anfernee Hardaway, they dream of a career in the NBA, then they work day after day, honing their skills, building their strength and stamina, competing against others with the same dream—and they make it happen. Like Walt Disney, they dream of a wonderland where the impossible happens before our eyes, then they struggle and sweat and invest and risk, day after day—and they make it happen.

In her book *How to Put More Time in Your Life*, Dru Scott tells the story of her special friend, Margaret, who discovered at the age of forty-two that she only had a week to live. Margaret had been having a series of intense, unexplained headaches. By the time the doctors diagnosed the cause of the headaches as a brain tumor, there was nothing they could do to save her.

"I couldn't believe it," Dru Scott recalled. "I'd seen her just four weeks earlier. She had been as blithe and full of vitality as ever. She and her husband had an exceptionally happy marriage, two wonderful sons, rewarding careers—everything to live for. I couldn't believe that she would die so suddenly, in such a cruelly unexpected way."

Two days before Margaret's death, Dru talked to her on the phone. The pain medication slowed Margaret's speech but could not quench her spirit. "For some reason," said Margaret, "during these last six months, I've been thinking more about how I spend my time. I'd always thought of myself as primarily career-oriented, but I now realize that my family is most important to me. I've been concentrating on spending more time with them. . . . It's so much easier to face what I am facing now because I've spent my time doing what really counts."

Dru remembered visiting Margaret at her home, and Margaret had gestured to a messy desk in one corner. "I should feel guilty about this mess," Margaret had said, laughing, "but there are so many things more important to me than having a clean desk. The things that count come first." During her last months, even though she had not known that she was nearing the end of her life, Margaret had spent a lot of time with her husband and her young sons, doing fun things, building relationships, building family memories.

"As I sat by the phone, reliving my memories of Margaret," Dru concluded, "I thought over what she had said to me about doing what counts. I realized that if I were in a similar situation, I couldn't make that statement. I wasn't spending my time on the things that really mattered. I was allowing too much of it to slip away while I attended to things I felt guilty about. Were it not for Margaret's words, I might never have taken the time to discover what really counts in my own life and to do it every day. . . .

"Accept the full gift of this moment—you deserve it. Take hold of today. Use it, enjoy it in the most exciting, creative way you can. This is a day for you to do the things that are most important to you. This is a day to know how good it is to be alive."[4]

Make today pay off tomorrow. Make the future happen, and start right now. That was Walt Disney's first secret of success. That was the secret that separated him from the masses: He knew how to make today pay off for tomorrow. Everything he did was a positive, proactive investment in the future. Very few people have a handle on that principle—and the ones who do are the ones we call "success stories." The key to grasping and using this principle is to understand, clearly and accurately, what *time* truly is, and how it is to be used.

This day is yours. Invest it wisely. However you use it, whatever you do with it, today is a down payment on your tomorrow.

In the next chapter, we will examine that third block of time, the one where all your present efforts, expenditures, and investments will pay off: *Tomorrow.*

CHAPTER 4

Tomorrow, or, How to Build the Rest of Your Life

○ *The best way to predict the future is to make it happen.*
Alan Kay, executive, Apple Computers

○ *The pace of events is moving so fast that unless we can find some way to keep our sights on tomorrow, we cannot expect to be in touch with today.*
Dean Rusk, former Secretary of State of the United States

Amusement park?
When Walt Disney's staff heard him use that phrase, they thought they knew what he had in mind—a Coney Island–type carnival with bumper cars, Ferris wheels, roller coasters, and hot dog stands. To be sure, the Boss would add some special Disney touches, maybe have some painted pictures of

Mickey and Minnie on the plywood facades of the fun house, but other than that—hey, an amusement park is an amusement park. Nothing new there, right?

Wrong!

"As usual," Disney writer Charles Shows later recalled, "Walt was way ahead of us—and ahead of his time. He had his own unique and incredible ideas of what his Disneyland would be."[1] Walt Disney wasn't looking to the amusement parks of the past for his inspiration. He dreamed of a totally *new* kind of family amusement experience, something that had never existed before, the theme park of the future.

Soon after arriving at Disney Studios, another Disney writer, Bob Thomas, was introduced to Walt's vision of the future. Walt took Bob Thomas for a drive in his convertible on a cool April morning in 1955. The air along Harbor Boulevard was fragrant with the rich honey-blossom perfume from the orange groves that sprawled over most of Anaheim. That was in the days before Anaheim became an urbanized crazy quilt of hotels, motels, trailer parks, and fast-food restaurants, back when the main business of Orange County, California was, well, *oranges*.

Walt pulled the car into a huge parking lot—a vast expanse of blacktop marked off in freshly painted parking spaces, a testimony to Disney's unquenchable vision. He just *knew* that, come summer, those parking spaces would be filled—and so would his dream park. From the car, Bob Thomas caught his first glimpse of the now-familiar train station.

They got out of the car and strolled through the main gate. As they walked, Disney pointed out all the amazing features of this sparkling new entertainment village he had conceived, built, and lent his own name to: *Disneyland.*

"Look at that detail in the train station woodwork," he said. "We got hundreds of photographs and drawings of railroad stations in the last century, and we copied all the details."

Farther along, they came to Main Street, which was still unpainted and had much of its steel understructure exposed. But Disney didn't see any of the unfinished or incomplete aspects of his living tribute to Americana. He saw the future reality, that Main Street to be, the idealized and reconstructed vision of the little Missouri town of his youth. "Over there's the ice-cream parlor, with marble-topped tables and wireback chairs," he said. "And over there is a candy shop, where people can watch old-fashioned fudge-making and taffy-pulling. And there's the music store and there's the silent movie house."

They went on to Fantasyland, where Bob Thomas marveled at the sight of the blue-turreted Sleeping Beauty Castle—a piece of storybook fantasy in the middle of southern California. Then Walt led him to Frontierland, through Davy Crockett's stockade. They passed the Mark Twain riverboat and the Painted Desert and the emerald jungles of Adventureland.

Finally they came to a place that seemed to hold a special fascination for Walt Disney—a brave new world he called Tomorrowland. It's entirely fitting that one of Disneyland's main themes is tomorrow. Tomorrowland is a realm that expresses the spirit of its creator, for it is entirely devoted to dreams of the future. There, recalled Thomas, "a massive rocket pointed skyward. Inside, Disney said, visitors would enjoy the fantasy of being transported to the moon and back. Kids who dreamed of driving would be able to do so on a miniature freeway, operating gasoline-fueled cars."[2]

Even Disney himself, as visionary as he was, did not imagine the Tomorrowland attractions that lay beyond the horizon of 1955: Space Mountain, Captain Eo, George Lucas's spaceflight simulator Star Tours, and much more. Forty years later, Disneyland continues on and on into the future, growing and changing, spinning off even bigger versions of itself in places like Orlando, Tokyo, and Paris. In fact, even as I write these words, the Orlando Magic Kingdom is unveiling a totally reimagined, reinvented Tomorrowland featuring an all-new, high-tech "sensory thriller" attraction called ExtraTERRORestrial Alien Encounter.

We look at Disneyland today, with the advantage of 20/20 hindsight, and we say, "Of course! Just what the world needed! How could it fail?" In fact, however, *most* business and entertainment experts who looked at Disney's plans prior to July 17, 1955, were *predicting* failure, as I mentioned earlier. After all, though the Disney company's animated shorts and features had been immensely popular for some thirty years, the company had always struggled financially. In fact, Disney's animators had sometimes labored for weeks without a paycheck in order to bring a feature film to the screen.

But Disney's philosophy of the future was simple, powerful, and effective: "Think, believe, dream, and dare." After thirty years of laboring and battling for survival, always operating on the brink of financial ruin, Walt Disney finally experienced true financial success—and it was Disneyland that finally put Walt and his company solidly in the black. Disney proved it: You've got to think "tomorrow." He made sure that everything he did today had a payoff for tomorrow. And when his investment paid off, it paid off *big!*

THINKING "TOMORROW" IN THE WILLIAMS HOUSEHOLD

Around our house, we try to encourage our nineteen kids to think "tomorrow" and live in today. We try to build a "think, believe, dream, and dare" atmosphere within our family, so that our kids will be unleashed to go as far as they want to go. Here are just three examples:

• Our daughter Karyn had entered the Miss Teenage Florida pageant. At age fifteen, she was one of the youngest entries. A precocious, mature, levelheaded kid, Karyn is a good student and was captain of the J.V. cheerleading team at Edgewater High at the time. One of our four birth kids, she has had some wonderful breaks in her life, including the opportunity in the late 1980s to work with Carol Lawrence in the Epcot Christmas Show. Carol, of course, is an accomplished actress, dancer, and singer with an international reputation. With her enormous energy and enthusiasm about life, as well as her warm personality and strong values, she was a great role model for Karyn. Carol gave Karyn a big boost and helped her to see the wide-open possibilities of her tomorrow.

So when Karyn went into the Miss Teenage Florida pageant, she went in believing anything was possible. She made the top fifteen finalists—then was cut from the top five. She was disappointed. She cried. I gave her a couple of days to grieve her loss; then I sat down and talked to Karyn about her future. "Dad," she said, "I want to get back in that contest next year. You know, I could have three more years in the pageant. I really think I could win it! And you know what I want to do then? After high school, I want to go to the University of Florida, and I want to be a cheerleader there. When the Gators come running out on the field in September of '97—my freshman year—I want to lead them down the field doing front flips! And then I want to be Miss Florida. And then before I graduate, I want to be Miss America. And then I want to be an actress—just like Carol Lawrence."

I heard that and thought, *Wow! Here's a kid who knows how to think "tomorrow"!*

• Another of our birth children, Bobby, was born small and has fought an uphill battle of size all his life. Even so, he's a talented athlete, and baseball is his life. Bobby started playing Little League ball when we came to Florida nine years ago. It was obvious to me, even when he was ten or eleven, that Bobby had ability. It was obvious also that he had inherited his father's "wheels"—that is, he didn't run all that fast. So his best shot would be as a catcher, where running speed is not a critical factor. He showed a nice aptitude for that spot and got great coaching throughout middle school and high school.

Still, throughout his school years, he had a lot of doubts about his ability to compete—a lack of confidence based on his struggle with his size. At every level of competition, as he moved from J.V. to varsity, advancing grade by grade, advancing to tryout camps, even attending a fall tryout camp run by the Houston Astros, he demonstrated that he could compete—yet he continued to worry about the next level.

Finally, in November 1994, Bobby was approached by Bob Rikeman, the head baseball coach at Rollins College in Winter Park, Florida. "Bobby," he said, "you're the best high school catcher I've seen this year in the state of Florida. I want you at Rollins, and here is our scholarship offer to you." And it was a very substantial offer! A few days later, Bobby accepted the offer. Later, we had a talk, and Bobby described to me his thoughts about "tomorrow."

"Dad," he said, "here are my goals: I want to be drafted by a major league team this spring when I graduate, just to have it on my record. I'm still going to go to school. After college, I'm going to sign up with a team and play in the pros. After my big-league career is over, then I'll probably go into the front office . . . just like you."

What a thrill it was to hear that! Bobby may only stand five feet seven inches and weigh 150 pounds, but in his mind, he is shattering all the ceilings that used to hover over his life—ceilings of fear, ceilings of self-doubt, ceilings of self-limitation. He's thinking "tomorrow"—and he's working like crazy every day to sharpen his skills and build his endurance to make "tomorrow" happen!

Then there's Katarina.

• In 1991 a beautiful, preschool-age Romanian child, our Katarina, joined our big, happy family. I'll level with you: Kati is not the most talented of our nineteen children, and she's not a stellar student. She hasn't demonstrated any great prowess in sports (gonna have to work on *that!*). But she's a great kid, and even now, she is working on discovering herself and exploring her potential.

Just recently—while this book was being written, in fact—I sat down for a talk with Kati. I knew that she looked around at all the other kids in her family and compared herself with them. They were baseball players, swimmers, A students, or whatever, and Kati had started to view herself as a plodder. I didn't want her to have that kind of self-image, so I said to her, "Kati, let me tell you something. I'm gonna predict that—if you want to—you could go to New York and be a high fashion model. If that's the kind of future you really desire, you could be on the cover of magazines in about fifteen years."

Now, I'm not sure how much of that she understood, but I saw a light come on in her eyes. I had planted a vision of a possible tomorrow in her mind. Well, Kati took that vision and ran with it. Right away, she ran and told her brothers and sisters she was going to be a New York model. The next morning, I went in her room to wake her up, and she sat bolt upright in bed and said, "Am I still going to New York to be a model?"

I said, "If that's what you want, then absolutely!"

That afternoon, a note came home from her teacher at school: "Delighted to hear that Kati is going to New York to model." I wrote a note back: "Not real soon—we hope in fifteen years!" We later found out that the school bus driver was dialed in on Kati's future. At eight years old, this kid was thinking "tomorrow" and believing in herself.

Now, do I know for sure that Karyn is going to be Miss America, or that Bobby is going to catch in the major leagues, or that Kati is going to be a New York model? Of course not. There are no guarantees in life. Each of these kids still has a number of years to explore new possibilities and new avenues. They may each take some unexpected detours along the way. But they are no longer drifting toward a murky future out there in the fog. They are being drawn in a focused direction because a little bit of light has been shone on tomorrow. They are thinking positively about their futures, and when you think "tomorrow," it changes the way you live today. It motivates you. It inspires you. It lifts you. It calls forth your best efforts and unleashes you to be the best you can be.

What's more, you can be a success in life without having your picture on the cover of *Sports Illustrated, Forbes,* or *Elle.* I'll be proud of all my kids, no matter what direction they take their lives, no matter what level of achievement they reach. The important thing right now is that they have dreams, they have focus, they have confidence, they have belief in themselves. Once a kid is freed up to think "tomorrow," anything can happen!

FOUR "TOMORROW STRATEGIES" TO HELP YOU SHAPE YOUR FUTURE

In the previous chapter we saw that it is crucially important to stay focused on today, on meeting today's challenges, on solving today's problems, on getting today's work done. Why? *To build a better tomorrow,* that's why! Tomorrow is our goal; today is the distance we have to run in order to reach our goal.

But before we can get to our goal, we have to define that goal. We have to take stock of our lives, our dreams, our hopes, our desires, and our ambitions. We have to decide exactly what kind of tomorrow we want. Then and only then can we start working today to make our dreams of tomorrow come true.

Walt Disney summed up this principle in the simple phrase, "Think 'tomorrow.'" Stephen R. Covey, in his book *The Seven Habits of Highly Effective People,* expressed this same principle with the words, "Begin with the end in mind." He writes:

> To begin with the end in mind means to start with a clear understanding of your destination. It means to know where you're going so that you better understand where you are now and so that the steps you take are always in the right direction.
>
> It's incredibly easy to get caught up in an activity trap, in the busyness of life, to work harder and harder at climbing the ladder of success only to discover it's leaning against the wrong wall. It is possible to be busy—very busy—without being very effective. . . .
>
> How different our lives are when we really know what is deeply important to us, and, keeping that picture in mind, we manage ourselves each day to be and to do what really matters most. If the ladder is not leaning against the right wall, every step we take just gets us to the wrong place faster. We may be very busy, we may be very *efficient,* but we will also be truly *effective* only when we begin with the end in mind.[3]

In this chapter, we will examine four ways to "think 'tomorrow,'" to "begin with the end in mind," so that you can begin in an effective way to hammer your dreams of tomorrow into reality. Those four "tomorrow strategies" are:

1. Define your mission in life.
2. Define your core principles.
3. Set your priorities.
4. Make your plans.

Let's look at each of these strategies in turn.

Tomorrow Strategy No. 1: Define Your Mission in Life

I was recently invited to speak at a Fellowship of Christian Athletes rally at Lee Middle School in Orlando, where seven of our children attend. It's tough when kids know their dad is about to give a speech to their friends. They all wanted to tell me what I should talk about. "Tell funny stories, Dad!" said one. "Tell 'em about Shaq!" said another. "Tell 'em about me!" said another.

"You'll find out what I'm going to talk about along with everybody else," I said, with my most inscrutable grin.

So on the appointed day, I got up before a hundred thirteen- and fourteen-year-olds (including my own seven) and said, "Let me tell you something. You young men and young women are at a very crucial point in your life. You've got all your best years right in front of you. You can do anything you want with your future. But you need to start making some important decisions *right now.* God has given you certain talents, abilities, and dreams, and *now* is the time to explore all those gifts and to begin discovering your mission in life. Kids, you're not just a cosmic accident. God has an exciting future planned for you. He wants to use you in a big way. So I encourage you to find your purpose in life—call it your mission in life, call it God's will and plan for your life.

"You know, kids, many people get to the end of their lives without ever figuring out what their purpose was or why they were here. And that's really sad, isn't it? They say, 'If only I had made better choices when I was young . . .' or 'I never did what I should have been doing,' or 'I just did what other people expected of me,' or 'I just did what my parents wanted me to,' or saddest of all, 'I just drifted through my life and frittered it all away. I just never bothered to plug into my mission in life.'

"I'm sure you guys have all heard of Terry Cummings, a longtime NBA player who now plays for San Antonio. 'I've learned,' he once said, 'that knowing what God wants you to do in your life is like having a road map to a place you've never been before.' So I encourage you to reach for that road map, to seek God's will, to find your mission in life, because that mission will carry you unerringly into the future, into places you've never been before."

After that talk, I got to chat with many of those kids, and I was glad to see that most of them took what I said to heart. Sure, some wanted to know what Shaq is really like or to talk about what kind of year Penny Hardaway is having with the Magic. But most of them wanted to know more about defining their mission in life. And that gives me a lot of hope for the future of those kids.

I believe that all truly successful people have a mission in life. *All.* No exceptions.

How can I be so sure there are no exceptions? Because the only way anyone can *truly* be successful in life is if they are accomplishing their mission in life. Any undisciplined, unmotivated dunce with a dollar in his pocket can hit the lottery for $50 million and become filthy rich—but that doesn't mean he is successful. It just means he's a *rich* dunce. Such a person has no mission or purpose in life. Before he won the lottery, he was just taking up space on the planet; after winning the lottery, he's taking up space in the high-rent district.

To be truly successful, you have to be able to define and articulate your mission. You have to be able to write it down and keep it in front of you. A clearly defined mission in life gives you an objective yardstick. Your mission in life is a scorecard you can use so that when you get to the end of your day, or the end of another year, or the end of your life, you can look back and say, "I carried out my mission. I have been a success in life."

Why does the word *success* mean so many different things to different people? Because different people have different perceptions of exactly what their mission in life should be. What is Ted Turner's mission in life? Rich DeVos's? Bill Clinton's? Hillary Rodham Clinton's? Shaquille O'Neal's? David Letterman's? Kevin Costner's? Saddam Hussein's? Mother Teresa's? Rush Limbaugh's? Bill Gates's? Connie Chung's? Pat Robertson's? Stephen Hawking's? Whitney Houston's? Larry King's? Michael Eisner's?

I can't speak for any of those people, but I can tell you a little bit about Pat Williams's mission in life. First, I want to know God, because I think that's what we're here for as a human race. Second, I want to be the best husband and father I can be, because none of my other achievements means anything if I'm a failure in my own home. Third, I want to be the best sports executive I can be, because I deeply believe that all work is honorable, and I honor myself and I honor God when I do my job to the absolute utmost of my ability. Fourth, I want to use the gifts and the platform God has given me through speaking, writing, and professional sports to impact people, to carry the message God has given me, to improve the lives of as many people as possible, and to encourage as many people as possible to reach out to the lost and lonely kids in this world through such means as adoption. Those are my goalposts, and I'm charging toward 'em with every ounce of energy in my body. Some days I fall short, but I get right up and keep going, because I know which direction to run. I know where my goalposts are.

What about you? What's your mission in life? There are so many varieties of people, so many individual goals and dreams to be fulfilled, so many ways of completing the sentence, "My mission in life is . . ." Once you have defined your mission in life, you have defined what the word *success* means to you. The only way you can truly feel successful and satisfied in this life is if you have a set of goalposts to run toward.

Now, I don't want to mislead you when I talk about "goalposts." That metaphor only goes so far. In a real sense, a mission in life is not so much a set of *goalposts* but *guideposts,* because true success is not a destination but a journey. To be successful doesn't mean you've reached the finish line, that you've won the trophy, and that you can now go fishing for the rest of your life. Rather, being successful means you have achieved the ability to carry out your mission in life on a continual, effective basis. The person whose mission in life is to write novels and entertain millions is not going to be satisfied with one best-seller. To that person, "success" means arriving at a place where he can devote the rest of his life to doing what he loves and what he feels called to do. The same is true of the person whose mission in life is:

- To serve God full-time.
- To heal the sick.
- To perform on the stage or screen.
- To perform on the basketball court.
- To run a successful company.
- To lead a government.
- To build an emotionally and spiritually healthy family.

Most people equate "success" with "the lifestyles of the rich and famous." Personally, I don't think owning a mansion in Brentwood or having your picture on the cover of *People* magazine is a good indicator of true success. Otherwise, people like John Belushi, Kurt Cobain, and River Phoenix would still be alive. If you are rich and famous but completely miserable, then you have failed in the most important task in life: finding a sense of meaning, satisfaction, and joy in your life.

I'm not saying money is unimportant. But I would not encourage anyone to define his or her mission in life as "Make lots of money." Material riches can be taken away from you by thieves, con men, the IRS, bad breaks, bad investments, natural disaster, or catastrophic illness. *Real* riches—a relationship with God, a warm and loving family, closely bonded friendships, personal integrity, honor, a good name—these are riches that can never be taken away from you. Personally, these are the riches I've devoted my life to acquiring. I agree with the words of the great American psychologist-philosopher William James, who said, "The great use of life is to spend it for something that outlasts it."

How do you begin to define your mission in life?

Step 1: You begin by taking out some quality time for meditation and reflection. Clear your mind of all the externally imposed restrictions on your life, all the fears, shoulds, and oughts that keep you trapped in a place where you really don't want to be: "My parents always wanted me to be a _____." "My spouse says I should _____." "I've always done what I'm doing. It's too late for me to change." "I don't deserve to be happy." "I'm afraid of risk, change, and hard work."

Step 2: Ask yourself some hard questions, and give yourself some honest answers:

- What am I good at?
- What abilities and qualities do I possess?
- What abilities and qualities have other people, whose opinions I respect, affirmed in my life?
- What am I passionate about?
- If I could do anything I want with my life, what would it be?

- What is the one thing I could do in life that I could do eagerly and joyfully every day of my life?

This is the brainstorming and spitballing stage. Feel free to let your mind roam freely. Throw ideas out like sparks from a Roman candle, scribble them on a sheet of paper, no matter how crazy or impractical. Even a crazy idea may spark a brilliant one. Don't censor yourself. Don't stifle your imagination. All things are possible.

As you start to formulate answers to these questions, you may feel a nagging nudge of negative thinking: "I couldn't really do that! I couldn't devote my life to doing something I enjoy; I'd feel too guilty!" Tell that negative little voice to get lost. Don't discard any possibilities—at least not at first.

Step 3: After you have begun to clarify in your own mind what you'd like to do, what your ideal life would be like, then ask yourself:

"What would I have to do to make this dream a reality in my life? Go back to school? Move to another city? Change jobs? Start my own business? Sell my house?" This is the point in the process you begin to get sensible and practical. You weed out ideas that are clearly unworkable. And you start figuring out ways to put shoe leather to the dreams that *just might* have a chance of coming true.

Step 4: Work out a practical plan for achieving your mission in life. Figure out the logistics—how much money you need to save or borrow, where you are going to get the training you need, what part of the country (or the world) you need to move to. Then put your plan into action.

In order to stay focused on your goals for tomorrow, you need to keep your life mission always before you. But how do you do that? A friend of mine recently shared with me his plan for keeping faith with his vision of tomorrow. He maintains a daily discipline of prayer, meditation, and journaling, and he keeps his journal in a file on his computer. Every time he boots his computer at the beginning of the day, this journal file comes up on the screen, and at the top of the file is what he calls his "Personal Mission Statement." He shared this statement with me, so that I can share it here with you:

My Personal Mission Statement

Today, I commit myself to:
- Seek God's friendship and help.
- Be effective and successful as a husband and father.
- Be a self-controlled and self-disciplined person.
- Be orderly in all dimensions of life.
- Be proactive, not reactive.
- Be positive.
- Be a person who never compromises integrity and honesty.
- Plan tomorrow's work today.
- Live now.

Tomorrow Strategy No. 2: Define Your Core Principles

One man who had a profound impact on my early career in sports management was Mr. R. E. Littlejohn, the owner of the Spartanburg Phillies, then a farm club of the Philadelphia Phillies. Mr. Littlejohn was an astute businessman and an avid supporter of minor-league baseball. He was also a man of uncompromising principle.

Now, I was raised by parents who taught me right from wrong and encouraged good character traits. I already placed a premium on such principles as honesty and integrity even before I met Mr. Littlejohn. But when you're twenty-four and you're starting your career in the dog-eat-dog world of professional sports, trying to get to the top quickly, trying to become a big-time executive in your field, you look around you and you see a lot of people operating on the theory that you do whatever it takes to get the job done. So I'm grateful that Mr. Littlejohn got ahold of me when I was young. He not only modeled honesty and integrity to me, but he laid it out for me in no uncertain terms.

"Pat," he said, "there are a million one-time salespeople in this world. They'll do or say whatever it takes to make one sale. But the ones who make it in this business—or any business—are the ones who can go back to the same customers again and again because they are remembered as trustworthy and honest, because they are people of integrity. If anyone doubts your word one time, you can never get the trust back. If you lose people's trust, you're through." He loved to quote Mark Twain: "When in doubt, tell the truth." Those words of his still ring in my ears today.

I learned from watching and listening to Mr. Littlejohn that success depends on, first, defining one's core principles and, second, sticking to those principles. Honesty and integrity are principles that build trust, but there are other principles that are equally important in building us into people of success and genuine achievement. Some examples:

- Fairness (which generates equity and fairness)
- Human dignity (which prompts us to be cordial and respectful toward others)
- Service to others (which inspires us to make a contribution to our world)

We can see the importance of principle in our recent political history. When Ronald Reagan was elected president in 1980, no one had any doubt what he stood for: Reagan intended to cut taxes, strengthen the military, and stand up to the Soviet Union in a strong way. Whether you liked him or not, whether you agreed with him or not, Reagan defined himself clearly in his first hundred days, and throughout his eight years as president, his course never wavered. His principles were there for everyone to see: He kept his campaign pledges, he restored a high level of tradition and decorum to his office, and he managed to ram his tax cut proposals through an opposition-controlled Congress. Though Reagan clearly had his detractors, and the closing months of his administration were tainted by the Iran-Contra scandal, Reagan was widely perceived as a principled man—and that perception was what made him a successful, two-term president.

When George Bush was elected in 1988, he ran on a Reagan-soundalike pledge of "no new taxes." Two years into his presidency, he went back on his campaign pledge and signed into law one of the most massive tax-rate hikes in U.S. history. In 1992, a hostile public, feeling that Bush had broken the fundamental honesty principle, fired him from the job and hired a relatively unknown governor from a small state to run the country—Bill Clinton. Principle was the make-or-break issue in that election, and Bush's presidency broke against the principle of keeping faith with the electorate.

The issue of principle came back to haunt Bush's successor. Bill Clinton's approval ratings slid steadily downward as he increasingly became perceived as a man who waffled, reversed himself, changed his stories, and "clarified" previous statements. In short, he acquired a reputation as "Slick Willy," and the "slicker" he was perceived to be, the deeper his political problems grew. "Slickness" is just another name for lack of principle. The midterm elections of November 1994, which vaulted the Republican party to control of both houses of Congress for the first time in forty years, were widely viewed as a resounding personal rejection of Bill Clinton by voters who were weary of "slickness" and demanded a principle-centered government. Ted Koppel summed up Clinton's problems on *Nightline,* December 14, 1994, when he said, "The president's image is that of a man with no fixed compass, someone who cannot be trusted to keep a pledge."

In discussing these three presidents, I'm not endorsing any political point of view. I have a point of view, but it's totally beside the point I'm making here. I'm only talking about how these three presidents were *perceived* by the voting public, and how those perceptions affected their success (or failure) in office. Whether you are liberal, conservative, or moderate, regardless of your party affiliation, you *must* be a person of principle or you are doomed to failure.

What is true in politics is also true in every other arena of life—the sports arena, the business arena, the military arena, the church arena, and the all-important arena of the home. Our commitment to such principles as integrity and honesty should be rock-solid—so solid that when we leave the office at the end of the day, there should not even be one of our employer's paper clips in our pocket. Our commitment to fairness and justice should exceed that of a Supreme Court justice. Our commitment to human dignity should put us in the same league as Mother Teresa. As we daily renew our clear, uncompromising commitment to these core principles, we lay a solid foundation for success.

Tomorrow Strategy No. 3: Set Your Priorities

One of the greatest lessons I ever learned in sports management came at the end of my first year in the NBA, in the summer of 1969, when I was business manager of the Philadelphia 76ers. The phone on my desk rang. I picked it up and heard the voice of the team owner, the late Irv Kosloff, a Philadelphia businessman who operated a major paper company. I don't recall what he called about—some transitory matter involving the operation of the team, now long forgotten. But I will *never* forget one statement that he made—not in any conscious effort to teach me anything. It was actually more of an offhand statement, a footnote to our business discussion, yet his words etched themselves indelibly upon my mind.

"You know, Pat," he said, "in order to be successful in sports management, you've gotta ask yourself two questions, not just every day, but every minute of every day. First question: What am I doing right now to help the 76ers win more games? Second question: What am I doing right now to help the 76ers sell more tickets? If what you're doing doesn't fall under one of those two headings, you're on a detour, you're on a side road, and you better get back on track."

Wow! What a powerful insight! And every day since then, I've approached every task of my career with those two questions in mind, because that's what my business is about: winning and selling tickets. Without meaning to, without even trying to, Irv Kosloff taught me one of the most crucial lessons of my entire career: the importance of setting priorities.

I took that profound lesson about priorities and put it to good use in 1986 and 1987. Those were my first years in Orlando when I worked so desperately, along with a committed group of Orlando businesspeople, to build an NBA team in central Florida. It was a huge challenge, probably the greatest of my career, and we had to prioritize our tasks in order to beat the odds and get this incredibly huge job done. A project of this size must be broken down into step-by-step priorities or the sheer weight of it will break you. Here are the priorities we worked with in order to hammer our dream of a team into a court-stomping, sneaker-squeaking, backboard-pounding reality:

Priority One: Gather all the financial information possible to see if the business of pro basketball would work in Orlando. Jimmy Hewitt and his accountants were relentless in studying esitmated costs and income sources before deciding to go forward.

Priority Two: Get a strong ownership group together so we could *afford* the dream.

Priority Three: Rally the community, get the people of O-town excited, make them believe that Orlando could truly be a major-league basketball town.

Priority Four: Work with the city and county governments to get all the plans and preparations ready to build an arena—because without an arena, nothing could happen.

Priority Five: Brainstorm and design a team name, logo, and colors to give the community something that would be fun and exciting and real to relate to.

Priority Six: Sell Orlando to the NBA League office and the other team owners. We needed all these clubs to vote for us, so we pursued their vote shamelessly.

There were other priorities in descending order, but these six priorities came ahead of everything else. Without setting clear priorities, it would have been easy to get bogged down in minutiae, to major on the minor, to consume all our prime time on secondary matters. There were people in those days who wanted to focus on who the coach would be or what kind of players we should have—and those would be important considerations down the road. But when we were at the starting gate, we needed to focus on first things first. We had to set clear priorities. Jacob Stuart, head of the Orlando Chamber of Commerce, told me, "Focus on the macro and not the micro." We did that—and the Magic exists today as a testimony to the importance of priorities.

The ability to set priorities is the ability to organize your tomorrow. It is the ability to decide what is important and what is not, so that you can keep moving steadily in the direction of your goals. The ability to set priorities is a key ingredient of success.

"Unsuccessful people cannot set priorities," observes screenwriter, actor, and former White House speechwriter Benjamin J. Stein. "In the nation's capital, where I grew up, there's a man I went to school with. He's smart. He's handsome. His father is a big wheel. And he's miserable—stuck in a job as a manager of an apartment building. But if I suggest he study for the civil-service exam, he insists that he doesn't have time, that he's too busy with his hobbies. He's been telling me this since 1966!"[4]

Throughout our day, all of us are continually assaulted by distractions and interruptions that attempt to pull us off course, away from our dreams and goals. We easily forget that *urgent* matters are not always *important* matters. The telephone rings insistently, urgently. It impatiently demands to be answered, so we pick it up. That phone call may bring us a million-dollar deal—or it may be an automated sales call, a total time-waster. Successful people know how to say "no," how to stick to their own agendas, how to limit interruptions and intrusions. Successful people know how to fill their prime-time hours with productive effort and how to screen out the time-wasters and energy-drainers.

If we want to shape a better tomorrow, if we want to hammer our dreams into reality, then we *must* get a handle on today's priorities.

Tomorrow Strategy No. 4: Make Your Plans

If you were to visit the reception area of our Orlando Magic offices, the first thing you'd see is a big, metal plaque hanging on the wall. On the plaque are the words of the Magic vision statement, which our staff wrote several years ago to direct us in our mission as an NBA team. Here are the words we wrote:

> The vision of the Orlando Magic is to be recognized as the professional sports model of the twenty-first century by exemplifying the principles and practices of a championship organization in both the sport and business of basketball. We intend to achieve world-class status as a franchise through unwavering commitment to integrity, service, quality, and consumer value, while emphasizing the partnership among our community, our fans, our coaches, our players, our staff, and our owners.

Each year, as an organization, the Orlando Magic sets goals and objectives. The most recent set of goals and objectives we adopted were:

1. Uphold high standards of quality.
2. Maintain a maximum level of profitability.
3. Achieve a level of 100 percent customer satisfaction for all customer groups.
4. Achieve a level of 100 percent employee satisfaction.
5. Be recognized as a charitable and community leader.
6. Win an NBA World Championship.

Those were our goals, our priorities, for 1994. Once those goals were set, it became much easier to make our plans for the year. Take the goal of an NBA World Championship, for example. That's a big goal. We took a hard look at our team and realized that one thing had to happen in order for us even to have a chance to win that championship: We had to fill a hole on our team, the power forward slot. It just so happened that as we began looking to fill that position, a free agent power forward became available: Horace Grant's contract with the Chicago Bulls had just expired.

Problem: Horace Grant was an experienced player with a big rep, so a lot of teams were clamoring for his attention—including the Bulls, who didn't want to lose him. We needed and wanted Horace Grant in Orlando, but the man had plenty of options to choose from.

We spent the summer of 1994 working our plan. We started by bringing Horace down to Orlando to let him see the operation and meet the people. We squired him around Orlando, put him up in a Disney hotel, and gave him a real taste of the central Florida community. We also took him out to Holland, Michigan, to spend some time with the owner of the Magic, Rich DeVos, in July 1994. Horace had made it known that he didn't just want to be a cog in a big basketball machine; he was looking for a family-type atmosphere. The attitude and feel of an organization obviously starts from the top, and nobody is more family-oriented than Rich DeVos. Rich and Horace hit it off right from the start.

The effort to convince Horace Grant that the Magic was his new home was spearheaded by our president, Bob Vander Weide, and our director of basketball operations, John Gabriel. They did a fantastic job of planning the plan and working the plan. The end result was that Horace was able to see all that the team and the community had to offer, and when he made his decision, Horace actually accepted considerably less money to come to Orlando than other teams were offering! Obviously, he wanted a chance to play alongside Shaquille O'Neal and Anfernee Hardaway, two of the hottest tickets in the NBA. But I truly believe it was the community and the caring family atmosphere of the Magic that really sold him.

From that moment on, Horace blended right in with the rest of the team. We immediately noticed a difference—not only because of his play as a strong rebounding defensive-oriented forward, but also because of his leadership skills. Horace already has three NBA Championship rings in his possession—mementos of his days with Chicago—and he's clearly out to win more rings for Orlando. Nothing speaks louder than accomplishment, and his three championships with the Bulls are evidence of that. Though he's essentially very quiet, he's not afraid to speak his mind when something's out of line. The Magic is still a young team, so to have that kind of veteran leadership in the locker room and out on the court is very valuable.

Great sports teams don't just happen. A championship team isn't just a bunch of guys who can run and shoot and hang from the hoop by one hand. Planning is everything. A championship team is a Rubik's cube of moving parts that interact in complex and constantly shifting ways. A level of strategy and thought goes into the building of a team that makes a game of chess look like tic-tac-toe.

When you get right down to it, the same is true of whatever you are trying to build: Your career. Your family relationships. Your church program. Your business. Your novel. Success in any of these endeavors takes careful planning. A failure to plan always shows in the final result.

Some of us are driven by habit and routine. Others of us seem to lurch from crisis to crisis. Those who are successful make plans to succeed. Those who fail to plan—well, Bernard Baruch put it best when he said, "Whatever failures I have known, whatever errors I have committed, whatever follies I have witnessed in private and public life, have been the consequences of action without thought." To which pastor and seminary president Charles R. Swindoll adds, "The easiest thing in the world is to drift through life in a vague, thoughtless manner. God says there's a better way. He tells us to take time by the throat, give it a good shake, and declare: 'That's it! I'm gonna manage you—no longer will you manage me!'"[5]

The Bethlehem Steel Corporation was founded in 1904 by forty-one-year-old Charles M. Schwab, who was mentored by the great financial magnates of the late nineteenth century, Andrew Carnegie and J. Pierpont Morgan. (If Schwab's name sounds familiar, it's probably because his great-grandson of the same name is the founder-spokesman of the stock brokerage firm that bears his name.) Under Schwab's leadership, Bethlehem was a middling-successful company, but Schwab wasn't content with middling-successful. He wanted to be *mega-successful*. So he turned to management consultant Ivy Lee for advice on how to make his operation more efficient and profitable. "Show me how to get more things done with my time," said Schwab, "and you can name your price. I'll pay you anything within reason if you can give me advice that works."

Lee accepted the challenge and wrote out a plan—a plan so brief that it fit on a single sheet of paper with plenty of white space to spare. Ivy's plan was this:

> Write down the most important tasks you have to do tomorrow. Number them in order of importance. When you arrive in the morning, begin at once on No. 1 and stay on it until it is completed. Recheck your priorities, then begin with No. 2. Then No. 3, and so on. Make this your habit every working day. Pass this plan on to those who work under you. Try it as long as you like, then send me your check for what you think it's worth.

This one idea completely revolutionized the management style at Bethlehem Steel, and within five years Schwab's company had grown even larger and more profitable than industry giants Carnegie Steel and United States Steel. Within the first year, Schwab gratefully wrote a check to Ivy Lee for $25,000. Lee's simple secret: Plan tomorrow's priorities today, then stick to your plan and attack those priorities in order. The individual—or the company—that can follow this simple recipe is guaranteed to move closer toward the goals and dreams that spell success.

Life is full of pressures and stresses, and we easily allow ourselves to be rushed or panicked into bad decisions. We think, "I don't have time to plan. I have to act now!" But planning is indispensable, even in tight-pressure situations. A noted surgeon once said, "If I knew I only had five minutes to perform a delicate operation, I would spend the first two minutes planning the procedure." There is a lot of wisdom in the old carpenter's adage, "Measure twice, cut once." In other words, slow down and study the situation. Look at all the angles. Before you act (and regret your actions), take time to pray, prioritize, and plan.

But when you plan, be flexible and sensitive to changing realities. Theodore Levitt of Harvard Business School once made this observation on how to be an effective planner and manager in a fast-changing environment: "Most managers manage for yesterday's conditions, because yesterday is where they got their experiences and had their successes. But management is about tomorrow, not yesterday. Tomorrow concerns what *should* be done, not what *has* been done."

INVESTING IN A BETTER WORLD

This, then, is how you effectively handle those three blocks of time in your life, so that you can move steadily toward your goals and hammer your dreams into reality. Yesterday is a canceled check—don't stare at it. Today is your special day— live it, feast on it, use every last drop of it in pursuit of your dreams, wring all you can out of it. Tomorrow is your goal, your target, your bull's-eye—and if you want to reach that goal and hit that bull's-eye, you need to define clearly the ideal shape of your tomorrow and make realistic plans for getting there. To do that, you must:

1. Define your mission in life.
2. Define your core principles.
3. Set your priorities.
4. Make your plans.

As you consciously, deliberately, repeatedly practice these steps, you will soon find that you have become the kind of person who "thinks 'tomorrow'"—and who makes tomorrow's dreams happen today.

What is your mission in life? One of the most crucial dimensions of my own mission in life is to be the best husband and father I can possibly be. That's an even higher priority in my life than being the best NBA general manager I can possibly be. And it's a tough challenge. I mean, most guys have to pull off this fathering thing one, two, three, maybe four times in a lifetime. I've got to pull it off *nineteen* times! But I'm not complaining, because to me, fatherhood is the most fun and satisfying challenge a man can undertake.

I truly believe that the most important way to think "tomorrow," the most important investment in tomorrow anyone can make, is to invest in the life of a child. When you invest in the life of a child—when you pour your own time and love into that child, when you empower that child to believe in himself or herself, when you teach that child the right way to live—then you make an investment that will pay off tomorrow in your own life and in that child's life. But more than that, it is an investment in making tomorrow's world a better place. A child who grows up feeling loved, who grows up believing in his own ability to make a difference in the world, is a gift we give to the world, a little bit of light to brighten up one of the world's dark corners.

Let me tell you two little stories about just one of the nineteen investments in tomorrow that I have made. The name of that investment is Caroline, and she comes from Brazil. She became a part of our family in December 1993 when she was ten years old, and she is a real sweetheart, a very tender and sensitive child.

One summer afternoon, about six months after Caroline had come into our home, I was sitting with her and several of our other kids, watching a rented video of the movie *Annie,* the story of the comic strip character Little Orphan Annie. The movie ended, and the kids all got up and ran out to go swimming—all, that is, except Caroline. She ran over to me, threw her arms around me, and just started sobbing her heart out.

"Hey, what's the matter?" I said. "Why are you crying, honey?"

For a long time, she just kept sobbing and couldn't speak. Finally, she calmed down a little and I heard her say, "I'm so glad I've got a daddy!"

Ooh! I tell you, my heart felt like a nuclear meltdown at that moment. I realized afresh what a change this young lady's life had undergone. Watching that movie, with its depiction of Depression-era orphanage life and the street life of homeless children, had brought back a lot of memories for Caroline—*recent* memories of life on the streets and in the child welfare institutions of Brazil. After all, she had only been a part of our family for about six months! Her life had changed incredibly in that short period of time. She had gone from being an abandoned street kid in a Third World country to life in an American suburb, attending a good school, getting love, attention, and three squares a day. Her horizon had been transformed from one of mere day-to-day existence and survival to a genuine *future,* filled with hope and promise. And I have to tell you, straight from my own heart, it's an awesome, humbling feeling to know God has used you to make this kind of difference in the life of a child.

A few months later, Caroline and I were at a playground near our home in the Orlando suburb of Winter Park. Caroline was on the swings, and two swings over was a little boy. A few steps behind him were his parents. I took them to be from another country—it turned out they were from Puerto Rico—and I walked over and engaged the couple in conversation. I introduced myself and discovered that they were Orlando Magic fans and recognized my name.

"We have one other son at home," the woman said. "Do you have other children?"

I laughed and said, "Do I have other children!" Her eyes got as big as saucers when I told her exactly how many children I have. We talked about family and adoption for a few minutes.

"With two boys," she said, "we've always wanted to have a

little girl. But I can't have any more children. We've talked about adopting, but they put you on a waiting list, and it takes years to get a child."

"You've been trying to adopt in America, right?"

"Yes . . ." she said.

"Well," I replied, "your problem is you're looking in the wrong country!"

"The wrong country?"

"Sure! If you want a little girl, the place to look is Brazil. That's where we found Caroline. There are thousands of little girls in Brazil. You can make that dream come true!"

Well, Caroline was still swinging a few yards away, and I didn't think she had been listening to our conversation, but just then her little voice piped up and she said, "And those little girls need mommies and daddies too!"

Caroline's got a bright tomorrow ahead of her. A lot of other boys and girls in this world are not so fortunate. I just keep hoping and praying that a lot more people will begin to share this dream of tomorrow. It's a dream of a world in which *all* children—including children in Latin America, Eastern Europe, Africa, Asia, and inner-city America—have the mommies and daddies they want and the love they need.

What is your dream? What is your idealized vision of success? What is your mission in life? We have just looked at the first step, the first of Walt Disney's five magical secrets of success: Think "tomorrow." In the next chapter, we will explore the second secret behind a magical kingdom, a magical basketball team, and a magical, miraculous way of life: *Free the imagination!*

MAGICAL SECRET

NUMBER 2

Free the Imagination

CHAPTER 5

Blue-Sky Thinking

○ *Nothing limits achievement like small thinking; nothing expands possibilities like unleashed imagination.*
William Arthur Ward, poet

○ *Minds are like parachutes—they only function when open.*
Thomas Dewar, chemist and physicist

○ *Don't listen to those who say, "It's not done that way." Maybe it's not, but maybe you'll do it anyway. Don't listen to those who say, "You're taking too big a chance." Michelangelo would have painted the Sistine floor, and it would surely be rubbed out today.*
Neil Simon, playwright

Something incredibly exciting happened to me on Saturday night, January 21, 1995—while this book was being written, in fact! That night, I was honored at the sixtieth annual awards banquet of the Touchdown Club at the Washington Hilton in D.C. It was an amazing evening in many ways. The climax of the night, and the most humbling moment for me, was when I was presented with the Hubert H. Humphrey Humanitarian Award—an honor that, since 1978, has previously been given to luminaries such as Bob Hope, Jerry Lewis, Danny Kaye, Danny Thomas, Jack Klugman, Johnny Carson, Burt Reynolds, Gene Autry, and Harmon Killebrew, among others. It's an awesome thing to be included in such stratospheric company!

Though it was incredibly moving to be the recipient of such an honor, I think the real highlight of the evening for me was sitting at the head table next to one of my sports heroes, Florence Griffith Joyner, recipient of the Outstanding Olympic Achievement Award. Florence, better known as Flo-Jo, is the first American woman to win four medals in one Olympic year—three gold and one silver at Barcelona in '88. She holds world records in the 100- and 200-meter events. She has not only speed but style. She is famous for her one-legged track outfits and her six-inch-long, intricately adorned nails, and she currently serves as cochair of the President's Council on Physical Fitness and Sports. Flo-Jo is a beautiful, sweet, humble, gracious young lady, and she also does extensive humanitarian service on behalf of the United Negro College Fund, the American Cancer Society, and the Multiple Sclerosis Foundation.

I told her about my fourteen-year-old daughter, Daniela, who had developed a real talent in track (I'll tell you all about Dani in a moment), and I asked Flo-Jo if she would sign a picture to Dani and mail it to her.

"I'd love to," she said enthusiastically. I gave Flo-Jo my card and she tucked it in her purse.

"I sure appreciate it," I said. "There's no telling how important that could be. You never know what one word of encouragement at the right time can mean in a person's life."

"Don't I know it," she replied. "Let me tell you what happened to me. I was one of eleven children growing up in south-central Los Angeles. I didn't have much going for me. In fact, you'd have to say there was not much of a future for me. But when I was eight years old, I got a chance to meet Sugar Ray Robinson, the former boxing champion."

My jaw dropped. Sugar Ray Robinson himself! Probably the best boxer, pound for pound, of all time! "What did he say to you?" I asked.

"Sugar Ray looked right in my face and said, 'It doesn't matter where you come from, what your color is, or what the odds are against you. What does matter is that you have a dream, that you believe you can do it, that you commit to doing it. It *can* happen, and it *will* happen!' Right there, at just eight years old, I was sold. I was fired up with what my future could be. I saw Sugar Ray from time to time over the next few years, and he kept encouraging me and reinforcing me. That's what launched my career."

Would Flo-Jo be where she is today without the blue-sky thinking of Sugar Ray? I doubt it. I'm convinced (and so is Flo-Jo) that Sugar Ray Robinson opened that little girl's mind to the possibilities of a limitless future. Today, she takes the encouragement she received from Sugar Ray and passes it along to other young people. In fact, about a week after I met Flo-Jo in Washington, D.C., our daughter Dani received a package in the mail. It contained not one but *two* signed photos and a handwritten letter on Flo-Jo's letterhead. Here's what Flo-Jo wrote to Dani in the letter:

> Dear Dani,
> I wish you all the best in athletics and school. If you set a goal, work hard and believe in yourself. You will accomplish anything you believe in!! If you ever have a moment or two, I'd love to hear from you. Take care, Dani, and always follow your dreams!
> Love,
> Florence Griffith Joyner
> Flo-Jo

And on one of the photos she wrote:

> To Dani
> You have the potential within you to reach the stars! Believe in yourself and don't allow anyone nor anything to stand in your way. Believe you are the best!
> Love,
> Flo-Jo

"WHICH OLYMPICS CAN I RUN IN?"

Now let me tell you about Dani. She arrived from Brazil in late February 1993, and we immediately got her involved in a lot of activities. Some of the activities she attempted just didn't register. She struggled with different sports, arts, and musical activities, trying to get a handle on who she is and what she's capable of doing. Nothing seemed to click. Finally, one of the coaches at school said to her, "Dani, why don't you go out for track?" She didn't see much point in it, but she shrugged and said, "Okay." (I think she agreed to try track primarily to get out of swimming practice.)

We didn't go out of our way to make it easy for her. Frankly, I wasn't too crazy about Daniela quitting swimming just because she found it too challenging. I told her, "Dani, we don't have enough drivers to get you back and forth to track practice. If you want to go out for track, fine, you can do it, but you've gotta find a ride home after practice. We just don't have enough chauffeurs." She agreed, and she did it.

Her first junior high track meet, Dani ran the mile and absolutely dominated the event. I was thunderstruck! I had tried to encourage Daniela athletically, but I hadn't been able to get her to run from one end of the backyard to the other. Yet here she was at her very first meet ever—*and she won by a full lap!* Go figure.

Well, that was just the beginning. She went on, meet after meet, and won every last one of them with a string of outstanding times! Local track coaches took note of her performance, and she got involved in a summer track program. The next thing we knew, she was running well enough to qualify for the National Junior Olympics, where she gave an outstanding performance.

Here was a kid who started running primarily to escape swimming—but she took the opportunity, had some success, got her imagination freed up about her own inner potential and possibilities, and *zoooom!* Off she went! Now she's sprinting toward a college track scholarship, and she recently said, "Dad, do you think I can run in the Olympics someday?"

"Hey," I said, "once your mind is freed up, who knows?"

"When?" she persisted. "Which Olympics can I run in? Is '96 in Atlanta a little too soon?"

"Well, Dani, I think running in the Olympics at age fifteen may be a little premature. Let's shoot for Melbourne, Australia, in 2000. If you're ready to run when you're nineteen, I promise we'll buy you a plane ticket."

Daniela's successes have begun to free up her mind. The letter from Flo-Jo has taken her freed-up imagination to even greater heights. After reading the encouraging notes from Flo-Jo, she immediately sat down, took out a sheet of Mickey and Minnie stationery, and wrote,

Dear Flo-Jo,
Thank you very much for your letter and pictures. I was born in Brazil in 1981. I grew up with my mother till I was 8 years old then she put me an orphan. I stayed there till I was 12. Then Pat & Jill Williams came to see me. They liked me and decided to adopt me. When I was living with my real mother I had no brothers or sisters. But when I got here I was amazed.

When I came here I didn't speak any English but now I know how to it. I came to America in Feb. 22nd in 1993. I like my parents a lot. They are really cool.

When I came here my dad put me in softball. Then for a while I didn't like it so I quit. Soccer season had started at my school so I tried out then I made it. I play in whole season then soccer was over then basketball. I tried out for it but the 1st year I didn't make it. I tried out also for volleyball. I didn't make it. So volleyball season was over.

I tried out for track. My dad thought I couldn't run neither. Because when I came here I couldn't even jog a 100 meters. So my dad thought I couldn't do it. So I ran the mile and I won. So a teacher went and told my dad that. Then I kept winning every race that I ran. Middle school was to easy for me, so my dad put me in a track club. I ran there for a while. I went to the nationals. I didn't do that good but my dad was there all the time. I was sad but you can't never win every race. Track season was over then I start doing cross-country. I won all most all the races. My dad was always proud of me. I was really happy.

My fastest time for the mile is about 5:28 and for the 5 k is about 19:58. I would like to be just like you. I will follow all my dreams and I will be rooting for you in the 96's Olympics. I hope to meet you. One of these days, I hope I will be in the Olympics too. I feel special because you are the fastest female runner and you are my friend.
Love
Daniela Williams

There's the proof. When the mind is freed up to blue-sky thinking, there are no limits.

Blue-Sky Thinking in Orlando

I started freeing up my imagination the minute I arrived in Orlando in June of 1986. Remember at that time we had no team, no arena, no community interest, and no NBA encouragement.

Most of my time was spent speaking at service clubs, business meetings, conventions, and churches. If three people showed up, I'd join them for a fourth at the bridge table!

I worked out a little routine. I'd say, "Folks, when we get our team and it runs out on the floor of the new arena, you'd better have your tickets. When Bird and Jordan and Magic come to town, you don't want to be on the outside with your nose pressed against the glass doors, waving and yelling at me, 'Get me in. Open the doors.' All I'll be able to say is, 'You should've ordered your seats back then.'"

Many people responded to my pitch. Many didn't.

But my mind was freed up, and I could picture the sold-out building we now have for every game and the waiting list of three thousand people.

It's amazing what can happen when your imagination runs wild, and your mind is freed up to blue-sky thinking! Many successful Americans have adopted blue-sky thinking, using such spurs as birdcages of the mind.

BIRDCAGES OF THE MIND

The next time you get in your car, turn the key, and hear that engine roar to life, you just might want to say, "Thank you, Charles Kettering."

Kettering was the Ohio-born engineer-inventor who first imagined—and then invented—the electric starter, a device that revolutionized the development of the modern automobile. His invention was first introduced on the 1912 Cadillac, and the starter on the car in your driveway is only a refined version of Kettering's original invention.

But that's not all you may want to thank the spirit of Charles Kettering for. This great and imaginative man, who passed away in 1958, gave us a long list of innovations that have made our lives better and easier, including:

- quick-drying lacquer finishes for cars,
- improved high-intensity automobile headlights,
- anti-knock fuels,
- the high-speed, two-cycle diesel engine,
- the high-compression internal combustion engine, and
- the first electric cash register.

Kettering also developed the first guided missile in history—a propeller-driven vehicle with a two-hundred-pound bomb payload. This missile was used in World War I.

Kettering's imagination and passion for science extended far beyond the realm of mechanical contraptions. Many of the advances in the modern detection and treatment of cancer come from the research facility that bears Charles Kettering's name: the Sloan-Kettering Institute for Cancer Research in New York City.

What was it about Charles Kettering that made him such a prolific, productive, and successful individual? One of the most important factors in his life and career was his *wide-open imagination!* Everything was possible to Charles Kettering, and he preached his belief in the wide-open possibilities of life everywhere he went. Here are a few of my favorite "Ketteringisms," which he spoke at various points in his long and illustrious career with such corporations as National Cash Register Company, Delco, and General Motors:

- "The opportunities of man are limited only by his imagination. But so few have imagination that there are ten thousand fiddlers to one composer."
- "It's amazing what ordinary people can do if they set out without preconceived notions."
- "There will always be a frontier where there is an open mind and a willing hand."

- "There are very few dead ends to anything except in people's minds."

Kettering sometimes referred to creative thinking as "hanging birdcages in the mind." He vividly illustrated this concept one time when he made a bet with a friend. "Joe," he said, "I bet you a hundred dollars that I can make you buy a pet bird within a year from today."

"Now, Charlie," said Joe, "what in the world would I do with a pet bird?"

"Well, is it a bet or isn't it?"

"You're on."

A few days later, Charles Kettering arrived at Joe's house with a gift—a beautiful, ornate birdcage handcrafted in Switzerland. "This," he explained, "is for the bird you're gonna buy."

"But I tell you, I'm not gonna buy any bird!"

"We'll see," said Kettering.

Joe took the birdcage and hung it in his dining room, near the table. Every time Joe entertained people in his home, his guests would ask him, "When did your bird die?"

And Joe would be forced to reply, "I never had a bird."

His guests would look puzzled and say, "Well, what have you got a birdcage for?"

After this scenario took place three or four times, Joe finally went out and bought a parakeet. The bird cost him $102—two dollars for the pet shop and a hundred for his smug friend, Charles Kettering. "It was easier to just buy the bird," Joe explained as he paid off his wager, "than to keep explaining that stupid empty cage you gave me."

Kettering later reflected on this incident and said, "If you hang birdcages in your mind, you eventually get something to put in them." The things we put in those "birdcages of the mind" are called ideas. No one knew the power of ideas better than Walt Disney.

THE POWER OF IDEAS

Walt Disney was in his late thirties when the idea of Disneyland first occurred to him. His daughters were young, and he enjoyed taking them to the amusement park on Sundays. His girls loved the carnival atmosphere of the park, with its exciting rides and games of chance and strange exhibits. Though he was glad his daughters enjoyed it, Walt didn't have any fun at these places. Instead, he sat on the bench, watching his daughters, munching on peanuts, and thinking. He thought about how much fun amusement parks were for kids and that there was nothing for adults to enjoy, nothing for the whole family. He thought about how ugly, dirty, and litter-strewn the typical amusement park was, and he wondered if it really had to be that way. Most of all, he thought of ways to build an amusement park that would be bigger, brighter, cleaner, and more fun for the entire family—not just for kids.

It took fifteen years for Disney to make his idea a reality, and he was a fifty-three-year-old grandfather when it happened. Even his closest associates had a hard time envisioning the breathtaking scope of Disney's ideas, and his own brother, Roy, thought the entire undertaking was "a screwball idea." Walt was plagued by problems and obstacles, and he stood many times at the brink of financial ruin before it was achieved. But by the time the theme park opened in 1955, the reality was every bit as big and exciting as Disney's dream. It was just as he had pictured it: a totally new kind of family entertainment park.

Disneyland was an amazing success—so successful, in fact, that it single-handedly put the Walt Disney Company in the black. Disney himself had never drawn more than a very modest middle-class salary throughout some thirty-plus years of struggle. Finally, the father of Mickey Mouse was a resounding success!

Within a few short years, however, Walt realized that his "big idea" was not nearly big enough! Sure, he and his company were making a lot of money from his hugely successful theme park—but so were a lot of other people. Despite its 160-acre size, Disneyland had become a small island in a sea of hotels, motels, shops, restaurants, gas stations, and car-rental agencies—and all of them were making money off the crowds that *he* had attracted to Anaheim! Property values in the Disneyland area shot up over 1,000 percent—practically overnight! Even though Disneyland itself was a gleaming jewel of a vacation spot, much of the surrounding area was a cheap and tawdry rip-off of his vision. He vowed that the *next* time he built a theme park ("Here we go again!" groaned his brother Roy), he would make sure he had control of the *entire* environment of the park.

When he envisioned his second park, Walt Disney World in Orlando, Florida, he started with a much bigger idea and a much bigger piece of real estate. Though his first dream park consisted of 160 acres in Orange County, California, Walt Disney began his second dream park by purchasing *28,000 acres* of Orange and Osceola Counties, Florida. In just a few years, the scope of his vision had increased by 17,500 percent!

Walt Disney didn't live to walk down the Main Street of his new Magic Kingdom or to stroll from pavilion to pavilion in Epcot Center. He died in 1965, almost five years before Walt Disney World opened. On the day the Florida park opened, someone commented to Mike Vance, creative director of Walt Disney Studios, "Isn't it too bad Walt Disney didn't live to see this?"

"He did see it," Vance replied simply. "That's why it's here."

One example of how the Disney team was inspired by Walt to achieve the impossible is illustrated by a story from Disneyland's first year of operation. The park was already open, but several attractions were not yet completed and open to the public. One of these was the Rainbow Caverns Mine Train in Frontierland (which was later replaced by the Big Thunder Mountain Railroad roller-coaster ride). Inspired by the Oscar-winning Disney True Life Adventure *The Living Desert,* the Rainbow Caverns attraction featured a leisurely train ride through a re-created desert of the great American Southwest.

Walt wanted the train to enter the caverns, where a fluorescent waterfall would glow in rainbow colors under black light. The plan was to add fluorescent dyes to the flowing water itself, each color in a separate trough to keep the rainbow colors from mixing and turning into fluorescent mud. Claude Coats, the Disney artist who was given the job of making the waterfall glow, checked with chemists and engineers who told him it couldn't be done. Coats reported this news to Walt. "They say it's impossible," said Coats. "You can't keep the water from splashing and mixing and turning fluorescent gray within a week."

"Well, Claude," Walt replied with a merry lack of concern, "it's kinda fun to pull off the impossible, isn't it? I'm sure you'll find a way."

So Claude Coats went back to the drawing board. He got together with another Disney artist, John Hench. After a few weeks of experimentation, they came up with an arrangement of braided glass fibers in the water channels that almost completely eliminated the splashing and kept the Rainbow Caverns as dazzling as their name.

Not too long ago I had a fascinating talk with Bob Matheison, a recently retired Disney exec who worked side by side with Walt Disney during the 1950s and 1960s. "Walt was a visionary," Bob told me. "He was filled with curiosity and ideas. He was always thinking five projects ahead of the one he was working on."

"Would Walt be surprised," I asked him, "if he could come back and see how Walt Disney World has turned out?"

"Not at all!" Bob responded. "In fact, he'd say, 'Why isn't this project or that attraction finished? You guys are five years behind where you oughta be!' Of course, he'd say it with a twinkle in his eye and an impish grin on his face, he'd say it in fun—but he'd also mean it! He would never, ever say anything is impossible! He impacted all of us with his belief that anything we could imagine, we could do. We continually attempted and accomplished things we thought were just plain impossible, because Walt's belief inspired all of us to believe!"

Walt Disney was a man of ideas, imagination, and vision. "Vision," wrote Jonathan Swift, "is the art of seeing things which are invisible." Disney saw the invisible, and he made it visible. He envisioned the impossible and made it possible. He was an extraordinary man—yet he came from totally ordinary beginnings, as Bob Thomas notes:

His parents were plain people who moved from one section of the country to another in futile search of the American dream. Young Walt showed no brilliance as a student; he daydreamed through his classes. Cartooning proved his major interest, but his drawings were uninspired; as soon as he could hire better cartoonists, he gave up drawing entirely. It seems incredible that the unschooled cartoonist from Kansas City, who went bankrupt in his first movie venture, could have produced works of unmatched imagination—and could even have undertaken the creation of a future city.[1]

Such an ordinary man, and such extraordinary achievements! How did he do it? I believe that when you free up your imagination, *anything* is possible.

Advertising writer Dick Kerr described the life-changing power of ideas in some ad copy he wrote for United Technologies Corporation: "The person sitting in a shack in the valley may look up at the big house on the hill and wonder how the other people got there. They probably got there with an idea and the guts to see it through. Some of our nation's best ideas have come from people of modest means and education. Spend some time each day thinking about something that will find a ready market. Remember, someone had to invent the paper clip, contact lenses, and the clothespin. Your clothespin may be waiting around the corner."

That's the power of an idea. That's the power of blue-sky thinking.

UCLA psychologist Lawrence Morehouse uses a golf analogy to demonstrate the importance of a freed-up imagination to success: "In the sand trap, the difference between the novice and the champion is that the novice thinks, 'I hope it gets on the green,' whereas the champion visualizes the flight of the ball, how it will land on the green and run into the cup." Successful people are able to envision and see their successes. Their imaginations effervesce with thousands of tiny bubbles called "ideas." Their minds are constantly engaged, and their energies are continually bent toward making the invisible and the impossible come true.

Success is just an idea away! Free up your imagination and anything—literally *anything!*—can happen. At the very least, you can change your life. But who knows?

"Not to engage in the pursuit of ideas," said educator-philosopher Mortimer Adler, "is to live like ants instead of like men." But as we pursue our ideas, we must remember to handle them with care. It takes conscious, deliberate effort to properly plant, nurture, grow, and harvest ideas. Ideas are:

- *Fragile.* "A new idea is delicate," said Charlie Brower. "It can be killed by a sneer or a yawn. It can be stabbed to death by a quip, and worried to death by a frown on the right person's brow." We need to create an atmosphere in which ideas are encouraged—both our own ideas and the ideas of those around us.
- *Disturbing.* We don't like to admit this about ourselves, but most of us are more comfortable with the same old ways of doing things, the same old ways of thinking, the same old categories and pigeonholes. New ideas upset our equilibrium and force us to change our thinking. The human mind often acts like the body's immune system, attacking new ideas in the same way that a macrophage or a lymphocyte attacks an invading virus. We need to *retrain* our minds so that they will welcome new ideas. I admire former UCLA basketball coach John Wooden. He said, "Don't let what you can't do keep you from doing what you can."
- *Self-reproducing.* Ideas breed more ideas. Creativity begets more creativity. "Ideas are like rabbits," said Nobel and Pulitzer prize-winning novelist John Steinbeck. "You get a couple and learn how to handle them, and pretty soon you have a dozen."
- *Free.* Ideas cost nothing to produce, and they often produce millions! Some ideas can be patented, some can be copyrighted, some can be trademarked, but most are just out there in the public domain where anyone can use them. Ideas are contagious and infectious. It's exciting and exhilarating to be around people of ideas. Creative people spark creativity and enthusiasm in the people around them, and often throw off more ideas than they themselves can use. "Many ideas grow better," observed Oliver Wendell Holmes, "when transplanted into another mind than in the one where they sprang up."

"WHERE DO YOU GET YOUR IDEAS?"

The number one question asked of writers is "Where do you get your ideas?" Fact is, successful writers seldom have to struggle to find ideas. Most have trunkfuls of ideas and will never live long enough to turn even a tenth of them into books. Their heads are constantly whizzing with ideas. Why? Because they have learned the secret of creativity. They continually feast on ideas. They immerse themselves in ideas. They wallow in ideas. And all those ideas have a tendency to collide and split like atoms inside their brains, causing a chain reaction of imagination, setting off one explosive new idea after another.

You may be thinking, "But I never have any ideas! I'm just not creative and I never will be!" Hogwash! We are *all* creative. The Bible says we are made in God's image, and the very first verse in the Bible says, "In the beginning, God *created . . .*" God is creative, and we, being made in His image, are creative too! You just need to know how to unleash the God-given creativity that is already built into you!

That doesn't mean we are all creative in the same way. We are all creative *in our own ways*. You may not be able to write the Great American Novel, but you may have an extraordinary creative gift for starting an entrepreneurial business or leading a church ministry or working with children or helping homeless people. All of these activities require imagination and ideas. All the creativity you'll ever need is already there, right inside you, just waiting to be unleashed.

"But how do I unleash it?" you say.

Glad you asked. The following are six practical steps to unleashing your creativity. Each step is simple, each is doable, and each is *fun*.

Creativity Unleasher No. 1: Exercise Your Brain. (Think! Sounds so simple, but few of us do it.)

"The brain," said business consultant Robert Half, "is a mass of cranial nerve tissue, most of it in mint condition." Brains need regular exercise, and the only way to exercise your brain is to think!

"Thought," observed Helen Keller, "is great and swift and free. The light of the world. The chief glory of man." Blind and deaf, locked in the "sensory deprivation tank" of her own impaired body,

Helen Keller was still a woman of great vision. She lived in a world of silence and darkness; thinking was her sound and her light.

Why, then, do most of us avoid thinking? Because thinking is *work!* But all truly successful people know that thinking is a key ingredient of creativity and success. "All the problems of the world could be settled easily," observed IBM's founder, Thomas J. Watson, "if people were only willing to think. The trouble is that people very often resort to all sorts of devices in order not to think, because thinking is such hard work." Thomas Edison agrees: "There is no expedient to which a man will not go to avoid the real labor of thinking." So does auto magnate Henry Ford: "Thinking is the hardest work there is, which is probably the reason why so few engage in it."

We avoid thinking by surrounding ourselves with noise. We get in the car and immediately click on the stereo. We watch TV over breakfast and after dinner. Some of us even take a radio into the shower with us. All that racket and yakkety-yak drowns out the silent voice of our thoughts—and hinders our creativity. Ideas tend to arise when the mind is relaxed and at rest, focused on a problem that needs to be solved. Creative people know that some of their best ideas come to them while driving, lathering up in the shower, or waiting to fall asleep—because there are no distractions to interrupt the flow of ideas!

If you want to be creative and have lots of ideas, you have to teach yourself and discipline yourself to *think.* The more you think, the more your mind is stretched, and as Oliver Wendell Holmes observed, "The human mind, stretched to a new idea, never goes back to its original dimensions."

Creativity Unleasher No. 2: Read!

In 1964, a Danish engineer named Karl Kroyer faced a nightmarish problem. A freighter, the *Al Kuwait,* had capsized and sunk, hull upward, in the harbor of Kuwait City. The ship's cargo—six thousand sheep—had drowned in the disaster, and the carcasses were rotting in the holds. The submerged hull was located near the intakes of the city's desalinization plant—a facility that took in salt water from the ocean and processed it into salt-free drinking water. That plant was the only source of potable water for the city, so the city's entire water supply was in danger of being poisoned by the biological toxins from the decomposing cargo. Kroyer had to figure out some way of raising the ship without cracking it open and spilling its contents.

Kroyer's solution: He pumped Ping-Pong balls into the ship's hull—a total of 27 million balls!—so that the freighter slowly and gently came back to the surface.

Where did Kroyer get his idea? Some time earlier, he had read a Donald Duck comic book to his children. In that story, Donald's boat had sunk, and he raised it by pumping it full of Ping-Pong balls! A completely wacky solution—never meant to be taken seriously. But it worked in real life, and the drinking water of an entire city was saved—*saved by a Walt Disney comic book!*

Have you ever stopped to consider what a book truly is? It's a piece of a human mind sitting on a shelf! You can take it down, crack it open, and suddenly you are linked—mind to mind, soul to soul—with another human being. The author might even have been dead for centuries, yet the moment you begin to read, he or she comes instantly to life in your hands and begins speaking to you: telling you a story, relating great events of the past, unraveling the mysteries of life and the universe, or describing how to build a birdhouse. Any fact you want to know, any place you want to visit, any life you want to live is there in a book. "It is not true that we have only one life to live," said S. I. Hayakawa. "If we can read, we can live as many more lives and as many kinds of lives as we wish."

Now, I know that there are some people who just don't like to read. I submit that such people make a choice to cripple themselves. You wouldn't want to be illiterate, would you? Well, you might just as well be if you choose not to read! "The man who *does not* read good books," said Mark Twain, "has no advantage over the man who *cannot*."

As Sam Ewing, the noted philosopher, once observed, "If more people used their library cards like they use their credit cards, we'd have a country full of Albert Einsteins."

All the successful people I know are people who read. One example: Ed Bradley, a correspondent on CBS's *Sixty Minutes*. "As a child," he recalls, "I lived to read books. The library was a window to the world, a pathway to worlds and people far from my neighborhood in Philadelphia. Even today, as I travel around the world shooting stories for *Sixty Minutes,* I often visit places I used to dream about because of the books I'd read. The library made a difference in my life."

I have to tell you: Pat Williams is a voracious reader. I'm a black hole for reading matter, sucking up every bit of printed material I can get my hands on. I figured out long ago that my mind is a muscle. I've always had an intense desire to exercise all the muscles in my body, but I never figured out a way to hook up a Nautilus machine to the muscle of my mind. There's only one way I know to strengthen my mental muscles: reading. So I read about fifteen to twenty magazines and trade journals a week—sports- and basketball-related magazines, news magazines, fitness magazines, motivational newsletters, and Christian literature. I read the *Orlando Sentinel* and *USA Today* from cover to cover every morning. And I have at least six books I'm working on at the same time: devotional books, motivational books, Civil War histories, biographies, and books on the history of baseball.

Where do I find the time to read? For one thing, I keep books in the car with me. Just in the course of a year, I can get through a couple of books just waiting at red lights. (If you try this, be sure and put the book down when the light turns green!) I use every bit of time I spend waiting in doctors' offices and for other appointments to read books. I look forward to airline travel because I know I'll have several hours with nothing to do but read. And the best time to read is during kids' sporting events, during the time when someone else's kid is at bat. I can get through volumes a year while I'm there watching games. Sometimes I "read" a book-on-tape instead of listening to that drive-time chat station on the radio.

Reading one book a month will help put you in the top 1 percent of all people in the world. Reading one book a week in your field will make you one of the most competent people in your generation. Reading five books in your lifetime on any one subject will make you a world-leading authority on that subject.

Walt Disney loved to read. He once said, "There is more

treasure in books than in all the pirate's loot on Treasure Island, and best of all, you can enjoy these riches every day of your life."

I've saved a few other quotes about reading that have really motivated me:

Andrew Carnegie said, "A man's reading program should be as carefully planned as his daily diet, for that too is food, without which he cannot grow mentally."

And Earl Nightingale observed, "Books have meant to my life what the sun has meant to the planet Earth."

Someone once said, "Trees give us two crucial elements for survival: oxygen and books." How true! If you want to succeed, if you want to be a person of ideas, you must be a person who *reads*.

Creativity Unleasher No. 3: Be Observant!

Most people go about their lives with their minds turned off. They absorb input without sifting or analyzing it. Creative people are always looking at ways to improve their world. When they watch TV, they think, "How could that have been done better?" When they read a book, they think, "How could that have been written better?" When they work on their car, they think, "How could this have been engineered better?" They exercise their creative faculties all the time, wherever they are, whatever they are doing. They continually ask themselves, "How could this be improved, adapted, or modified? Would I have done it this way? Is there a better way to do it?" To be creative, adopt the curious, tinkering mind-set of creative people.

One of my favorite people in sports is Mike Krzyzewski, the basketball coach at Duke University. I think Mike expressed this concept perfectly when he said, "If you put a plant in a jar, it will grow to take the shape of the jar. Let it grow by itself, and it may grow so twenty jars cannot hold it."

Creativity Unleasher No. 4: Spend Time with Creative People!

One of the best ways to spark your own creativity is to bask in the glow of other creative people. "In a fireplace," says Marc Maurer, president of the National Federation of the Blind, "one log by itself, regardless of how big, will almost certainly fail to burn. There must be at least two. The flame from one is reflected by the other. The brightness and heat come from the space between the logs, the reflection of the flame. As it is with the flame, so it is with ideas."

Surrounding yourself with creative people is helpful not only in inspiring creativity but in helping to ensure that human energy is added to good ideas in order to make those dreams come true. "A new idea has only a limited time to take fire, to catch the imagination of the public and burn," adds Maurer. "And if the flame is to be reflected—the kindling point sustained—more than a single person is required. There must be two, five, ten—at least a handful—to build the heat and speed the process. Regardless of its merit, if an idea once ignited fails to reflect the flame of group interaction, its time will soon pass, and it will disappear into insignificance and be forgotten. . . . If the idea is to live and prosper—if it is to make a meaningful difference in the lives of people—all of the elements must be present: the idea, a leader, and at least a handful to reflect the flame."

Creativity Unleasher No. 5: Brainstorm!

One of the things I would love to do is sit in on a Disney "imagineering" session. In those sessions, the top idea people of the Disney organization get together in a room and do nothing but imagine possibilities and design the ultimate—the ultimate in theme park attractions, in television specials, in movies. In these sessions, there are no mental limits, no horizons. The Disney organization has created an atmosphere that is completely idea-friendly, a climate and a culture that honors the imagination and unleashes creativity—and the results are obvious in everything Disney does.

In the Magic organization, we have blue-sky sessions where we take a subject or a goal and just call out and write down every crazy, impossible idea we can think of. For example, every year we have a session where we brainstorm every conceivable way we can increase revenues. No matter how silly, we write them all down—no editing, just brainstorming to the sky. (Stephen Dougles of Campus Crusade For Christ says, "Most ideas are lost if they are not written down within ten seconds. Write it down.") One guy may say, "Have Disney make a feature film about the adventures of our mascot, Stuff!" Another will say, "Sell seats on the team flights for away games!" One idea I came up with: "Paint Magic logos on the bottoms of every swimming pool in Orlando so that when planes are landing from all over the world, the passengers see all these thousands of Magic logos! Everywhere they look!" You may get five hundred ideas, and only two will be good and doable—but those two ideas will be absolutely phenomenal, because people had the freedom to dream their dreams without any limits, without any ceilings.

I like to kid some of our newer employees at the Magic, "Look, if you don't produce at least one new idea per day, your job is in jeopardy!" People around here understand that crazy ideas and impossible possibilities are encouraged and even demanded. That's part of the magic of the Magic!

In our offices, classrooms, locker rooms, churches, and homes, we must create a blue-sky, anything-goes, shoot-for-the-moon mind-set. What's more, we must learn to have blue-sky sessions in our own minds, in the privacy of our own thoughts, so that we can reach our individual goals. We need to grab a piece of blue sky. Here's how to do it, step by step:

1. Start with a notepad, Post-It pad, or some other stack of scribble sheets. Put your pad and pen down on a table with plenty of working space; then sit down at the table and make yourself comfortable.
2. Take a few moments to relax your mind. Meditate on a peaceful image, read Psalm 23, pray—whatever helps you to get into a calm, centered, optimistic mood.
3. Set a timer—an egg timer, a watch with a beep-alarm, an oven buzzer—for three or four minutes, no more than five.
4. *Brainstorm!* For the next few minutes, let your mind roam. Think about the goal you want to reach and free-associate. Let your thoughts bubble to the surface without censoring, criticizing, or doubting. No idea is too crazy or outrageous.

You'll find that desires, dreams, wishes, goals, and ideas will begin to emerge, one after the other. Scribble them down in just a word or two, no more than three or four words per idea. Be as quick and brief as possible—doodle a little picture if that's faster than writing. As soon as you scribble one idea, rip off that sheet of paper, toss it aside, and scribble the next. Ideas will come to you in a flood of creativity, they will peak, and then, after a couple of minutes, they will begin to diminish.

5. Stop. By the time your timer beeps or buzzes, you will have a stack of ideas. Some will be terrible—and that's okay, because others will be flashes of genius. Even the terrible ideas often serve to spark a great idea.

6. Now that the brainstorming, blue-sky session is over, it's okay to be critical and discerning. Sift through your ideas, keep the great ones, toss the clinkers. Organize your ideas into categories and priorities. Use these ideas as a foundation for your plan of action. Once you have a plan, post it in a place where you will be constantly reminded of it: your car's dashboard, your refrigerator, your desk, your computer's electronic "wallpaper" or start-up file, your bathroom mirror, your devotional notebook.

7. Make a regular habit of going back to the drawing board and holding private "blue-sky sessions" at least once a month to keep yourself on course and to keep your thinking fresh, creative, and focused.

Creativity Unleasher No. 6: Turn Ideas into Action!

"Everyone who's ever taken a shower has an idea," says Nolan Bushnell, founder of Atari. "It's the person who gets out of the shower, dries off, and does something about it that makes a difference." Ideas are absolutely worthless—*unless and until we convert them into action!* An idea without action behind it is just a fantasy, an idle daydream, a speculation. An idea empowered by action becomes a force for change.

Here are some ways you can turn your ideas into action:

1. *Focus your ideas.* Concentrate them like laser beams. Give them coherence and cohesion. Intensify and consolidate them until you can state them in a single sentence that will generate excitement and enthusiasm in those who hear your ideas. "If you can't write your idea on the back of my calling card," said David Belasco, "you don't have a clear idea."

2. *Communicate your ideas.* Most ideas require a group effort, not just an individual effort, in order to produce success. If you can't communicate your ideas to others, you will never get other people to join you in making your ideas become reality. "You can have brilliant ideas," said former Chrysler CEO Lee Iacocca, "but if you can't get them across, your ideas won't get you anywhere."

One day a little boy asked Walt Disney, "Do you draw Mickey Mouse?"

Walt had to admit, "I do not draw anymore."

"Then you think up all the jokes and ideas?"

"No," Disney said. "I don't do that."

Finally the boy looked at Walt and said, "Mr. Disney, just what do you do?"

"Well," Disney said, "sometimes I think of myself as a little bee. I go from one area of the studio to another and gather pollen and sort of stimulate everybody. I guess that's the job I do."

To communicate your ideas effectively, you have to be like Disney. You have to inspire, ignite, coax, and motivate your listeners. You must be passionate. You must be persuasive. You must be persistent. "Good ideas are not adopted automatically," said Admiral Hyman G. Rickover. "They must be driven into practice with courageous impatience." A good idea is like a stone on top of a hill. Once it starts moving down the hill, it will build a momentum of its own—but it's not going anywhere until you *push* it!

3. *Take risks for your ideas.* Disney's screen classic *Snow White* was an enormous risk. Disneyland and Disney World were also huge risks. If you want to succeed—and succeed *big!*—you have to be willing to take a chance and leave your security blanket behind. Stretch a rope across your front lawn and walk it from one end to the other, and nobody will care. Stretch that same rope

between the two towers of the World Trade Center and walk across it, and you'll draw crowds and make the evening news on every network. Playing it safe is boring. Taking a risk is exciting. Be willing to risk—not recklessly, but with calculated boldness, so that your accomplishments will be visible and memorable.

Field Marshal William Joseph Slim is the British general who turned back a Japanese invasion of India and who defeated Japanese forces in Burma during World War II. He knew that too much caution can lose the war. "When you cannot make up your mind which of two evenly balanced courses of action you should take," he said, "always choose the bolder."

I recently saw with my own eyes the unfolding of a story that says a lot about the limitless possibilities that are open to us all if we will just free up our imaginations and reach for that big blue sky. The end of this story has not yet been written, but I'm so excited about it that I wanted to share it with you here. (In a few years, I'll come back and tell you how the story turns out!)

This is the story of a boy I'll call James. He attended middle school with some of my own kids, is now a freshman in high school, and is a standout basketball player for a fourteen-year-old. He's black, lives in a low-rent section of Orlando, and comes from a broken home. Now, I've been acquainted with James for several years, and he's a nice kid. His mother has tried to do a good job of raising him and giving him good values.

Not long ago, I got word from one of James's teachers that he is ineligible to play on the freshman basketball team because his grades have been poor. He's a bright kid with a likable personality, but he's been spending a lot of time running with the wrong crowd. After the teacher explained this to me, I said, "Have his mother call me. I want to see him."

The mother called, and I set up a time for James and his mom to come over to the Orlando Arena and watch the team practice. James arrived that morning wearing a Magic jersey with a big number 1 and "Hardaway" printed on the back—a duplicate of the jersey worn on the court by Anfernee "Penny" Hardaway. When I remarked about the jersey, he grinned and said, "Penny Hardaway is my man! He's the coolest!"

It was a game date for us, so there was a lot of adrenaline

flowing as the team got prepped for the game that night. I could see James sitting in the stands, soaking up the energy of the squad as they went through their paces in the morning practice.

After the practice, I took James down to the locker room and led him from player to player, making introductions. "James, I want you to meet Donald Royal . . . Brooks Thompson . . . Coach Brian Hill." With every introduction, James's eyes got a little bigger. "Dennis Scott . . . Nick Anderson . . . Brian Shaw . . . Horace Grant." By the time we got to Shaquille O'Neal, his eyes looked like they were going to pop right out of his head, like a character in an animated cartoon. "James, this is Shaquille O'Neal," I said. Figuring there was no percentage in beating around the bush, I got right down to it. "Shaq," I said, "James has two problems: His grades aren't any good, and he's running with the wrong crowd. Can you talk to him?" So Shaquille talked to him for a little while, and then I said, "James, there's one more person I want you to meet."

James followed me down a row of lockers, and there, sitting on a bench with a towel around his neck was The Man himself, James's idol, the player with the big blue number 1 on his back. James whispered his name in a voice filled with awe:

"Anfernee Hardaway! Wow!"

"Penny," I said, "I want you to meet my friend James."

Now, Penny Hardaway comes from a very rough background in Memphis. He grew up under his grandmother's tutelage, he's lived in the mean streets, he's seen urban violence firsthand. In fact, he was once shot as a youth and ended up in the hospital with a bullet in his foot. Penny has been around the wrong crowd, and he's emerged from it. He has had problems in school, and he's overcome them. He knows where James comes from—and where he is headed. "Penny," I continued, "James has a great future. He could be a terrific basketball player, but here's what he's up to. His grades are down and he's scholastically ineligible. He spends too much time around people who are going to get him in a world of hurt. Do you have a few minutes to talk to him?"

Penny grinned at James, motioned to the bench with those great big talented hands of his, and said, "Hey, man, let's talk."

There was an instant electrochemical connection between

them. It was clear that Penny knew the world that James lived in. They sat there face to face, practically nose to nose, and they talked. I didn't want to eavesdrop, so I got out of the way and busied myself with other things—but every once in a while, I just had to glance over at the bench. I could see that these two guys, each with a big number 1 on his back, were locked in intense conversation. Penny not only talked, he listened. I don't know what was said, but I assume they talked about school, about home, about basketball, about winning in life. James devoured every syllable that Anfernee Hardaway spoke.

I left them for a few minutes, ran upstairs, grabbed a glossy color photo and brought it back down. When I got back they were still talking—and by the time they had finished, they had spent a good twenty minutes together, one on one. They stood up, Hardaway placed one arm around James's shoulder, and they walked over toward me. I said, "Penny, would you sign this picture for James?" He grinned and said, "Sure!"

Penny got an indelible marker and labored over that picture for about five minutes—writing a little, then pausing to think, then writing some more. When he had finished, he handed the photo to me so that I could give it to James. As I was taking it over to James, who was standing by his mother, curiosity got the better of me and I read what Penny had written:

> To James,
> Never forget what I told you today. Remember, you control your own destiny, not your friends. Stay strong and be good to your mom.
> Anfernee Hardaway

I got a lump in my throat when I read this. I handed it to James, along with a couple of tickets to the game that night, and James showed the photo to his mother. I watched them walk out of the Orlando Arena, and I thought, What an experience this boy has had. Maybe this is one less statistic we'll have to read about someday. James had his mind freed up that day as a result of a nose-to-nose talk with his hero. He can go on and live to his full potential—or he can throw it all away. The choice is up to James.

But I believe James is going to make the right choice. I think he turned a corner that day in early December 1994—because about six weeks later, in January of 1995, James and his mom came back. He had his report card in his hand, and each grade had gone up by one full letter, all across the board! In fact, one grade had gone up two letters! He was now eligible for the basketball team and had already played in three games. James's mother was beaming. "His teachers can't figure out what got into James," she said, "but they're delighted!"

I took James down to the locker room, and Penny welcomed him with a big hug. James showed him the report card, and Penny grinned. "All riiiiight!" said Penny, high-fiving the boy. "I'm really proud of you, man! I knew you could do it! But don't stop here, James! You can go beyond even this!"

James turned to me and said, "If I get all A's, can I be a Magic ball boy?" All A's! Here was a kid whose mind was totally freed up!

"James," I said, "if you get all A's, I'll see what I can do for you! Meanwhile, I want you to get me a copy of your report card every single quarter, okay? I'm going to make sure Penny sees every one of them."

When James and his mother left the arena, both of them were walking about eighteen inches above the floor—and frankly, so was I!

We read all the time about various evils and problems in sports, from strikes and labor disputes to drugs and gambling. But athletes like Penny Hardaway can have an enormous impact for good on America's youth. Here is just one boy, and it looks like his whole life may have been turned around and redirected by a twenty-minute talk with a basketball star. That's a powerful statement about the value of positive role models to free up the imaginations of our young people, to open up to them a great future filled with possibilities. But there are so many other kids like James whose minds are still bound up and whose horizons are still limited and barren. I hope and pray we can reach more of them before it's too late.

Now the question is: *How about you?*

My friend, I urge you to free up your imagination. Catch a

glimpse of the limitless horizons that await you. Throw your mind wide open and reach for the blue sky. There's no telling what will happen. You can *be* anything. You can *do* anything.

Turn the page, and I'll prove it to you.

CHAPTER 6

You Can Do Anything!

○ *The difference between what we do and what we are capable of doing would suffice to solve most of the world's problems.*
Gandhi

○ *You must do the thing you think you cannot do.*
Eleanor Roosevelt

○ *If we did all the things we are capable of doing, we would literally astonish ourselves.*
Thomas Edison

○ *Man is made so that whenever anything fires his soul, impossibilities vanish.*
Jean de la Fontaine, seventeenth-century French essayist

Walt Disney had a wide-open, anything's-possible attitude. Where did he get it? Nothing in his Missouri farmboy background points to the creative, imaginative genius he later displayed.

He started out sketching chickens, pigs, and cows on his father's farm, worked on a newspaper route with his brother Roy when he was ten, and drove an ambulance in France during World War I (when he was only fifteen). He returned from the war and hired on as an apprentice commercial artist in a Kansas City ad agency at age nineteen (earning the princely salary of fifty dollars a month). He soon formed his own advertising company, where he experimented with a brand-new art form: animated cartoons. His one-minute "Laugh-O-Gram" 'toons were filmed on a nonexistent budget in an unheated garage, but they became enormously successful in theaters across the country.

He improved his animation techniques and came up with an imaginative innovation: combining animated cartoon images with live-action footage. He introduced this approach in a series called *Alice in Cartoonland,* and this technique was later refined and perfected in such films as *Mary Poppins* and *Who Framed Roger Rabbit?* Produced on a shoestring budget, his *Alice* films were sold to distributors for a big $1,500 an episode. At age twenty-two, he moved to Hollywood and established himself as a major force in the animated cartoon world.

His next character, Oswald the Rabbit, was an overnight success. Unfortunately, Disney neglected to protect Oswald by copyrighting him—and the rights to the character were stolen out from under him. Disney learned from his mistakes, developed a new character—a big-eared mouse with a girlfriend named Minnie—and proceeded to make him a star. Originally, he wanted to call his mouse "Mortimer," but Walt's wife hated the name—so Mickey Mouse was born.

The first Mickey Mouse cartoon, *Steamboat Willie,* was a silent film, like all other films then being made. But about the same time Walt was finishing animation chores, "talkies" made their debut. *What a great idea!* thought Walt. *Cartoons that talk!* So he added a sound and music track to *Willie*—and the cartoon went on to win an Academy Award!

More cartoons brought more imaginative innovations: color, original songs, visual effects, sound effects. Many of Disney's Mickey Mouse and Silly Symphony cartoons were more popular than the feature films they were shown with. Walt was always looking for new ideas, always reaching for the outer edge of the fantastic.

Disney was not afraid of daring, risky experiments: 1937's $1,500,000 feature-length gamble *Snow White;* his startling and unprecedented animated symphony *Fantasia* (as commercially daring today as it was in 1940); his bold 1954 plunge into a new and untested medium called television; his landmark live-action film *20,000 Leagues Under the Sea,* released in 1955; and, of course, Disneyland. Everything he did was a grand celebration of imagination and wonder. His dreams were all "impossible dreams" that he patiently, steadfastly hammered into reality.

Pure imagination was the rarified air Walt Disney breathed. From his freed-up mind came cars, trains, and tugboats with personality and human problems; princesses and fairy godmothers and wicked witches; and a duck in a sailor suit with a baaaaaaad attitude! He wielded magical power through the art of animation, achieving the impossible on a regular basis with apparent ease.

Disney was always looking for new ideas, new techniques, new technologies to push the envelope of his art form. He surrounded himself with creative people, and his Burbank studios were a hothouse of imagination where new ideas bloomed daily. "Walt was always way ahead of any of us," said Disney animators Frank Thomas and Ollie Johnston in *Disney's Animation: The Illusion of Life.* He was always "searching for new procedures, new forms of entertainment, and we never can think of the future without remembering how he turned ideas over in his mind."

One of the ideas that fascinated Disney was the legend of Hiawatha. Thomas and Johnson recall that Disney wanted to find some completely new and never-before-imagined way of bringing the legend to life:

> He kept bringing it up over the years, trying to find the right way to do something with it. He said to us, "There's something there, y'know? Something we could do—something that's right for us. I don't know what it is or how we'd do it. Don't think of a film, don't even think of a show—don't limit your thinking to a regular theater. Maybe it's something out in the woods, or on a mountain, maybe

the people are brought in—or—I don't know—but there's something there!" That is the way we view the future today.[1]

Hiawatha was one of the Disney dreams that didn't materialize before he died, but he had successfully transmitted his idea to his colleagues. On June 10, 1995, the Disney Company launched a film about Native Americans—not the story of Hiawatha that Walt envisioned, but a film called *Pocahontas*—in a bold and innovative new way that was much like what Walt himself tried to describe to Frank Thomas and Ollie Johnston so many years ago. The company invited 100,000 people to a free multiscreen outdoor premiere on the Great Lawn of New York's Central Park. The movie was projected on four eight-story-tall screens, and the sound enveloped the audience from 150 speakers. The event was, in Disney chief Michael Eisner's words, "a family Woodstock."

I think Walt would have been pleased with the grand scale of the *Pocahontas* launching in Central Park. But he wouldn't have stopped there. He would have kept looking for bigger and better ways to present his dreams. Walt Disney never let practical realities get in the way of his imagination. "It's my job to dream the dreams," he once said, chuckling. "But paying for 'em? That's my brother Roy's job."[2]

IS ANYTHING IMPOSSIBLE?

Some people say that nothing in life is impossible. I say that *almost* nothing in life is impossible—but there are a *few* things that are *clearly* impossible. For example, it is impossible to:

- dribble a football,
- get bubble gum out of an angora sweater,
- barbecue pancakes,
- lift a bald-headed man by his hair,
- slam a revolving door,
- twirl a baton in a mobile home, or
- get off Jerry Falwell's mailing list.

Other than that, everything else in life is pretty much wide open. The sky's the limit. Men like Kent Cullers prove that almost nothing is impossible.

THE UNIVERSE IS HIS!

Kent Culler came into the world a few months prematurely in 1949—and he wasn't breathing. The doctors quickly administered a heavy dose of oxygen in an effort to save his life. The oxygen enabled the Culler baby to breathe, but it also clouded the lenses in his eyes and permanently damaged his retinas. He was completely blind.

Kent's parents were determined that, even though their child had a permanent sight-impairment, he would not grow up with a *life*-impairment. Again and again throughout his childhood, they drilled one message into their blind son: "You can do *anything*."

As a boy, he did virtually everything sighted children did. He climbed trees (and fell out of them). He rode a bicycle (he sometimes hit parked cars and fire hydrants, but he would pick himself right up again). He went to public school right alongside sighted kids. He was a straight-A student and a Boy Scout.

Kent's favorite book was *The Golden Book of Astronomy.* As his father read that book to him almost every night, young Kent pictured the unlimited expanse of the universe, filled with red giant stars, white dwarf stars, pulsars, nebulae, galaxies, and unknown worlds. It filled him with a fascination for physics and astronomy. Kent Culler went on to become valedictorian of his high school class, was Phi Beta Kappa in college, and earned a doctorate in physics at UC Berkeley. In his early twenties, he submitted a computer model to NASA that demonstrated dramatic improvements that could be made to the space shuttle's radar system. NASA agreed with Culler, scrapped its original radar design, and hired Kent as a scientist.

Kent Culler is one of NASA's most creative and productive scientists. For NASA's Search for Extra-Terrestrial Intelligence (SETI) project, he designed special equipment that sifts through the background radio noise of the universe, looking for evidence of intelligent communication. His high-speed radio listening device is able to scan a volume of information equivalent to the contents of all twenty-nine volumes of the Encyclopedia Britannica—*in a single second!*

Whereas most of us think in gravity-bound terms, Kent Culler's mind is free to tour the outer planets. He's used to imagining the universe not just in terms of visible light that you and I can see but in terms of infrared, ultraviolet, gamma radiation, X rays, and microwaves. Not having the "handicap" of normal vision, Kent can "see" images of the universe that the rest of us are "blind" to!

A lot of blind people grow up believing they are handicapped, limited, shut up in a world of darkness. Kent Culler grew up believing—as his parents repeatedly told him—that he could do *anything* he wanted to do. As a result, the *whole universe* belongs to Kent Culler.

What about you? Do you believe you can do *anything* you want to? And what do you teach your children? Shouldn't you be giving them the same message Kent Culler's parents gave him?

YOUR ATTITUDE DETERMINES YOUR ALTITUDE

On the instrument panel of every airplane is a device called the *attitude indicator.* This instrument shows the pilot—even in conditions of rain, fog, or darkness—the airplane's true orientation relative to the horizon. Even if the ground is invisible to the pilot, he or she can know with certainty whether the plane is level or banking, and if the nose of the plane is pitched upward or downward—thanks to the attitude indicator. If the nose is pitched upward while power is applied, the plane will climb; if downward, the plane descends. The plane's attitude is a key factor in determining whether an airplane goes up or down—and the same is true of you and me.

Our attitude determines our altitude. We can go as high as our attitude will take us—and, if our attitude points us toward the ground, we can also crash and burn. Positive thoughts create constructive actions that lift us toward our goals. Negative thoughts breed destructive reactions that drag us toward the muck and the dirt of failure.

One of our Filipino sons, Brian, who is thirteen, is an outstanding swimmer. But like most kids that age he struggles through some of the grueling practices.

Brian's coach, Kevin Meisel, was putting him through ten tough intervals recently, and after just six of them, Brian stopped and wouldn't do any more.

As they were driving home afterward, Kevin said, "Brian, you can do that work. You could have done all ten intervals. You just have to push yourself."

Brian replied, "I know I can do the work, coach, but my head won't let me."

What a powerful statement! That's not just true with Brian but with most people. Our attitude determines what we can do.

"The greatest revelation of our generation," said the great philosopher-psychologist William James, "is the discovery that human beings, by changing the inner attitudes of their minds, can change the outer aspects of their lives." It was also William James who said, "We become what we think about"—a restatement of the biblical adage: "For as he thinks in his heart, so is he."[3] And Dr. Frank Crane put it this way: "Our best friends and our worst enemies are our thoughts. A thought can do more good than a doctor or a banker or a faithful friend. It can also do us more harm than a brick."

A lot of us think our happiness is determined by our circumstances. "If I just had enough money," or "If I just had the right marriage partner," or "If I just had the right career," or "If my childhood hadn't been so dysfunctional—then I would be happy." That just ain't so! Happiness doesn't come from our circumstances! Happiness comes from *the way we think* about our circumstances!

"A happy person," said ABC 20/20's Hugh Downs, "is not a person in a certain set of circumstances, but rather a person with a certain set of attitudes." And the father of positive thinking, Dr. Norman Vincent Peale, agrees. "Happiness," he said, "is not a matter of good fortune or worldly possessions. It's a mental attitude. It comes from appreciating what we have, instead of being miserable about what we don't have. It's so simple—yet so hard for the human mind to comprehend."

CHOOSE YOUR ATTITUDE

Science has shown that your attitude can have a profound effect on your physical health as well. Husband-and-wife research team Ronald Glaser, a virologist, and Janice Kiecolt-Glaser, a psychologist, did a study of forty Ohio State University medical students. In this study, blood was drawn from the students at various intervals during the school year. Amazingly, the blood work showed a dramatic and consistent drop in immune-system "killer cells" and interferon levels during exam weeks. The students also reported more viral infections during exam weeks. Conclusion: The mental stress of studying for exams seriously interfered with the natural functioning of the immune systems of these students, leaving them more susceptible to disease.

The British medical journal *Lancet* reported a similar effect of mental attitude on the physical health of cancer patients at King's College Hospital in London. In a long-term study of fifty-seven breast-cancer patients who had undergone mastectomies, researchers found that 70 percent of those who displayed a positive "I'm-gonna-beat-this" attitude survived ten years or more, whereas roughly 75 to 80 percent of those who resigned or stoically accepted their diagnosis were dead within ten years. Attitude was the number one factor in surviving cancer.[4]

Dr. John E. Anderson, president of the Center for Sports Psychology in Colorado Springs recalls similar situations in which mental attitude determined physical performance in sports. "I once asked a world-class athlete to guess the outcome of a major competition," Anderson recalls. "'I'll come in fifth,' he said. And that's exactly where he finished, even though he could easily have placed third or even second, since two other major contenders fared poorly.

"Contrast him with 'Flo-Jo'—Florence Griffith Joyner. Training a week before the 1988 Games, she wrote in her diary the time she expected to run and win the 100-meter dash: 10:54 seconds. When Flo-Jo crossed the finish line, the clock showed 10:54. She had not only seen herself winning, but called her winning time to the split second."

Your attitude can help you to overcome the worst imaginable circumstances in life. In his book *The Winner's Edge,* Denis Waitley tells the story of Air Force Colonel George Hall, who was shot down and captured in North Vietnam. Colonel Hall spent five and a half years in solitary confinement as a prisoner of war. The boredom and sensory deprivation of that dreadful existence destroyed the minds and the lives of many other brave men—but George Hall found a way to survive.

Though he was barefoot and dressed in his black prison pajamas, and even though he was shut up in a claustrophobia-inducing little cubicle, Hall discovered that he had an amazing freedom. He was able to leave his prison cell clad in a golfing outfit and clean white golf shoes. Underneath his feet was the thick green carpet of a plush fairway on the Pebble Beach golf course in northern California. At his side, an eager young caddy carried his clubs. The sun was shining, and there was a gentle, salty breeze wafting in from the Pacific Ocean. Colonel Hall proceeded to play each hole, beginning with the first, and on in succession to the eighteenth. He studied each shot, measured each swing, felt each blade of grass between his fingers as he replaced every divot, noted the texture of the sand in each bunker, chipped well-placed shots onto each green, pulled out each flag and handed it to his caddie, then checked the lay of the green to determine which direction the ball would break, sank each putt, strode to the next tee—

All in his imagination.

Every day for five and a half years, Colonel Hall played a perfect game of golf on the Pebble Beach course. Why? Because he understood that he had a choice to make. He could either resign himself to the fear and hopelessness of his situation—or he could replay his happiest moments from the past, taking his mind out of solitary confinement and setting it free upon a beautiful golf course on the California coast.

At the end of his captivity, something truly amazing happened. Upon his return to the States, Colonel Hall couldn't wait to get back on the golf course—and when he did, he shot an eye-opening 76! Not a bad score for a seasoned professional—and an absolutely phenomenal score for an amateur duffer who had spent the last five and a half years shut up in a box in Vietnam. Asked how he accomplished such a feat, he replied, "In the past five and a half years, I never putted a green in more than two strokes." All those years of playing perfect games in his imagination had produced a near-perfect performance on a real golf course!

Do any of us really appreciate the power of our own minds to bring us the success we want?

In 1958, a nineteen-year-old pianist named Liu Shi-kum took high honors at the International Tchaikovsky Competition, placing second only to Van Cliburn. Liu returned to his home in Communist China, where he received the accolades of his countrymen and became a concert pianist. In the mid-1960s, however, Chairman Mao instituted his Cultural Revolution throughout China, in which any artistic expression deemed inconsistent with pure Chinese culture and with Marxism was automatically purged. Many artists and musicians were jailed or killed. Liu himself was caught up in the purges, since the classical music he played was considered an evil and corrupting Western influence. Called "an enemy of the people," Liu was jailed and beaten. His right forearm was fractured in one of the beatings, and he was shut up in a cell without anything to read, write on, or listen to. Worst of all, there was no piano. For six years, Liu was shut up in the worst prison conditions imaginable.

In the early 1970s, thanks to a thaw in Chinese-American relations, the Philadelphia Orchestra, under the direction of Eugene Ormandy, came to China on a goodwill tour. Ormandy, who remembered Liu's outstanding performance at the International Tchaikovsky Competition in 1958, requested that this talented pianist be permitted to perform in concert with the Philadelphia Orchestra. Embarrassed by the fact that this great talent was languishing in prison, the Chinese authorities promised that Liu would be able to perform, and Mao Tse-tung personally ordered Liu's release.

So Liu came out of prison for a command performance in Peking—but he had a problem. He had not touched a piano in six years. The broken bone in his arm had healed improperly, which caused pain when it was moved. How could this musician hope to perform competently, much less brilliantly, with such handicaps?

Yet the night of the concert, he delivered a performance that his listeners called "brilliant" and "astonishing." How was this possible? Because, like Colonel Hall in Vietnam, Liu Shi-kum had spent every day of his captivity doing what he loved—and doing it all in the freed-up realm of his imagination. In his prison cell, Liu practiced his music on an invisible piano, hearing the notes in the silence of his mind, keeping his talent alive within the disciplined confines of his own brilliant mind. It was a triumph of attitude over circumstances. He never gave up, he maintained his faith in his art, and he cultivated his dedication to excellence—even in the dark, brutal confinement of a prison cell.

Another man who conquered the horror of imprisonment—psychiatrist and Nazi death camp survivor Victor Frankl, summed up the achievements of Colonel Hall and Liu Shi-kum when he said, "The last of the human freedoms is the freedom to choose one's attitude in any given set of circumstances."

WHERE DO CHAMPIONS COME FROM?

New York Times sportswriter Tom Friend quoted then Dallas Cowboys coach Jimmy Johnson, who recalled the pep talk he gave his team before its 1993 Super Bowl victory. "I told them," said Johnson, "that if I laid a two-by-four across the floor of the locker room, everybody there could walk across it and not fall, because our focus would be that we were going to walk that two-by-four. But if I put that same two-by-four ten stories high between two buildings, only a few would make it, because the focus would be on falling. Then I said, 'Your focus right now has to be as if we're playing on the practice field in front of nobody. If you let it overwhelm you that it'll be the most watched sporting event in the world, that there'll be 3,000 media people here, how much money will be made—if you make it bigger than life, that will be a distraction. And that's the crux of this game.'" Johnson kept his team's focus on the will to win, not on the hoopla that surrounded the game—and the Cowboys went for the win and grabbed it.

One of the most famous games in World Series history is famous *precisely* because it is such a clear demonstration of the unquenchable power of a positive mental attitude. The game:

1932 World Series game three, October 1, 1932. The place: Wrigley Field, Chicago. The teams: the New York Yankees and the Chicago Cubs. It was a bitterly contested series, drenched in bad feelings between the two clubs. The Yankees had already won the first two games at Yankee Stadium, but now they were playing in hostile territory, surrounded by 49,936 loud and raucous Cubs fans.

Babe Ruth, the Yankee "Sultan of Swat," was incensed by the Cubs' ill treatment of his friend and former teammate Mark Koenig, who had recently been traded to Chicago. Koenig had been cheated out of half his share of the Series money by a vote of his teammates, even though his .353 batting average had given the Cubs the pennant in a tight National League race. Ruth was furious and wanted to punish the Cubs. "Hey, Mark!" he called out to his buddy from the dugout. "Who are those cheapskates you're playing with?"

Ruth was also furious with the entire city of Chicago because he and his wife had been mobbed by hostile Cubs fans outside his Chicago hotel. They had been spat upon and pelted by garbage. On the morning of the game, Ruth had been showered with lemons during batting practice by angry Cubs boosters. Even the Cubs trainer, Andy Lotshaw, took part in the abuse, hollering to Ruth, "If I had you on my team, I'd hitch you to a wagon, you potbelly!" More than anything in the world, Ruth wanted to slam a couple of home runs right into the grinning faces of those rude and rowdy Cubs fans and their favorite team.

He got his chance in the first inning, hitting a three-run homer. Lou Gehrig followed up with a homer of his own in inning three, bringing the score to 4–0. The Cubs fans roared and raged, throwing more lemons and pop bottles onto the field, urging their team to fight back. The Cubs responded by coming back in the fourth and tying the game 4–4.

The fateful inning, the fifth, was at hand. Ruth stepped up to the plate, and the crowd jeered with a ferocity reminiscent of a bloodthirsty Roman coliseum crowd. From the Cubs dugout, Ruth's opponents called out a steady stream of unprintable catcalls. From the mound, Cubs pitcher Charlie Root wound up and hurled a perfect strike over the plate. Ruth let it go by. The jeering from the stands and the dugout intensified. The Sultan smiled in the direction of the Cubs dugout and raised one finger, as if to say, "That's one!"

Root threw two more pitches—ball one and ball two. Then Root powered a fastball right down the center of the strike zone. Ruth eyed the ball amiably as it sped past. Strike two. The crowd exploded in cheers over Ruth's apparent poor judgment in passing up the ball. Ruth turned to Cubs catcher Gabby Harnett and said, "It only takes one to hit it." Then he turned back toward Root, and the two men, hitter and pitcher, traded remarks. No one knows what the two men said to each other because the noise of the crowd drowned out their words. But the look in each man's eye was clear: They were facing each other down, challenging each other, taunting each other.

Then came the pivotal moment, the demonstration of Babe Ruth's unquenchable attitude, his unconquerable will to win: He raised his hand and pointed off behind Charlie Root, toward the center-field fence. *He was actually calling his shot, telling Root where he intended to hit it!*

Root sneered, went into his windup, then released the ball, sending it on a curved trajectory, low and away. Ruth eyed the whizzing ball and swung his bat. Wood and horsehide connected with a resounding *whack!* It might as well have been a thunder-clap, for the crowds in the stands were instantly hushed. The ball soared over Root's head, over the head of the center fielder, into the center-field bleachers—*right where Ruth had said it would go!* It was one of the longest home runs ever hit at Wrigley Field.

Ruth loped leisurely around the bases, laughing and holding both hands together over his head like a championship boxer, grinning in the direction of the Cubs dugout as he jogged past. It was a triumph of attitude that helped propel the Yankees to a 7–5 victory over the Cubs—and which enabled the Yankees to sweep the entire Series.

Even the great Lou Gehrig, who hit two home runs in that same game, was awed by Ruth's winning attitude. The night of that game, Gehrig had dinner with a sportswriter, and all he could talk about was Ruth's "called shot" homer. "What do you think of the nerve of that big monkey," said Gehrig, "taking those two strikes, then calling his shot and hitting the ball exactly where he pointed?"

What is true in sports is true in every arena of life. "We can do only what we think we can do," said Robert Collier. "We can be only what we think we can be. We can have only what we think we can have. What we do, what we are, what we have, all depend upon what we think."

TEACHING OUR CHILDREN TO DO THE IMPOSSIBLE

A few years ago, it was impossible to fly to the moon. It was impossible to make a phone call from your car. It was impossible to run a mile in under four minutes. It was impossible to send pictures and documents over the phone. It was impossible to prevent polio and smallpox. It was impossible to turn on a TV, pop a tape in a VCR, and watch any movie you wanted. It was impossible to fly faster than sound. It was impossible for a baby to be born three months prematurely and survive. It was impossible to cure many kinds of cancer. It was impossible to turn black-and-white movies into color movies. It was impossible to send a spacecraft out of the solar system.

Today, all of the above things have been done and are being done. Routinely. Daily. We are living the fantasies of yesterday's science fiction—and we take it all for granted. We do the impossible without a second thought.

What are the "impossibilities" we face today? It's impossible to cure AIDS. It's impossible to cure the common cold. It's impossible to travel faster than light and visit other stars. It's impossible to end war. It's impossible to end poverty and homelessness. It's impossible to walk on air. It's impossible to live on the moon and Mars. It's impossible to live under the ocean. It's impossible to mine gold in the asteroid belt. It's impossible to balance the federal budget. It's impossible to make pollution-free automobiles. It's impossible to live to be five hundred years old. All of these things are "impossible"—today.

But tomorrow—who knows?

Question: Who will turn today's "impossibilities" into tomorrow's commonplace realities? Answer: *Our children.*

But if we want our children to do the impossible tomorrow, we have to begin teaching them today that *they can do anything.* We have to take every opportunity to practice Magical Secret No. 2 with our children, and free their imagination and creativity. We must show them that the wide blue sky has no limits, no horizons, no ceilings. They can fly as high as they want—to the moon, to Mars, to Alpha Centauri, to the Andromeda Galaxy, to infinity. The universe is theirs for the taking. Here's how Walt Disney put it: "Every child is blessed with a vivid imagination. But just as a muscle grows flabby with disuse, so the bright imagination of a child pales in later years if he ceases to exercise it."

As I see it, there are three deadly killers of creativity and blue-sky thinking running rampant in our society today. Our job as parents is to guard our children and fend off these killers and keep our children's minds wide open to the limitless possibilities that hide behind the word *impossible.* Those three deadly killers are teachers, television, and parents. Let's take a closer look:

Creativity Killer No. 1: Teachers

Most teachers are dedicated to opening a child's mind, and many do an absolutely fantastic job of inspiring blue-sky thinking in our children. Teachers who know how to free the imagination of our children are worth a million times what we pay them. They deserve a statue in the park and a library named in their honor. But not every teacher is dedicated, gifted, and inspiring. Some make it their goal to produce a classroom of well-programmed robots, thirty minds slotted into nice, neat little rows of pigeonholes. They don't inspire; they regiment. And they can kill imagination and creativity so quickly!

I don't advocate anarchy in the classroom. A certain amount of orderliness is necessary for learning to take place. But there has to be some allowance for the messiness, the spontaneity, the unruliness, and the enthusiasm of an imaginative child. You can't blame a teacher for liking little Josie who sits quietly in the front row, both feet on the floor, hands primly in her lap, eyes attentively on the teacher at all times. Josie's never a problem, and the teacher would love to have a roomful of Josies. I'm not knocking the Josies of the world, because we need them.

But I'm a little more concerned about Jamal and Jimmy and Juan in the back row, the kids who run windsprints on the ceiling, talk when they should listen, run afoul of the rules now and then, and think at right angles to the rest of their classmates. One of those kids in the back row could become the next Shaquille O'Neal or Billy Graham or Dave Thomas or Neil Armstrong or Colin Powell—or, depending on how he is handled in that classroom, he could become the next statistic to be claimed by the mean streets.

As parents, we should become involved in our schools, encouraging and supporting those teachers who draw out the dreams and creativity of our kids. We should make sure our kids are being mentored by that kind of teacher. We need to protect our kids from the creativity killers and steer them toward the creativity enhancers.

Creativity Killer No. 2: Television

The Tube: as a technology, it's a wonder. You can now receive a virtually unlimited number of cable or satellite channels, you can watch anything you want at any time you want, you can plug video games and VCRs into it. And that's why it can be such a creativity killer: You can sit in front of it forever and be endlessly, mindlessly entertained. I'm not talking here about the violence, the degraded morality, the gutter language, and everything else that the Tube offers today—as bad as all that is. All of that is a given.

I'm talking about the *medium of television itself* and the hypnotic, addictive power it has to suck the mind, the imagination, and the irreplaceable gift of time from a person's life. Television has a seductive voice that reaches out to young and old alike and says, "Sit down, veg out, let your mind go limp, let me entertain you." Remember the Control Voice that started each episode of the old *Outer Limits* sci-fi show? It said, "There is nothing wrong with your television set. Do not attempt to adjust the picture. We are controlling transmission. For the next hour, just sit quietly and we will control all that you see and hear . . ." What is really chilling about that little speech is that it is *not* science fiction! *That is what television actually does to our minds!*

We have a very simple rule in the Williams home: *No TV*. Pat Williams controls that box, not the nineteen minor-age inmates of our household. We've tried all the gimmicks you've probably tried in your family: only so much TV per day, or a reward of so much TV if the chores get done, or you can't turn it on till your homework's done—but none of this stuff works! So we adopted a very clear policy: the Tube stays dark. Sometimes we'll rent a movie or make room for a special program, and then TV becomes a family entertainment (or educational) event. But those are exceptions. "No TV, period!" is the rule.

The hypnotic power of TV is nothing short of amazing. If the set is on and a child or teenager walks through the room, you can actually see that kid get magnetized by the Tube. It's as if energy beams leap out of those cathode-ray tubes and zap the child's mind like a ray gun. The kid will veer toward the set, cross the floor, drop to his knees before that flickering icon, and completely zone out. The eyes glaze over. The kid is so riveted to that Tube, he even forgets to blink. If allowed to, he will remain there in front of the set for six, eight, or ten hours.

Our kids are involved in all sorts of productive, fun, exciting activities—sports, music, the arts, hobbies, games, and more. There are hundreds of imaginative, creative, stimulating ways they can and do spend their time. Our kids are enthused about—and successful in—so many of these different activities. Yet, given a choice between all these terrific experiences and just sitting and watching TV, I honestly believe they would choose couch-potato-hood.

TV is a killer. Kill it before it kills you and your kids.

Creativity Killer No. 3: Us!

That's right. Parents like you and me can be the worst killers of creativity and imagination of all! We suppress the possibilities of our children in many ways:

- With harsh, critical words: "Where are your brains?" "Can't you do anything right?" "You can't do it like that!"
- With indifference, inattention, and neglect: "Not now!

Can't you see I'm busy?" "Uh-huh, that's nice, now please stay outta my way."

- With lack of affirmation and positive feedback: "You didn't make the sky the right color." "Six A's and a C minus in math, eh? How come you're doing so lousy in math?"
- With controlling behavior: "Here, let me do that. You don't do it right."

These three deadly creativity killers need to be put in perspective. And so do our children's unique creative abilities, their "red threads."

RED THREADS

There is a verse in the Bible that says, "Train up a child in the way he should go, and when he is old he will not depart from it."[5] Some people think this verse means we should send our kids to Sunday school, teach them the Ten Commandments, have them say grace at mealtimes and pray at bedtime, and they will turn out to be good kids. But people who have read this verse in the original language tell me there is a much deeper meaning embedded there. A more complete translation of this verse might read, "Train up a child *according to his own unique characteristics,* and when he is older he will become all he was intended to be." In other words, we are not supposed to pour our kids into a mold or stamp them out with a cookie cutter. We are to discover and develop the unique traits and abilities of each of our children.

One concept that has meant a lot to me as a parent is the "red threads" concept. A "red thread" is that one aptitude, passion, or interest that stands out among all the rest in a person's life. In a child, it may be difficult to discern, but in an adult, it is a trademark, a stamp of identity. The child who spends all his before- and after-school time running a paper route, a lemonade stand, and a lawn service may grow up to become a go-getter entrepreneur. The child who loves to read may become a renowned author. The child who loves tinkering with CO_2-propelled toy rockets may become a NASA engineer. The child who is eager to learn the piano may one day be a composer, a performer, or even an executive in the music business. These early interests and abilities are a child's "red threads." They are the richly colorful aspects of that child's being that stand out against the background of gray and brown threads that he or she finds less interesting and exciting.

My "red thread" was sports. My whole life is athletics. I love every sport there is. As a boy, I played baseball, basketball, football, every kind of ball I could get my hands on. Emerging into my twenties, I tried my hand at pro baseball for a couple years. Even though I didn't make it into the majors, my "red thread" still showed its true color. As a boy I thought I was an athlete, but it turned out that my real talent was as a sports manager and promoter. You never know where red threads will lead, so you have to do all you can to identify them and nurture them, knowing that they are the keys to a child's future.

The goal of the "red threads" concept is to allow our children's individuality to bloom and mature. When we discover and emphasize the "red threads" in our kids, we accentuate the positive in their lives. Many negative forces seek to tear kids down, so it's crucial to continually find "red threads" that enable them to feel confident, involved, motivated, and interested in life. If our children reach adolescence without any activity they enjoy or skill they excel in, then we have failed as parents. The child who has no "red threads," who sees his life as a pattern of dull grays and browns, is an ideal candidate for drugs, illicit sex, cultism, occultism, and the other lures and dangers of our age.

In order to discover and nurture our children's "red threads," we have to get to know our kids, individually and deeply. We need to know their strengths, abilities, emotional makeup, needs, goals, ambitions, likes, dislikes, and drives. That means we have to spend *time* with our kids—not so-called "quality time" but honest-to-gosh *quantity time*. You've heard of "quality time"—and it's a myth. The idea is that a few well-chosen, well-planned moments of togetherness can take the place of a real, long-term, time-intensive relationship with your kids—and that's just an out-and-out hoax! What do kids know about "quality time"? Kids want to talk to you, wrestle with you, play ball with you, climb all over you, be tickled by you, and in general get as big a piece of you as they can!

Kids want your time—a lot of it! They want *you!* They aren't thinking "quality time." They're thinking *time,* period.

I remember a poem I once read in a newspaper, attributed to "Author Unknown," called "To My Grown-Up Son." It hit me right between the eyes the first time I read it:

> My hands were busy through the day
> I didn't have much time to play
> The little games you asked me to.
> I didn't have much time for you.
> I'd wash your clothes, I'd sew and cook,
> But when you'd bring your picture book
> And ask me please to share your fun,
> I'd say: "A little later, son."
> I'd tuck you in all safe at night
> And hear your prayers, turn out the light,
> Then tiptoe softly to the door.
> I wish I'd stayed a minute more.
> For life is short, the years rush past.
> A little boy grows up so fast.
> No longer is he at your side,
> His precious secrets to confide.
> The picture books are put away,
> There are no longer games to play,
> No good-night kiss, no prayers to hear.
> That all belongs to yesteryear.
> My hands, once busy, now are still.
> The days are long and hard to fill.
> I wish I could go back and do
> The little things you asked me to.

The purest, sweetest joys I've ever known have been experienced in the quantity of time I've spent with my kids. Quantity time is the only way really to observe, understand, and get to know a child in all of his or her wonderful, God-given uniqueness. Quantity time spent with your children is the *only* way you can "train up a child according to his own unique characteristics." It's the only way you can find his or her "red threads."

Now, I'm going to share with you a secret, a nugget of deep wisdom. I'm going to share with you one of the most effective ways you can use a big quantity of your time to bring out your child's unique interests, talents, abilities, and possibilities: *Get behind the wheel and drive.* If you want to free your child's imagination and introduce him or her to all the many possibilities that life has to offer, you have to be willing to chauffeur that child all over the known universe—from school to the YMCA to Little League to church youth group to soccer to swimming practice to voice lessons to summer activities at the zoo to the dance studio to gymnastics to tae kwon do lessons to snow trips to beach trips to mountain trips to summer camp to—

Well, to wherever that child's interests and imagination may lead!

You may need to get a station wagon. In my case, I invested in a fifteen-passenger van (and sometimes, I have to charter a Greyhound!). If you are not willing to drive your kids from here to there and beyond, then they will never get the opportunity to realize all they might become. Every parent must manage to keep his or her child involved in activities.

And while you're being a great parent to your own kids, you might want to look around and see if there are any other kids you could be "Dad" or "Mom" to. I once had a long talk with Reggie White, the Green Bay Packers football star who is also a Christian minister and a leader in the black community. I'll never forget one thing Reggie told me. "Pat," he said, "I could solve the problems of the inner city real quick if I just had enough sports facilities and drivers and people who cared about getting those kids involved in activities and doing things with their lives. There is unlimited musical, artistic, athletic, and educational talent all over the inner cities. Those kids just need a chance. They just need people who will take the time to care and show them the possibilities life has to offer."

Goethe said, "Treat a man as he is, and he will remain as he is. Treat a man as he can and should be, and he will become as he can and should be." I would paraphrase that to say, "Treat a child according to his or her unique, unlimited potential, and that child will grow into that potential and do the impossible!" Our job is to believe that our kids are capable of anything, even the impossible. We must free up our own imaginations, and then we can free up theirs.

UNCHAINING THE IMAGINATION OF A NEW GENERATION

Dr. James Dobson, psychologist and host of *Focus on the Family,* once recalled a TV documentary he saw on the training of elephants. He described how these magnificent beasts were subjected to a stressful, even cruel form of "brainwashing" in order to take the fight out of them and make them useful for work. First, these extremely social animals were placed in total isolation for three days. This made them psychologically vulnerable to the next stage, in which they were brought out in the middle of the night to a place where there was an awesome, blazing bonfire. There they were surrounded by men who screamed at them and shook sticks at them. Hours later, when the sun came up, these beasts were so terrorized and abused that their wills were broken. Man had become the master, and the elephant had become the slave. "Even though I understand the economic need for working elephants in India," concludes Dobson, "there is still something sad about their plight. . . . Their fragile emotions are manipulated to destroy their independence and curb their individuality."

I do a weekly radio talk show in Orlando, and one of the most fascinating interviews I ever did was with Gunther Gebel-Williams, the famed animal trainer for the Ringling Brothers-Barnum and Bailey Circus. I was talking to him about elephant training, and he told me in his thick German accent that when elephants are trained for the circus, they are initially held in place by a massive chain that is firmly attached to a sturdy banyan tree. They spend the first few days or weeks tugging and tugging on that chain, trying to get free—but the chain and the tree are too strong. Later, that banyan tree is replaced by a small stake, and the massive chain is replaced by a smaller, lighter chain. With a single flick of its trunk, the elephant could yank that stake right out of the ground—but he doesn't know it. He has learned that a chain means bondage, and it is useless to fight it. His will is broken, his mind is broken, he is completely imprisoned by that puny chain—even though he has all the power he needs to break free!

The point of these two elephant stories is that children are often broken in much the same way as these elephants. Many kids are isolated and ignored one moment, then screamed at and abused the next. They may become docile like the elephant—or they may become embittered and antisocial. They learn to think of themselves as limited—as either stupid or untalented or ugly or imprisoned by circumstances. In reality, there is no limit to how far they could go—but they don't know it. Their imaginations have been chained and their future has been shut down. I've seen many such kids, and I grieve for every one of them.

I want to find ways to break the chains that enslave the imagination of this new generation. In my own small way, with my nineteen kids, I am trying to make a difference. And I tell you, it is absolutely thrilling to have seen again and again, right in our own home, what a freed-up imagination can do.

In November 1988, I adopted four Filipino brothers at one swoop. Their ages were nine, eight, seven, and four when we got them. At the time, I already had eight kids, and I knew an instant 50 percent increase in the brood would be a big jolt to the family system. Our family is compassionate, so we gave these four boys a whole day to adjust to their new situation; then we threw them right into American life. Their immediate reaction to almost everything we exposed them to was, "We can't do that!" They had been in an orphanage in Mindinao, the southernmost island of the Philippines, and they had never had much opportunity to do anything active or creative with their time. They had never been challenged to compete in athletics, and they didn't want to be challenged. Every new experience we tossed at them was met with the reaction of a chained, enslaved little mind: "We could never do that!"

One of the first experiences we exposed these four boys to almost immediately was youth swimming, which is very popular in central Florida. We took them to the Rollins College pool and handed them over to veteran coach Harry Meisel and his son, Kevin. Those four boys went into the water, kicking and screaming, and as they were going down for the third time, we could hear them glubbing, "We can't swim!" And they couldn't. But hey, like I said, we're compassionate people. We threw an anvil out to each of them. (Just kidding!)

Harry and Kevin challenged these boys to attempt what they had never attempted before: *to do the impossible.* In a few days, these boys began to discover they had previously undiscovered gills and fins. They began doing the impossible—swimming—and they were loving it! Year by year, their skills, strength, and stamina as swimmers have grown—so much so that in the summer of 1994, three of the boys, Peter, Brian, and Sammy, qualified for the Junior Olympics in Florida. These boys who said, "We can't swim!" are now some of the top youth swimmers in the state!

Because their imaginations have been freed up, they have an unlimited future in that sport—and in life. Their minds are freed up. They learned that they could do anything, even the "impossible." Now, they obviously had good coaching, and (ahem!) tremendous parenting—but in the end, they did it all themselves. They did it with lots of hard work, lots of practice, and the wide-open, no-horizons, blue-sky belief that there are truly no limits, no ceilings in life.

I just told you how the stories of three of those four Filipino boys turned out: Peter, Brian, and Sammy became standout swimmers—but what about the fourth boy, David? He's the oldest and a good swimmer, but he's not as passionate about that sport as his brothers. His freed-up imagination took him in a different direction. Here's David's story.

The week David and his brothers arrived, I immediately put a baseball glove on him to check him out. (Whenever we bring new kids into the family, we have them run a few windsprints with a stopwatch to clock their speed, throw 'em a ball to see if they can throw, catch, dribble, and shoot—you know, the basics. If they pass the preliminary test, we keep them, and if not—okay, okay, I'm just kidding again.) So we handed David this baseball glove, and he didn't know if he was supposed to wear it on his hand, his foot, or over his face. But with a lot of encouragement from his new dad, he began plugging away at it.

About three years after he joined the Williams household, not knowing which end of a baseball glove was up, twelve-year-old David was pitching in the Little League district tournament when he pulled off what is an exceedingly rare accomplishment at any level of baseball: *He retired eighteen straight hitters and pitched a perfect six-inning game.* Everyone at that game was amazed by what they saw—but no one was more amazed than David himself!

At the end of the game, we walked to the car together, and I put my arm around him and congratulated him. He was wearing a grin so wide it had to be continued on the next face. He looked up at me and said, "Dad, I'm doing pretty good, aren't I?" What an understatement! I looked back at him and said, "Yeah, David, you sure are."

Now what do you think lies ahead for that boy? Anything at all! It's fascinating to peek inside his mind and see what he thinks he can do. David is fifteen as I write these words, but in his mind, he's already an athlete in his early twenties, out on the diamond in "the house that Babe Ruth built," leading off for the legendary New York Yankees, or maybe pitching or playing second base. Nothing is impossible for David, because his imagination has been freed up.

A DARING ADVENTURE

One more story from the Williams family scrapbook, and then we're finished with Magical Secret No. 2:

Williams Kids No. 17 and No. 18 arrived on Christmas night, 1993. Caroline, age ten, and Alan, age eight, arrived from Brazil, and we immediately threw them both into the Williams household routine of school, fun, chores, family devotions, and sports—lots and lots of sports. I grabbed Alan and enrolled him in the basketball program at the Y.

The first basketball game he ever saw was a game he played in. So, as you can imagine, his approach to the game was a bit unusual. In fact, each of the kids on that hardwood court had his own unique theory of how roundball is to be played. The game was vaguely reminiscent of basketball as I've always seen it played: I mean, there was a round ball and two hoops, but that's where the similarity ended. The rest of the game was a potpourri of volleyball, soccer, football, and wrestling, and it all took place on the basketball court at the Winter Park Y. None of the participants let the rules get in the way of athletic creativity.

Somehow in the middle of this melee, Alan got out in front of the crowd and dribbled, ran, drop-kicked the ball toward the basket. Somehow or other, he jumped up in the air and threw a ball up in the air. By some miracle known only to the angels, the ball bounced off the backboard, danced around the rim a few times, then slid through the net. Alan was one ecstatic little eight-year-old. For hours after that two-point shot, he was a bundle of adrenaline moving at the speed of light.

I brought him home from the Y so that he could tell everyone about the game. He didn't speak a word of English—he had only been in the country a couple of weeks at that point—but he was talking a hundred miles an hour in nonstop Portuguese, describing what he had done on the basketball court. I understood a little Portuguese, but I was completely lost while he talked. Then I caught this one phrase: "Quasi Michael Jordan!"

He had just said, "I'm almost Michael Jordan!"

That really hit me hard. A few weeks before, Alan was running in the streets of Sao Paulo, with no future, no concept of the big wide world beyond his grimy little horizon. Suddenly, he has a moment of glory and his imagination is so completely freed up that he is saying, "I'm soaring, man! I'm gonna be the next Michael Jordan!" Maybe he will, maybe he won't. But with his blue-sky, no-horizons, freed-up imagination, he has a chance to be everything he's capable of being. He can do anything he wants to—even the so-called "impossible."

What's the impossible thing you want to do? Reach for it. Risk for it. Pop the lid off your mind and shoot for the moon! Don't let any fear or trepidation hold you back. "Security is mostly a superstition," said Helen Keller. "It does not exist. . . . Avoiding danger is no safer in the long run than outright exposure. Life is either a daring adventure or nothing." So leave your security blanket behind, strap on your rocket-pack, and aim for the big blue sky.

Believe it, live it, and teach it to your kids: *You can do ANYTHING!*

Next stop on our road to success: the third secret behind a magical kingdom, a magical basketball team, and a magical, miraculous way of life: Strive for lasting quality!

MAGICAL SECRET

NUMBER 3

Strive for Lasting Quality

CHAPTER 7

"Good Enough" Never Is

○ *Do what you do so well that those who see you do what you do are going to come back to see you do it again and tell others that they should see you do what you do.*
Walt Disney

○ *The road to business success is paved by those who continually strive to produce better products or services. It does not have to be a great technological product like television. Ray Kroc of McDonald's fame did it with a single hamburger.*
G. Kingsley Ward, poet

In August 1989, I was invited to a business dinner at one of the Disney hotels in Orlando. I found myself seated next to Dick Nunis, at that time the top Disney executive in Orlando. Dick is a former football player at USC who started with Disney right out of college in the 1950s and worked alongside Walt Disney for a number of years. I was eager to learn all I could about Disney, so I asked Dick for his firsthand impressions of the man. "What were the qualities or characteristics of Walt Disney that made him so unique, so successful?"

Fortunately, as Dick responded to my question, I had the presence of mind to jot down his reflections on a napkin. I've had those notes all these years. "There are so many qualities that made Walt Disney such a special individual," said Dick, "but I think you can chalk up his success to nine great character strengths:

"One, he had integrity. You could absolutely trust the man.

"Two, he had creativity. He was a true visionary.

"Three, he had administrative ability. He knew how to get the very best out of people.

"Four, he was a motivator. He was like a great coach—not easy to work for, but he pushed you to the limit, and once you had delivered your best effort, you were grateful that he drew it out of you.

"Five, he was willing to gamble. He was a calculated risk-taker.

"Six, he listened well. He was willing to learn from anyone.

"Seven, he wanted people to challenge him.

"Eight, he did his homework. He was constantly looking at problems from various angles, studying, learning, improving.

"Nine—and this is probably the most important—he was fanatically committed to excellence. He continually reached for an intangible quality called perfection. Obviously, imagination and creativity were very important to Walt, and he liked new ideas. But he was just as pleased if you could take an existing idea and really perfect it, really buff and polish it into something of quality. In fact, he used to say, 'There are no new ideas. You just take a good one and improve on it.'"

Dick Nunis had a lot of firsthand experience with Walt Disney's fanatical commitment to excellence during his days with the Disneyland theme park in Anaheim. He was a training supervisor when the park opened in 1955. At that time, Walt felt his own organization lacked experience in certain aspects of theme park operation, so he contracted with outside companies to handle many Disneyland operations, including security, custodial maintenance, food service, parking, and crowd control. The problem was that the outside companies didn't understand Walt Disney's commitment to quality. The custodians didn't keep the park clean.

The security staff was rude and overbearing. The parking and crowd-control people actually hollered at the customers—the very people Walt considered his *guests!* Appalled, Walt fired the offending companies.

Dick Nunis had been in charge of training all the attraction operators, and they had all performed beautifully—a pleasant, efficient, smiling band of people who gave the customers a true Disney-style welcome. So Walt put Dick in charge of training Disney staff to handle all the other aspects of the park as well. Walt's commitment to quality was total and all-encompassing, and he expected excellence from everyone who represented the Disney name—even the parking lot attendants and custodians.

In the late 1950s, Dick Nunis was put in charge of Adventureland. His principal responsibility was to maintain a high level of quality in the centerpiece attraction of Adventureland, the Jungle Cruise. On one occasion, Walt Disney made a surprise appearance at the attraction. He boarded one of the boats along with the paying customers and set off on a cruise. When he returned to the dock a short time later, Dick was anxiously waiting for him. Walt was not happy.

"How long is that trip supposed to take, Dick?" he said, frowning.

"Seven minutes, sir," Dick Nunis replied.

"Well, the trip I took lasted just over four minutes, by my watch," said Walt. "We shot through there so fast, I couldn't tell the hippos from the elephants!"

So Dick Nunis went right to work. He put each of his cruise operators through a crash course in cruising. He rode boat after boat, repeatedly timing each cruise operator with a stopwatch, drilling them until they could practically run the entire course with their eyes shut! Dick expected Walt to come back at any time for another surprise inspection—and this time he planned to be ready.

About three or four weeks after the first inspection, Walt showed up again. Dick lined up his very best cruise operators in the first couple of boats, figuring that Walt would take the cruise once, maybe twice, and be satisfied with the improvement. But Walt didn't just take the first couple of boats. *He rode each one of those boats and timed each one of those cruise operators!* And every last one of them gave Walt a seven-minute ride, right on the dot. From then on, everyone knew that Disney was the Czar of Excellence. He was dead serious about giving the Disneyland customers a quality experience.

That story is an eloquent demonstration of Walt Disney's commitment to Magical Secret No. 3: *Strive for Lasting Quality.* He preached it, he lived it, and it shows in every product with the Disney name on it. To Walt Disney, "good enough" never was. Quality—the relentless striving for excellence and improvement—was clearly one of the cornerstones of Disney's enduring success. And striving for quality is the key to your success and mine.

The Cost of Disney Quality

Ward Kimball, one of Disney's legendary Nine Old Men of animation, remembers that Walt Disney's total dedication to quality once cost Kimball eight months of his life. Kimball was hired by the studio in 1934. He was just out of art school, only twenty-two years old, and he was given a major role in Disney's most ambitious project, *Snow White and the Seven Dwarfs.* He spent eight months working on a very funny four-and-a-half-minute sequence in which the dwarfs attempt to cook some soup for Snow White. Kimball completed the entire sequence in pencil animation, and his drawings were filmed, matched to the soundtrack, and projected in the screening room for Walt's approval before being inked and painted onto cels. After viewing the penciled footage, Walt called Kimball to his office.

"Ward," said the Boss, "I want you to know that you've done an absolutely beautiful job on that soup sequence. So it makes it really hard for me to tell you that we're going to have to cut it from the picture."

Ward Kimball was devastated. "Cut it! But why?!"

"I know how this hurts," said Disney, looking almost as pained as Kimball. "I love that sequence. I truly do. But it gets in the way of the story."

Kimball went home, depressed and dejected. He had spent the better part of a year on that sequence, and it was going to end up in a filing cabinet, instead of up on the screen where it belonged! That night, he pondered that sequence and thought about how it fit into the story as a whole. And the more he thought about it, the more he realized—Walt was right!

That is perhaps the highest expression of a commitment to quality—a willingness to sacrifice the work of hours and hours, a willingness to leave all that labor on the cutting room floor, if it does not contribute to the absolute perfection of your product.

Quality. Excellence. Striving to be the best. This is the goal that propels athletes and teams to success in the sporting arena. Pat Riley, head coach of the Miami Heat and one of the winningest coaches in NBA history, said, "Excellence is the gradual result of always striving to do better." And Vince Lombardi, legendary coach of the Green Bay Packers, put it this way to his team: "After the cheers have died and the stadium is empty, after the headlines have been written and after you are back in the quiet of your own room and the Super Bowl ring has been placed on the dresser and all the pomp and fanfare have faded, the enduring things that are left are: the dedication to excellence; the dedication to victory; and the dedication to doing with our lives the very best we can to make the world a better place in which to live."

Quality. Excellence. Striving to be the best. This is the attitude that propels companies to success in the business arena. Everything we do can be done better—and the better we do it, the more successful our business enterprises become. T. J. Rodgers, CEO of Cypress Semiconductor in California, expresses it simply: "Most companies don't fail for lack of talent or strategic vision. They fail for lack of execution—the routine blocking and tackling that great companies consistently do well and always strive to do better."

The need to produce quality and constant improvement doesn't just apply in the realm of high technology, either. Excellence is the recipe for success even when you are producing something as simple as a bag of popcorn or a bottle of pickles. That's the message Orville Redenbacher preaches in his slogan, "Do one thing and do it better than anyone," and it's the goal set by the "Pickle King," Henry J. Heinz, when he founded his Heinz "57 Varieties" food-canning company back in 1869: "Do the common thing uncommonly well."

"Quality isn't about money, it's about caring," says Hap Klopp, president of The North Face, the world's largest producer of outdoor adventure equipment. "It's about wanting to be the best because there is personal pride at stake—an individual declaration of identity with the product. There is always a market for the best, all over the globe. It's an obvious and well-known fact that mountain climbers don't like to buy discounted climbing ropes. And there's the joke about the parachute offer: 'For sale—cheap, slightly irregular, but used only once.' When something is as important as life and death—and all business decisions should be—quality is irreplaceable."

Quality. Excellence. Striving to be the best. This is the energizing principle that propels employees to success and promotion in the ranks of their organizations. Mark Basich, a worker at a Matsushita Quasar plant in America, wrote a definition of quality that is now posted on the wall of that plant: "Are you proud enough to buy what you build?"

Quality in business is something consumers expect and demand—quality products and quality services. Somewhere along the line, however, most of us have accommodated ourselves to a very low level of quality from our government. We expect that time spent at the Department of Motor Vehicles will be unpleasant. We expect our mail service to be slow. We expect our legislators to be incompetent at best, and possibly out-and-out crooked. "Close enough for government work," seems to excuse anything and everything. When we encounter someone at a government office who is courteous and efficient, or when we discover a legislator who truly does care about the deficit or the environment or lower taxes, we are not only pleased, we are astonished!

Some people in government, however, want to restore a standard of excellence and an expectation of quality to public service. "The first principle of this Congress should be quality," said Congressman Robert H. Michel of Illinois. "We need to make quality a distinctly American characteristic once again. In the increasingly competitive and ever-changing business world, a quality product will always be in demand. In a turbulent and unstable political world, a quality government will always remain the leader. We must face up to the changing world, not by relying on shortsighted measures and instant gratification, but by making a concerted effort to restore quality to our society."

Quality begets quality. People who strive for excellence in one area of life tend to express that same drive for excellence in other areas. The discipline of striving to do our best tends to make us better parents, better citizens, better neighbors, better people—and those who do good work will generally be rewarded with a better, richer, more satisfying life.

SELL ON QUALITY, NOT ON PRICE

Phil Crosby is a quality control consultant who lives in Orlando. He gives corporate training seminars all around the country, and our own organization received a big motivational lift recently when he spoke to our Orlando Magic administrative staff. "The cost of quality," he says, "is found in the expense associated with doing things wrong. If things were done correctly the first time, companies could do away with rework, sharply reduce inspections, tests, and complaint handlers, and thus enjoy real bottom-line savings. Quality isn't something you pass off to somebody to do for you; it has to be the way you live, work, and run the company. It isn't a business of hanging up a whole bunch of signs and doing a whole bunch of things; it's a matter of instituting new policy, telling everyone this is the way we are going to do it."

Whether you are buying quality or delivering quality, the best is always a bargain. Poor quality is always expensive. If you *buy* inferior products to save a few pennies, they will perform poorly, break down, need servicing, and cost you more in money and aggravation in the long run. If you *sell* inferior products or services, you will lose your customers, your reputation, and your livelihood—and deservedly so! Whether you are buying or selling, whenever you have to choose between the best price or the best quality, always go for quality. If you are in a tight race for customers against a tough competitor, don't be in too big a hurry to undercut your competitor's prices; instead, deliver better quality and better service. "It costs a lot to build bad products," says Norman Augustine, CEO of Martin Marietta and author of *Augustine's Laws.* He's right. So excel at excellence—that's the way to win.

In the *Think and Grow Rich Newsletter,* I read about a sales manager for John Deere who wears a tie-clip with the initials SOQ/NOP engraved upon it. Those initials stand for "Sell On Quality, Not On Price." That sales manager has a story to back up that slogan.

Some years ago, he was trying to land a major sale of Deere equipment to a fleet buyer. The customer had narrowed his choices down to Deere and one of Deere's competitors. The John Deere sales manager was called into the customer's office, and the customer told him, "I'm sorry, but I'm going to give the order to your competitor. Your prices are simply too high, compared to what your competitor is offering us."

The sales manager got up to leave, figuring he had simply lost the sale and that was that. But as he stood up, he noticed something that gave him an inspiration: the customer was wearing a pair of very expensive-looking boots. "Say," the sales manager said, "that's a great pair of boots you have on."

The customer grinned and began talking about the boots— about the leather and the construction, and how they were the best pair of boots he had ever owned, although they were also the most expensive boots he had ever owned.

"I see," said the Deere sales manager. "So what made you buy these boots instead of taking a pair off some shelf at a discount store?"

The customer opened his mouth to say something, then shut it again. He looked down at his boots, then up at the sales manager and said, "You know, you've got a point there!" Then he stuck out his hand to shake. "Okay," he said grinning broadly, "the sale is yours."

Always sell on quality, not on price. Make excellence your goal. Strive to be the best. These are different ways of saying one thing: *Build for lasting quality.* Successful people are quality-oriented people. I have found that all the successful people I have met seem to possess four attitudes that are focused on lasting quality. Those four attitudes are:

1. "I strive for perfection."
2. "I pay attention to details."

3. "I constantly try to improve."
4. "I give it all I've got."

In the rest of this chapter, we will take a closer look at each of these attitudes.

Quality Attitude No. 1: "I strive for perfection."

Over the years my children have had wonderful opportunities at Disney. As a teenager, my oldest son, Jimmy, performed in a show at Epcot with Mr. Rogers. My son Michael has done any number of things, including a lead role in a Christmas Day network special. Karyn has been on a committee of teenagers from around the country that has published a book for young people giving kids' reactions to the Disney World attractions. Bobby and Karyn have both performed in the Epcot Christmas show featuring Carol Lawrence.

During these past few years, I have made numerous trips driving the children back and forth to rehearsal at Disney, to the point that the car knew the way all by itself. I was deeply impacted by a sign on the front door leading into the rehearsal area, a sign I've seen scores, maybe hundreds of times, whenever I took my kids to Disney for their rehearsals.

> "When we consider a project, we really study it. And when we go into that new project, we believe in it all the way. We have confidence in our ability to do it right. And we work hard to do the best possible job."—Walt Disney

And I believe the words on that sign express Disney's continual striving for quality.

Are you 95 percent effective in everything you do? That sounds like a very high rating, doesn't it? Well, if you bat .950 in baseball, you can bet they'll put up a statue in your honor in the Baseball Hall of Fame. But batting .950 in just about any other enterprise is a sure prescription for failure.

In the early days of World War II, a defense contracting company was batting .950—and the results were *deadly!* Why? Because that company manufactured parachutes for American paratroopers! When their product was tested, nineteen out of twenty chutes opened. Every twentieth trooper might as well have jumped from a plane with a laundry bag strapped to his back!

The government told this defense contractor it would have to increase the quality of its product or lose the contract. So the manager hit upon an idea: He turned all of the chute packers into product testers. He took them up in a plane and had them strap on their own product and jump! Instantly, quality rose to 100 percent. The parachute packers had learned the importance of *striving for perfection.*

Ninety-five percent isn't good enough. In fact, I would submit to you that even 99.9 percent is not good enough. The only "good enough" that's truly good enough is perfection. *Insight,* an in-house publication of Syncrude Canada, Ltd., once published an article entitled, "Strive for Perfection . . . *Or Else!*" According to the article, if 99.9 percent is good enough, then . . .

- 103,260 income tax returns will be processed incorrectly this year
- 22,000 checks will be deducted from the wrong bank accounts in the next 60 minutes
- 1,314 phone calls will be misrouted every minute
- 12 babies will be given to the wrong parents each day
- 5,517,200 cases of soft drinks produced in the next twelve months will be flatter than a bad tire
- Two plane landings daily at O'Hare International Airport in Chicago will be unsafe
- 18,322 pieces of mail will be mishandled in the next hour
- 291 pacemaker operations will be performed incorrectly this year
- 880,000 credit cards in circulation will turn out to have incorrect cardholder information on their magnetic strips
- 20,000 incorrect drug prescriptions will be written in the next twelve months
- 107 incorrect medical procedures will be performed by the end of the day today

Sure, we're all human, everybody makes mistakes, nobody's perfect: These are truisms, these are a given. But the fact that we are all imperfect and make mistakes is what makes it so important for us to *strive for perfection.* There's a saying, "You shoot for the moon, you get over the fence." If you don't strive for perfection, if you don't shoot for the moon, you won't even rise to the level of mediocrity. Look at the truly successful people in this world and you will see people who have set very high standards for themselves—standards that are difficult or impossible to meet, standards of perfection.

Take my friend Bill Russell, for example—the legendary former star center for the Boston Celtics. Bill used to keep a personal scorecard for himself, and he graded his performance after every game, using a scale of one to a hundred, with a hundred being perfection. The very best game Bill Russell ever played, he scored a sixty-five on his personal scorecard. *Sixty-five!* Out of more than twelve hundred games, that was the highest score he ever gave any of his performances on the hardwood court. Yet he was unquestionably one of the five best basketball players who ever lived! Why? Because his goal was not "good enough," it was not 95 percent or 99.9 percent. His goal was nothing less than *perfection.* Though he never achieved perfection, he did achieve something that few other people have known: true and lasting *greatness* in his chosen field of endeavor.

This striving for perfection has been a part of the Disney organization from the very beginning. Walt's perfection-oriented attitude drove Disney as he took his film production company in a totally new direction: live-action feature films. And he didn't just "get his feet wet" in the feature film business—he took the plunge! His first try was a big-budget adventure film with far-flung location shooting, underwater photography, expensive special effects, and a major big-name cast (Kirk Douglas, James Mason, and Peter Lorre, to name a few). The film: Jules Verne's *20,000 Leagues Under the Sea.*

One of the most important scenes of the film involved a hand-to-tentacle battle between Verne's antihero, Captain Nemo, and a monster squid on the deck of Nemo's submarine, the Nautilus. For this scene, a massive water tank was constructed on the Disney sound stage, and an amazingly realistic supersquid was constructed with molded rubber skin and a complex wire-and-pulley control apparatus. Massive wind machines and wave-makers churned up the water, creating a stormy sea around the *Nautilus*. This single scene cost Disney $250,000 to shoot.

In his book Walt: Backstage Adventures with Walt Disney, former Disney writer Charles Shows describes sitting in the screening room with Disney and a couple of dozen other Disney staff members, watching the dailies from the previous day's filming. Shows recalls,

> Soon Walt arrived. The lights went out. The room was filled with nervous silence. The action began. The great scene was projected on the screen in front of us.
>
> It was fantastic. In saving the submarine *Nautilus* and its crew, brave Captain Nemo battled both the giant squid and the violent battering from the colossal waves created by the tempest. When the sensational scene was finished and the lights went on, the room exploded with applause. Every voice agreed that the scene was "the greatest"!
>
> Walt was silent—an ominous sign. One by one, the others observed his noncommittal stare.
>
> "Well, Walt, how did you like it?" someone asked.
>
> "Great, huh?"
>
> Walt said nothing. He just stared down at the floor. At last the crowd started uncomfortably toward the door. As they did, Walt shouted to the projectionist, "Let's take another look at that scene. I thought I saw a wire in one shot."
>
> Quickly, we all resumed our seats. The lights went out. The giant squid scene projected a second time.
>
> When it was over, a jittery aide leaned toward Walt. "What do you think?"
>
> "Like I said," Walt shook his head, "I *thought* I saw a wire in there."
>
> Then, kissing a fortune good-bye, Walt announced his final verdict: "Shoot it again!" Those three words were to cost Disney Studio about a quarter of a million dollars!
>
> Probably no other producer would have paid that price for perfection. But then, that's why there have been thousands of film producers—but only one Walt Disney![1]

The same perfection-oriented attitude that drove Walt Disney to reshoot a $250,000 scene in *20,000 Leagues Under the Sea* in

1955 is still at work in the Disney organization today. If you go to the Magic Kingdom in Orlando, which has been operating for almost twenty-five years, you'll see a place that looks as sparkling clean and freshly painted as if it was opened last week. They built the Magic Kingdom to endure and to be the finest fun environment anywhere, and they maintain it to standards of exacting perfection.

As a result of the high standards set by the Disney organization, something amazing has happened in central Florida: Other organizations in the Orlando area are aiming for the same standards of perfection! The city government, the county government, the hotels and restaurants, the nightclubs and music spots, the gift shops, and all the other business enterprises in the area are competing with each other—and with Disney—to out-excel each other! Businesses that fail to build and operate at Disney-quality standards have found that they look so bad by comparison, they simply can't compete!

I believe that the city of Orlando makes a better first impression than any other city in America. It starts at the part of the city that most visitors see first: the Orlando Airport. Considered one of the most beautiful airports in the world, it looks more like an entertainment complex than a mass transportation facility. Many people get off their plane, walk into the airport concourse, and mistakenly think they're already at Walt Disney World! The same striving for perfection can be seen in the design and construction of Orlando's other major buildings—the Convention Center, the new City Hall, entertainment centers such as Sea World and Universal Studios, and of course, the Orlando Arena, home of the Orlando Magic.

Let me tell you a little bit about the arena. There is no other sports complex like it in the world. Built at a cost of $100 million, it has hundreds of artistic touches that you just don't find on other buildings of similar function: a million hand-laid serpentine bricks on all the outside walkways, a terrazzo finish on the main concourse, and imported red Mexican tile covering all the major support beams. None of these touches was necessary. You could play basketball in a big building made of bare steel beams and gray concrete, and it will be every bit as functional—but it won't be perfect, and it won't make a statement of excellence and quality.

Contrast the Orlando Arena with a sports facility that was built at the same time just a few hundred miles away: the Miami Arena. Not only is the Miami Arena not as attractive as the Orlando Arena, but it was not built for lasting quality. *Within one year* after the Miami Arena opened, the outer walkways leading to the main entrances were crumbling and had to be ripped out and relaid. *Within one year,* the tile on the inner concourse had buckled and had to be reattached. *Within one year,* the rest rooms all needed to be overhauled. When you build for lasting quality, the thing you have built should not need overhauling in the first twelve months; it should stand for a thousand years.

Quality Attitude No. 2: "I pay attention to details."

There is one attraction in Disneyland that many people have never heard of, and are completely unaware of, even if they have been to the Magic Kingdom dozens of times. The attraction has been part of Disneyland since 1961, yet it is tucked away in a shady, secluded area that most visitors seldom see. It consists of a set of Italian marble statues in the form of Snow White and the Seven Dwarfs, arranged in a woodsy setting with a waterfall and a wishing well. The statues were commissioned by Walt Disney at a very high price and were carved by European sculptors.

If your feet are tired and you want to escape the sounds of the rest of the park for a few moments, visit Walt's quiet little sanctuary, guarded by Grumpy, Doc, and Company. To find it, simply follow the crowds from Main Street to the Sleeping Beauty Castle—but instead of crossing the drawbridge with everyone else, veer right, along the castle pond. You'll find it a very peaceful and enjoyable place to spend a few moments—and there's no waiting in line to see it. It's just one of the special little details that Walt Disney was so conscientious about—so small and out-of-the-way that most people miss it, yet so perfect and exquisite that it truly makes the Disneyland experience complete.

In our own way, our Magic basketball organization has worked hard to match Walt Disney's drive for perfection in every detail. I believe our attention to the little things is one of the reasons the Magic receives so much praise for the way our home games are presented. Even in the very beginning, when we were still building our organization and we didn't have a great team, we knew where we were: Orlando, Florida, the entertainment capital of the world, the adopted hometown of Mickey and Minnie. We knew that the people in this town had spent twenty-odd years in the shadow of the Matterhorn and Cinderella's castle, and they demanded quality entertainment. We also knew that we were going to have to provide something to watch besides basketball, because we were not going to be winning a lot of games our first couple of seasons. In fact, we were going to be like opossums: We'd play dead at home and get killed on the road.

So we made a decision early on that we were going to present our games as top-quality, Disney-level entertainment. Whether the team won or lost, the fans would have an evening packed chock-a-block with entertainment. After all, a basketball game consists of a two-and-a-half-hour window of time, only forty-eight minutes of which is action. So what do you do with the rest of the time? That's where the details come in: The music. The lighting. The announcer. The dance team. The mascot. The magicians. The halftime shows. The indoor fireworks. The scoreboard graphics. All of these details are woven into a tightly orchestrated presentation with one mission in mind: to present the audience with the most exciting entertainment we can, and to do so at the highest level of quality we can deliver. That's the way we do it today, and it's been that way since the very beginning.

Here are just a few examples of the attention our organization pays to every detail of a Magic sports entertainment show:

The announcer. We went through a year of auditions to get just the right announcer. We finally settled on a broadcaster from Tampa named Paul Porter. He auditioned for us several times throughout that year before we finally said, "This is the guy!" Our patience and Paul's persistence paid off. He's become a folk hero in Orlando with his distinctive voice, enunciation, and enthusiasm. Today, there are kids all over Orlando imitating Paul Porter. In fact, if you go to high school and junior high games, you'll hear announcers doing Paul Porter's shtick: "Shaqueeeeeeel Oh-Neeeeeeeeal! Annnnn-Ferneeeeeeeee Haaaaaarrrrdaway!"

The dance team. We spent a full year putting our dance team together, holding extensive tryouts all over the region, recruiting dancers from around the state. We called the team the Magic Dancers, and we carefully cultivated a certain style: a group of appealing, upbeat, energetic, yet wholesome girl-next-door types—a family entertainment act to suit the central Florida mores and tastes, not something out of Las Vegas. The dance routines are very athletic, so we continue to hold auditions every year, making sure that we have the twelve finest female athletes in the field of dance to present to our fans as part of each game.

The mascot. We spent a full year working on a costume and a concept for our mascot. We hired several different designers to produce ideas and sketches, including character designers who had worked with Disney and with Jim Henson's Muppets. We considered dozens of designs from top showbiz costumers—a top-hatted rabbit, several varieties of magicians and sorcerers, a number of weird Muppety creatures, a touristy-looking character with stars for eyes, and even a big bean with eyes and legs ("A bean?!" we all wondered, scratching our heads and puzzling over the artist's state of mind). Finally we settled on a magical green dragon named Stuff—a pun on "stuffing" a basket and a certain magic dragon made famous by Peter, Paul, and Mary.

Many sports teams figure you can put anybody in a mascot suit and who's gonna know or care? But I knew better. I had seen two different mascots—Big Shot and Hoops—fall totally flat during my days with the Philadelphia 76ers. Heck, I had even worn that hot, sweaty suit myself, so I knew it wasn't easy! Finally, I hired a truly talented performer, Dave Raymond, to put on the Hoops suit and perform during one game—and suddenly Hoops was a hit! My Sixers experience taught me that you've got to have the right talent in that suit, or all the time and money you spent designing the character is wasted.

So we tried out at least a dozen people to find the right performer to fill the suit of Stuff. Finally, we zeroed in on an energetic, enthusiastic young man (his identity is a secret!), and he has been the animating personality behind Stuff ever since. He was an instant hit with fans and sportswriters, including then-columnist for the *Orlando Sentinel,* Bob Morris, who gave our mascot the following plug after the unveiling:

> Stuff, the Magic Dragon
> Lived by the court
> And frolicked as a PR tool
> For O-town's big league sport!
> Little Pattie Williams
> Loved that mascot, Stuff
> He made the 10,000 ticket goal
> A job not quite so tough.
> Together they would travel
> The rubber chicken trail
> Pat would trot out Stuff to help
> Him make a ticket sale.
> Fat cats and corporations
> Wrote checks wherever they came
> Yes, football-mad Floridians
> Paid to see a round-ball game!

The magicians. Here was a detail that just fell into our laps. Before we even played our first game, we were approached by two magicians who had an act they were already performing. They said they wanted to be the magicians for the Orlando Magic. We had them work a few events for us, and they did a nice job. We kept them on, and they developed new tricks, new angles, new touches that really added to the entertainment value of our show.

Pretty soon, it became clear that something new had come into being: sports magic! They worked the crowd with all kinds of gimmicks—contests, games, and outrageous stunts. They came up with the giant slingshots (now being used by other teams) to send tee-shirts and other items hurtling all over the arena, even to the fans in the upper decks. The fans love it, and it has been a key component of our overall entertainment effort. In fact, the Magic magicians are performing for many pro teams in all sports all over the country. That's how big they've become.

There's no law that says that a basketball game has to consist only of basketball. In Orlando, we have made basketball an all-encompassing entertainment experience by focusing on the details, by making sure every component of the evening is a quality component, and by fitting them all together into a well-orchestrated mix of magic and excitement.

There is a famous saying in politics: "The devil is in the details." Many great endeavors are torpedoed by the little things that go unnoticed until it's too late. Business writer John L. McCaffrey put it this way: "The mechanics of running a business are not really very complicated when you get down to essentials. You have to make some stuff and sell it to somebody for more than it costs you. That's about all there is—except for a few million details." If you don't pay strict attention to those little details, your business, your project, your dream, and even your family or career may fall short or fall apart.

I once spoke at a convention in Orlando, and after my presentation, a woman came up to me and we chatted a bit. She was a businesswoman from Gainesville, Georgia, and as we talked, she handed me her business card. It had the usual information—name, title, address, and phone—but it also had a line in quotes that left a big impression on me: "I'm in charge of the little things." Those little things are so important—and I was glad to meet someone who understood the importance of the little things.

The great men of sports know the importance of small details. "I believe it's the little things you have to take care of," said Yankees owner George Steinbrenner, "and then the big things take care of themselves. But if you neglect those little things, the big things go to pieces on you." And former Dallas Cowboys coach Jimmy Johnson put it this way: "If a person is going to be disciplined enough to do the little things, then I feel that will carry over into his performance in other areas."

The Ted Williams Museum was recently given a bat that a collector paid twenty thousand dollars for because it was used by Ted in 1941, the year he hit .406. Before Ted saw the bat he closed his eyes and started squeezing the handle of the bat. Then he blurted out, "Yeah, this is one of my bats. In 1940 and 1941 I cut a groove in the handle of my bats to rest my right index finger. I can still feel the groove. It's one of my bats all right." Wow! You talk about paying attention to the little things.

And the great leaders in other fields also know the importance of small details. "I probably spend 99 percent of my time on what others may call 'petty details,'" Admiral Rickover once said. "Most managers would rather focus on lofty policy matters, but when the details are ignored, the project fails." Former NBC news anchor John Chancellor put it more concisely: "Genius lies in the details." And Marian Wright Edelman, founder of the Children's Defense Fund, said, "We must not, in trying to think about how we can make a big difference, ignore the small daily differences we can make which, over time, add up to big differences that we often cannot foresee."

March Fong Eu, the former California secretary of state, knows how important the little things can be. In a 1984 speech, she listed some of the "little things" that have directed the course of great events:

- In 1645, one vote gave Oliver Cromwell control of England.
- In 1649, one vote caused Charles I of England to be executed.
- In 1776, one vote gave America the English language instead of German.
- In 1845, one vote brought Texas into the Union.
- In 1868, one vote saved President Andrew Johnson from impeachment.
- In 1876, one vote changed France from a monarchy to a republic.
- In 1876, one vote gave Rutherford B. Hayes the presidency of the United States.
- In 1933, one vote gave Adolf Hitler leadership of the Nazi Party.
- In 1960, one vote change in each precinct in Illinois would have denied John F. Kennedy the presidency.

As coach Lou Holtz once said at Notre Dame, "If two seminars were held at the same time, one conducted by successful teams and one by losing teams, the similarities between the two would be amazing. The offensive and defensive theories both employed would be virtually identical. The amount of time they spent practicing wouldn't vary by more than a few minutes and their practice format would be the same. The main difference would be attention to detail. In the successful organization, no detail is too small to receive attention. No job is minor, and everyone takes great pride in realizing they are important and their responsibilities are critical to the unit's success."

I have seen the truth of these words in our own Orlando Magic organization, and in my own life and family. Even though I manage a big sports organization, and even though I manage a big family, I try to live by the slogan expressed on the business card of that woman from Gainesville, Georgia: "I'm in charge of the little things."

Quality Attitude No. 3: "I constantly try to improve."

The great English military strategist of the seventeenth century, Oliver Cromwell, knew it way back then: "He who stops being better stops being good." In more recent times, Donald Peterson, former chairman of the Ford Motor Company (where "Quality Is Job One"), put it this way: "The principle by which we live and die is that once we can do something well, we have to figure out how to do it even better." Being good is not enough. The key to maintaining quality and excellence is to be relentlessly committed to growth and improvement.

I've seen the truth of this principle again and again in the coaching profession. Coaches have to constantly strive—*not* to maintain current levels but to *exceed* current levels. If coaches don't constantly push their players for improvement, then things begin to slip: attitudes, work habits, effort, determination, and even the coach's own preparation. If one player begins to go lax, to give a little less effort, to express a negative attitude, to neglect good training habits, then his attitude and behavior soon begin to affect the next player. If it goes unchecked for long, a coach can lose his whole team, and the whole season can unravel very quickly. Inattention, pessimism, laziness, and bad habits are contagious and can only be prevented by a relentless commitment to improvement. Coaches, teachers, parents, entrepreneurs, and managers must not only maintain *consistently* high standards, they must continually press for improvement.

One of the things we do in the Orlando Magic to maintain a

constant emphasis on improvement is a concept we call Magic University. It's an idea that was conceived and implemented by Rich DeVos and the DeVos family after they purchased the Magic in 1991. Here's how it works:

Every September, we take the entire Magic Organization (every employee except players) away from the office for a two-day session of instruction and inspiration designed to improve the quality of everything we do. We bring in a speaker who gets our adrenaline pumping and shows us ways to increase the level of excellence throughout our operation. We lock the doors and spend intensive time together in classroom sessions, rap sessions, and workshops. Between each annual Magic University session, we have periodic satellite classes designed to maintain our focus on improvement throughout the year.

Our philosophy at the Magic is that you never arrive at quality. Instead, we believe that quality is a *continuous, relentless, never-ending* commitment to improvement. Champions never see themselves as always at their best; they can *always* become better than they are. Only the mediocre are always at their best. Charles Swindoll tells a story that makes the point:

> When the Ritz-Carlton Hotels won the Malcolm Baldrige National Quality Award, I had the opportunity to congratulate the owner of that outstanding organization, Mr. William Johnson, my good friend who lives in Atlanta, Georgia. In typical humility and his wonderful "Southern drawl," Bill gave others the credit. He added that now that they had won this prestigious honor, they would need to work even harder to earn the respect that came with it. "Quality," he said, "is a race with no finish line."
>
> He is correct. Competitive excellence requires 100 percent all of the time. If you doubt that, try maintaining excellence by setting your standards at 92 percent. Or even 95 percent. People figure they're doing fine so long as they get somewhere near it. Excellence gets reduced to acceptable, and before long, acceptable doesn't seem worth the sweat if you can get by with adequate. After that, mediocrity is only a breath away.

If you are engaged in an individual effort to achieve an important goal—for example, if you are writing a novel or preparing for a marathon—then set a series of graduated goals for improving the level of your performance. Link up with another person or group of people who will hold you accountable for your progress and improvement—people who will check in with you and ask you tough, probing questions about your performance.

If you are engaged in a corporate effort to achieve an important goal—building a sports team or a company—then set an example for the entire organization. Let the entire team see your focus on improvement. If your people see you compromising, they will compromise. If they see you sprinting flat-out for ever-higher goals, they will follow your example and increase their own efforts.

Quality Attitude No. 4: "I give it all I've got."

With nineteen children in the house, my children are expected to keep their rooms neat, to put their laundry away, to get their bathrooms picked up, and to tend to their own clothing or sports equipment. Each child is responsible for two or three morning chores—sweeping, cleaning, dusting, doing windows, carrying out garbage—and an equal number of evening chores to help keep the family system humming. The child who slacks off or decides to do a halfhearted job is likely to find himself or herself swimming laps in the pool, doing push-ups, or doing the job over until it's done right. Do our kids like it? No way! They often balk, gripe, or cut corners. I don't want to give you the wrong idea, because they're great kids, they have generally positive attitudes, and do their jobs well most of the time. But they're kids, and kids will slack off if you don't maintain and reinforce standards of excellence.

As a parent, I can tell you it's easy to let things slide, to say, "Heck, it's simpler to just wipe that counter again myself," or "I'll just let it slide this time." But if you let it slide one time, it will slide even further the next, and the next—until suddenly you realize you have no control. It's much more effective—and ultimately much easier—to maintain standards of excellence than to try to recapture and restore the standards you have lost.

While this book was being written, I had a conversation with my friend Jerry Jenkins, a gifted and prolific writer who has worked with me on six previous books. Jerry told me about his father, who has been a police chief for more than forty years in Illinois and Michigan. While in Kalamazoo, Michigan, he was in charge of the Justice Bureau for Juvenile Delinquency. He told Jerry in a recent conversation, "The bottom line of all the juvenile delinquency I've dealt with over the years comes down to two things: 1. Alcohol. 2. The drug called SFN."

As Jerry was relating this conversation to me, I thought, *SFN? What's that? I've heard of PCP, LSD, and LS/MFT, but what's SFN?* Then Jerry went on to explain, "SFN means 'Something for Nothing.'" According to Jerry Jenkins's father, this attitude—"I can get something for nothing"—is an addictive drug that pulls young people into the self-destruction and degradation of crime. It is an attitude that says, "If I can just pull off this one robbery or this one big swindle, I'll be set for life and I won't ever have to work again!" But that, concludes Jerry Jenkins's father, is not reality, it's not life. "You've got to work for it," he adds. "Work honestly, work smart, and above all, work hard. Give it all you've got."

Back in 1963, when I began working in the Phillies front office, assisting with the Miami farm club, I became immersed in the business of publicizing our team. We promoted our team any way we could, and one of the ways we got publicity was to get our managers on local radio shows. There was a young radio talk show host who broadcast his local late-night show from a houseboat off Miami Beach. He had a big following, and it was always great exposure to get on his show. I would make the arrangements, then accompany our manager—former big-leaguers such as Andy Seminick in '63 or Bobby Morgan in '64—out to the end of the dock where the houseboat was tied up. The boat was called *Surfside 6* and was the very boat used in the TV series by that name. We'd get aboard the boat, our guy would do his hour-long interview, and I would sit and watch.

That talk show host has come a long way since the early 1960s. In fact, you may have heard of him. His name is Larry King.

Over the years, I've bumped into Larry a number of times at different functions, he's endorsed a book for me, he's had me on his radio show, and I've had him on my local radio show in

Orlando. I've enjoyed watching him work from the time he was a local host on a Miami network right up to his present success aboard the international news network, CNN. Larry is a quality guy who turns out a quality product. In fact, I truly believe that quality products can *only* come from quality human beings with quality attitudes. They come from people who never give anything less than 100 percent of who they are, no matter what situation they are in.

In his new book, *How to Talk to Anyone, Anytime, Anywhere,* Larry tells the story of another quality human being, entertainer Danny Kaye. It's a story about Larry's TV call-in show when Danny was the featured guest. It was a situation in which Danny could have easily given 40 or 50 percent, and no one would have thought any less of him. But being a quality human being, Danny Kaye gave 100 percent, and the result was moving and memorable. Larry recalls the situation in these words:

> You couldn't help loving Danny, and like so many performers whose greatness comes in large measure from their genuineness, Danny Kaye was exactly the same person off stage and off screen as he was on.
>
> Once, when he was a guest on my radio show, a woman called from Toledo and told him, "I never in my life thought I'd talk to you. I don't have a question for you. I just want to tell you a story: My son loved you. He wanted to be like you. He imitated you, and his whole world revolved around you."
>
> Then she delivered the clincher: "He was killed in Korea when he was nineteen years old. He was in the navy during the war over there. The navy sent me a picture among his personal effects, and it was of you—the only picture he had in his footlocker. I framed it along with the last picture I had of him. I've dusted your picture and his every day for thirty years. I thought you'd like to hear that."
>
> Danny was crying in the studio, and so was I. And so was she. Then he said, "Did your son have a favorite song?"
>
> She said, "Yes. 'Dena.'"
>
> Then Danny Kaye sang one of his most famous songs to this Gold Star mother of the Korean War, with no band, no piano, just his voice, through the tears.
>
> It was one of the greatest moments I've ever experienced in

broadcasting, because it was such a human one. And Danny made it happen by his openness—not, in this case, a willingness to talk about himself, but a willingness to empathize, and to show emotion himself, that many people would not be ready to share.

Danny Kaye didn't have to sing that song. He could have simply said, "Thank you for sharing that," and gone on to the next call. Instead, he gave a big piece of himself—his feelings, his tears, his vulnerability, and his big, generous heart—to comfort and thank this woman. That's the mark of a quality human being.

A CULTURE OF EXCELLENCE

Excellence is not a policy decision. It is a mind-set, an attitude, a way of thinking and behaving. We create a mind-set of excellence in our businesses, our sports teams, our churches, and our homes not merely by demanding excellence or preaching excellence, but by *modeling* excellence, just as Walt Disney did. Once we have created a climate where quality is not just something we do but a feature of *who we are* as an organization, then the people in our organization will be inspired to go far beyond policy, far beyond duties and job descriptions, in order to maintain the organization's reputation for excellence.

An example of this principle comes (not surprisingly) from the Disney organization. In a recent speech, Valerie Oberle, a Disney vice president in charge of management training, relates the following story:

> Not too long ago, a guest checking out of our Polynesian Village resort at Walt Disney World was asked how she enjoyed her visit. She told the front desk clerk she had a wonderful vacation, but was heartbroken about losing several rolls of Kodacolor film she had not yet developed. She was particularly upset over the loss of the pictures she had shot at our Polynesian Luau, as this was a memory she especially treasured.
>
> Now, please understand that we have no written service standards covering lost luau snapshots. Fortunately, the hostess at the front desk understood Disney's philosophy of caring for our guests. She

asked the woman to leave her a couple of rolls of fresh film, promising she would take care of the rest.

Two weeks later, this guest received a package at her home. In it were photos of the entire cast of our luau show, personally autographed by each performer. There were also photos of the parade and fireworks in the theme park, taken by the front desk hostess on her own time, after work. I happen to know this story because this guest wrote us a letter. She said that never in her life had she received such compassionate service from any business establishment.

Heroic service does not come from policy manuals. It comes from people who care and from a culture that encourages and models that attitude.

Walt Disney built for lasting quality, and his commitment to quality continues to be lived out by the dedicated people in the Disney organization. The Disney corporate culture is a culture of excellence. That standard of excellence should be yours and mine as well. "Good enough" never was, never is, and never will be. *Strive for Lasting Quality* is a magical secret that leads to success and to realized dreams.

In the next chapter, we will explore the fourth secret behind a magical kingdom, a magical basketball team, and a magical, miraculous way of life—a concept Walt Disney called "Stick-to-it-ivity."

MAGICAL SECRET

NUMBER 4

Have "Stick-to-it-ivity"

CHAPTER 8

Stubbornness with a Purpose

○ *If you believe within your soul*
Just hold on tight and don't let go
You can make it happen
Mariah Carey, singer-songwriter, "Make It Happen"

○ *In life or in football, touchdowns rarely take place in*
seventy-yard increments. Usually it's three yards and
a cloud of dust.
Rush Limbaugh

○ *Success is on the far side of failure.*
Thomas J. Watson, founder of IBM

○ *Press on. Nothing in the world can take the place of*
persistence.
Ray Kroc, founder of McDonald's

My daughter Daniela was on the soccer team at Lee Middle School in Orlando. Not long ago, the Lee team played Meadowbrook Middle School. Throughout that game, Daniela's team was on the offensive. They totally dominated the play, whereas the Meadowbook team spent most of the game vainly trying to get the ball downfield. Amazingly, even though Lee had total dominance of the field, they were unable to score. The reason: the tenacious, persistent Meadowbrook goalie. Daniela and her teammates must have hammered fifty shots at that poor goalie, but she hung in there and stopped every one of them. During the same time, Meadowbrook didn't even get one shot at the Lee goalie.

As the game drew down to the final minute, it was a scoreless game, zip to zip. The clock ticked down to fifty seconds, forty, thirty . . .

With twenty seconds left in the game, the Lee girls forced their way downfield and took another volley at the beleaguered Meadowbrook goalie. She stopped the ball and punted it over the heads of the Lee team. It looked like a football punt—it must have sailed forty yards in the air. It came down at midfield and started rolling, and a Meadowbrook player came in and started dribbling the ball straight down the middle of the field. After spending the entire game standing around, just looking pretty, the Lee goalie crouched and tensed. In the final few seconds of the game, the ball was actually coming her way!

The Meadowbrook player moved that ball with grace, speed, and power. Daniela and the entire Lee team had been crowded down at one end of the field. Suddenly, they were all scrambling like mad to catch up to the ball that was now at the *wrong* end of the field! But there was just no way to get there.

The Meadowbrook dribbler kicked with all her might. The ball sailed. The Lee goalie leaped to intercept it, but the ball flew just over her fingertips, coming down behind her and nestling in the net of the goal, just like a mother hen laying an egg in her nest. Two seconds later, the gun sounded. Meadowbrook had won, 1-0.

I saw that game with my own eyes, and I was amazed. It was a heartbreaking loss for my daughter Dani, but whoever won or lost, the drama of that game was something to behold. And the lesson of that game is instructive for us all: The key to success is to *hang in there until the final gun sounds.* "Fall seven times, stand up eight," says the ancient proverb—and it's absolutely true.

Meadowbrook won the game in the last twenty seconds, proving that the only failure is the failure to keep trying.

We have all of our kids involved in many activities. Lots of different sports, but also acting, dance, modeling, and so forth.

The kids like what they do, but there are times when I hear, "Dad, I want to quit baseball," or "Dad, when can we stop going to swimming?" or "Dad, I don't like the soccer coach. I'm going to quit." My answer is always the same: "No, you're not going to quit. You're not allowed."

I learned my lesson years ago with our daughter Karyn. She was involved in gymnastics for years and was always an eager, enthusiastic, talented participant. But then I noticed Karyn began dragging and complaining and finally demanded to stop gymnastics altogether. Against my better judgment, I went along with her, and at age twelve her career was over.

Karyn had just finished her sophomore year in high school and was doing very well as a cheerleader. And guess what? Gymnastic skills play a big part in cheering. So Karyn was back regularly at Brown's Gymnastics Club in Orlando working out again.

I was driving her home from a class recently and Karyn asked me a question. "Dad, why did you ever let me quit gymnastics?"

I said, "Because you were moaning and groaning and making all of our lives miserable."

Karyn replied, "Well, you should have made me stick with it. You shouldn't have let me quit. So don't let the other kids quit their stuff either."

I think the whole gymnastics experience taught both of us a good lesson.

Perseverance is more important than brains, more important than skill, more important than talent, more important than strength, more important than luck. If you fall down a thousand times, then success means *getting up a thousand and one times.*

One of my first and most memorable lessons in the importance of persistence came during the summer following my eighth grade year. I tried out for a semipro baseball team on which all the other players were much older than I. I made the team, but I was nervous and worried about whether I could really perform at that level.

On the way to my first game, I rode in the back seat while my mother drove. Sitting in the front seat next to my mother was my grandmother. We were talking about my prospects with the team as we drove. "Well," I said at one point, "if it doesn't work out, I can always quit."

With a suddenness that startled me, my grandmother whirled about, jabbed one finger in my chest, and looked me sharply in the eye. "You don't quit!" she said sternly. "Nobody in this family quits!"

I got the message. And I didn't quit.

Since that day, I've seen it proven over and over: No matter what arena you choose in which to fight the battles of your life—in sports, in the arts, in business, in ministry, in family life—one of the absolute requisites to achievement is a quality called *persistence*. As my friend Rich DeVos, the cofounder of Amway, often says, "Persistence is stubbornness with a purpose."

STICK-TO-IT-IVITY

Back in 1986, when I was trying to launch the Orlando Magic, I got a firsthand lesson in the language I call "Disneyese." I was at Disney World for the theme park's fifteenth anniversary. Present that day as Disney's invited guests were a lot of heavy hitters from various fields of endeavor—entertainers, sports figures, and corporate bigwigs. I bumped into Buell Duncan, the chairman of SunBank, and we got to talking about bringing NBA basketball to Orlando. "You know," he said, "the guy you need to talk to is Michael Eisner."

Yes, I agreed, the head honcho of the entire Disney organization would be, ahem, a helpful contact.

"Well, I'll introduce you," said Buell. He took me over to the American Pavilion in Epcot, where Eisner was on a platform, flanked by Sen. Ted Kennedy, Supreme Court Chief Justice Warren Burger, and various other luminaries.

"Gee," I said, "he looks kinda busy—"

"Just hang around," said Buell. "He's almost through. I've got somebody else to meet, so I'll see you later!" Poof! He was gone, and I was on my own.

A few minutes later, Eisner wrapped up his speech. I waded

into the crowd of hand-shakers and autograph hounds that immediately surrounded him. With a lot of persistence and perseverance (important words!), I got close enough to make eye contact with him. I thrust out my hand and said, "Mr. Eisner, I'm Pat Williams, and I—"

His eyes lighted up. "Pat Williams!" he said, pumping my hand. "You're just the man I want to talk to!"

"I am?" I said, a little shocked. (Okay. More than a little.)

"Tell you what," said Eisner, "I've got another engagement right now, but I'll meet you at nine o'clock in Paris."

"Okay," I said numbly. Then I checked my watch. It was already eight o'clock. *Sheesh,* I thought, *I knew these Disney execs operated at a high level, but how am I supposed to get to Paris in an hour? Even the Concorde can't get me there in time—and they don't fly Concordes out of Orlando!*

And then it hit me: Eisner didn't mean Paris, France, or even Paris, Texas. "Paris" is Disneyese for the French Pavilion at Epcot!

An hour later, I met with Michael Eisner at the appointed place, and we had a very interesting meeting.

Disneyese originated, of course, with Walt Disney himself. He and the people around him freely invented terms like "imagineering," "Circarama," and "audio-animatronic." Whereas traditional carnival operators cynically referred to their customers as "marks," Disney made sure that visitors to Disneyland were referred to—and treated as—"guests." What the old-fashioned carnivals called "rides" Disney reinvented and renamed as "attractions" and "adventures." Disneyland attractions that carried a high volume of guests per hour were fondly (and privately) called "people-eaters" by Walt and his team.

When Disneyland celebrated its tenth anniversary in 1965, he switched two letters in the word "centennial" and called it a "Tencennial." There are no personnel offices or employees at Disney; instead, there is a "casting office" and every person who works for Disney (even the person who works in the kitchen or makes your bed in a Disney hotel) is a "cast member." The public areas of Disneyland are referred to as "onstage," while the behind-the-scenes parts that only "cast members" see are called "backstage."

My favorite bit of Disneyese, however, is a word Walt Disney coined to express his own brand of persistence and perseverance: *stick-to-it-ivity.* In their book *Disney Animation: The Illusion of Life,* two men who knew Disney well—animators Frank Thomas and Ollie Johnston, two of Disney's Nine Old Men—talk about the stick-to-it-ivity of their old boss:

> [Walt Disney] was not an immediate success. In fact, it is even surprising that he was able to get a toehold in this tough business of limited contracts and tight money. But Walt was a fighter and had great determination; he was no aesthetic artist living in a dream world. As he said, "I have been up against tough competition all my life. I wouldn't know how to get along without it." Any man with Walt's talents but without his spirit and tenacity would never have made it.
>
> There were constant battles, many defeats, endless disappointments: He lost the rights to his cartoon character, his staff, his contracts. And then when he finally began to achieve a bit of success, his studio became a prize to be taken over one way or another, or run out of business! Union jurisdictional problems plagued him as he developed new techniques, new equipment, and new ideas in entertainment. . . .
>
> Through those first years, Walt and his brother Roy struggled alone against the people who controlled the movie industry. In later decades when Walt's back was to the wall he had the strong support of his staff, whose loyalty and dedication to both their boss and their work kept them making sacrifices through days of uncertainty.[1]

The famous song from *Pinocchio* may tell us to "wish upon a star" to make our dreams come true, but Disney knew better. In the real world, if you want your dreams to come true you've got to be persistent, you've got to have fortitude, you've got to hang in there until the final gun goes off.

In his book *A Kick in the Seat of the Pants,* Roger Van Oech says that "as much as eighty percent of the creative process consists in doggedly plodding toward your objective. You're likely to get knocked down a few times along the way. If that happens, get up. Otherwise you'll end up with footprints on your back." Van Oech goes on to cite a survey of venture capitalists. These investors were asked what was the most important quality they looked for in an entrepreneur. Some of the qualities mentioned were market familiarity, demonstrated leadership ability, and a willingness to take risks. All of these were important, but the number one quality they prized was "the ability to sustain an intense effort"—in other words, *stick-to-it-ivity*.

The line between success and failure is extremely fine. Often, it is the difference between the person who hangs on by his fingernails for one second longer than all the rest. Often, it's the difference between the one who fights a little harder, runs a little longer, takes a little more punishment, endures a little more pain than the next guy. Many a game has been won or lost on the one-yard line or in the last second before the gun went off. Many people have given up on their dream when just a little more patience, a little more effort would have brought success.

A Singer with Stick-to-it-ivity

In October 1974, I was working on a major promotional effort as general manager of the Philadelphia 76ers. On Halloween Day, as we were getting ready to host a home game that night with the Knicks, I was completely swamped with details for our Halloween Night promotion—an apple-bobbing contest, a pumpkin-pie-eating contest, that sort of thing. The phone rang, and it was Barry Abrams, a record promoter who worked part-time at our games. "Pat," he said, "there's a young recording artist I'm working with who has just recorded a song. Could you play it on the P.A. system at the game tonight?"

"Gee, Barry," I said, "that's not the kind of thing we usually do—"

"You'd sure be doing this guy a favor, Pat. You'd be doing me a big favor too."

"Okay," I said. "Have him look me up tonight before the game." I hung up and completely forgot about it.

That night before the game, I was up to my neck in work when this skinny guy with a moplike head of hair came up to me. "Are you Mr. Williams?" he asked. "I think Barry Abrams called you today." I stared at him blankly, vaguely remembering I had talked to Barry, but with all that was going on at that moment, I couldn't recall what we had talked about. "I brought my tape," the fellow continued, holding up a cassette. "Can you play it at the game tonight?"

Then I remembered. "Oh, yeah. The guy with the tape," I said, regretting my promise to Barry. "Of all places, why did you pick a basketball game as a place to get your song heard? I mean, the acoustics are terrible in here, and nobody comes to a basketball game to hear music."

"Mr. Williams," he said, "I've got hundreds of these tapes, and I take them to radio stations, baseball games, basketball games, school dances, birthday parties, any place a bunch of people get together. If I get enough people to hear my tapes, then some of them are going to want to buy my records."

"Well," I said, shrugging, "I admire your moxie, anyway. Listen, we've got a lot going on tonight, and I'm really busy. But you see those guys up there in the sound booth? Go up there and talk to the electricians, tell 'em you talked to me and that I said that if you can work something out with them, it's okay with me."

"Thanks!" the guy said brightly. Then he turned and dashed off toward the sound booth. Once again, I promptly forgot about it and went about my work.

Soon the arena was full of fans, the teams came on-court for tip-off, and away we went. During one of the time-outs, I noticed a song on the P.A.—a smooth, easy-listening ballad. When it was over, there was a smattering of applause. I figured the guy had brought his mother and a couple of cousins for a rooting section.

About a month later, I heard the song again. This time, it was on the radio. The song was called "Mandy," and it was zooming to the top of the charts—and a young singer-songwriter named Barry Manilow was on his way.

That kind of success doesn't just happen. It happens because someone is dedicated enough and believes in himself enough to hustle from place to place, constantly shoving tapes in people's hands, constantly looking for a crowd to listen, and a stage on which to strut his stuff. It happens because someone has the stick-to-it-ivity to hammer a dream into reality. When we think of quitting, our example should be the postage stamp: It takes a licking, but it sticks to the job until it gets where it's going!

I've had many interesting guests on my weekly radio show:

Charles Barkley, Shaq, Bob Costas, Jerry West, Larry King, and even Tammy Faye Bakker. But one of my favorite guests of all was Bill Russell—former star center for the Boston Celtics, five-time NBA most valuable player, first black coach of a major American pro sports team, and a good personal friend. One of the topics we discussed on the show was his years coaching the Celtics, which as a player he had led to eleven NBA championships in thirteen seasons. I remembered a comment that was attributed to Bill in an article I once read. "Hustle," he was quoted as saying, "is a talent."

"What do you mean by that, Bill?" I asked.

"Hustle is drive, commitment, persistence, fire in the belly," said Bill. "The guy I think of when I think of hustle is John Havlicek, who played for me in Boston. We called him 'Mr. Perpetual Motion.' He played sixteen seasons and never gave an ounce less than 100 percent. He was there to play basketball. Man, did that guy have hustle! A Boston sportswriter once said to me, 'Well, all John Havlicek has is hustle.' I mean, he just tossed him off like that. I was blown away. I said, 'All he has is hustle! All he has? Listen, *hustle is a talent,* because not everybody does it! The guy with hustle is the guy who's left standing when it's over.'"

PERSEVERING AGAINST THE PAIN

Now, being a positive, optimistic, forward-looking guy, I always believe that today is better than yesterday, and tomorrow's going to be an even greater day still. But I'm also a realist. There's a lot of pain in this life. Sometimes life caves in on you, dumps on you, and leaves you broken and wounded. When that happens, what do you do? That is what the story of one of our players, Brian Shaw, is all about.

Early one Saturday morning in June 1993, Brian's father, Charles Shaw, was driving the family's Jeep Cherokee along Interstate 15, about nine miles south of Las Vegas. Also in the car were Brian's mother, Barbara, his twenty-four-year-old sister, Monica, and Monica's one-year-old daughter, Brianna, who was named in honor of her uncle Brian. The Shaws had traveled on vacation from their home in Oakland, California. It's not clear exactly what happened at 5:15 A.M. that clear summer morning in the Nevada desert. Perhaps Mr. Shaw fell asleep, or perhaps he was run off the road by another car. What is known is that the Cherokee ran off the road, flipped, and skidded on its top. Brian's parents and sister were killed; only little Brianna survived.

How do you go on after a loss like that? Brian's immediate family were all taken from him in a single moment. Brian's parents and sister were his heroes, his counselors, his friends, his rooting section. People who knew them called the Shaws "the perfect family."

Nearly two thousand people jammed the six-hundred-seat Taylor Memorial United Methodist Church in Oakland for the memorial service, including Brian's colleagues in the game, Gary Payton, Reggie Lewis, Mitch Richmond, and Tim Hardaway. People came to pay their respect to a great family and to offer consolation to Brian in his time of incomprehensible grief. Amazingly, it was Brian who seemed to be consoling everyone else!

He got up before the packed sanctuary, cleared his throat, and, in a voice that was strong though full of emotion, said, "Excuse me, but this is going to be my release." Then he gave a moving tribute to his parents and his sister—a tribute filled with reminiscences that were at times bittersweet and at times funny. The other mourners both cried and laughed along with this courageous young man. Brian shared about his father's love for the outdoors and memories of fishing trips in Alaska. He talked about the "sensitive side" of the family, his mother, who was director of a family development center in inner-city Oakland. He talked about the strength and beautiful spirit of his sister, Monica.

Finally, he talked about his infant niece. "All the great things you heard here today about my family," Brian concluded, "are alive in Brianna." And, I would add, in Brian himself.

"My family left me with an inner strength to deal with this," he says today. "I try to be positive about the memories, the many good times. Those thoughts are uplifting, even with the physical separation. I feel like my family is still present with me, watching over me. And I really want to make them proud."

I know Brian Shaw *does* make his family proud. He was playing with the Miami Heat at the time of his loss and now plays a valuable reserve role for the Magic. He's not a flashy player like Shaq or Penny, but he's solid, dependable, and consistent when the pressure is on. For many players, a tragic loss in life would be a distraction on the court. But Brian has not allowed his own suffering to cause his game to suffer. If anything, he seems to have immersed himself even more in his game, not so much to *escape* his pain as to make his family proud.

Brian Shaw is a marvelous human being—a warm, gentle, humble guy in a business where big egos are the norm. It takes enormous inner strength and character to persevere against such pain. I count it a privilege to know Brian, to watch him work, and to watch him courageously live out his life. He is a model to me, and to millions of fans nationwide, of the power of stick-to-it-ivity.

I want to add one other personal story about refusing to give up. In 1962, when I was a senior at Wake Forest, there was a freshman football player at school named Brian Piccolo, who went on to have an All-American career. After graduation, Brian signed with the Chicago Bears and launched his NFL career.

In 1969, I became the general manager of the Chicago Bulls and crossed paths once again with Brian. In the fall of 1969 the shocking story came out that Brian was suffering from an incurable form of cancer.

Brian died in June of 1970, but before he died he had a business card printed up and handed it out regularly. He gave me one of his cards, and I kept it for a long time. It said, "You can't quit. It's a league rule."

What a powerful example of hanging in there and living out stick-to-it-ivity.

PROFILES IN PERSEVERANCE

Irving Stone spent his career studying the great lives of history—Michelangelo, Freud, Darwin, Lincoln, Van Gogh. Then he wrote fictionalized biographies of their lives and times—books such as *Lust for Life, Clarence Darrow for the Defense, The Agony and the Ecstacy,* and *The Origin.* Stone was convinced that all the great lives he wrote about had something in common. "I write about people," he said, "who sometime in their life have a vision or dream of something that should be accomplished, and then they go to work. They are beaten over the head, knocked down, vilified, and for years they get nowhere. But every time they're knocked down they stand up. You cannot destroy these people. And at the end of their lives they've accomplished some modest part of what they set out to do."

Like Irving Stone, I have long been interested in stories of great lives and great persistence—people who have persevered against pain, heartbreak, obstacles, and setbacks in the relentless pursuit of their dreams. One such person was Bob Love.

I arrived in Chicago as general manager of the Bulls in September 1969. One of the players sitting on the bench was a forward by the name of Bob Love, nicknamed Butterbean. Butterbean Love had been in the pros a few years, but he had really never distinguished himself in the sport. He had started in Cincinnati, was traded to Milwaukee, was then traded to Chicago, and there he languished when I arrived on the scene as general manager. In fact, one of the first things I tried to do when I arrived was trade Butterbean to Seattle, but Seattle didn't want him.

Butterbean was a battler, he was determined, he hung in there and believed in himself. Finally, in the fall of 1969, he got his chance and the next thing you know he was off and winging. For the next eight years, he was an all-star forward, the greatest player to wear a Chicago Bulls uniform until Michael Jordan arrived.

It seemed that Butterbean was on his way, set for life—but there was one huge problem in his way: Bob had a severe stuttering problem. I recall one night when he was interviewed on WGN-TV after a Bulls game and his stuttering was so bad he could hardly get through the interview. It was one of the most embarrassing, humiliating things I've ever seen.

When his career ended in 1977, Butterbean wanted to stay in the game, primarily in coaching, but he was afflicted with this stuttering problem, and no one would hire him. So for the next seven years, Bob Love bounced from one meaningless job to another. Here was a guy who scored more than twelve thousand points in the NBA, and he ended up working as a busboy in a restaurant in a Nordstrom's department store in Seattle.

Still, Butterbean wasn't beaten. He worked hard as a busboy, never took a day off. He was always the first to volunteer to do extra work, and this made a deep impression on the people at Nordstrom's. They noted the pride and hard work ethic he possessed, and they eventually financed the speech therapy he needed to help him with this embarrassing problem.

The therapy was successful. Today, he is a public spokesman for the Nordstrom's store chain. He also works as director of community relations for his old team, the Bulls. He's continually out in the community, in schools, speaking and challenging young people, pointing them toward a brighter tomorrow, encouraging kids of all races, but with a deep impact on the inner city. His message is, "Prepare yourself today through education and sports. Develop your talents, so that tomorrow can be a productive period for you."

Butterbean is my first nomination for a profile of perseverance. Another one is Richard Nixon. When Nixon died in 1994, it was a time of mixed emotions for our nation. Many people revered him for his great achievements. Many others reviled him for his great disgrace in the Watergate scandal. But one thing that stood out in the comments of both his friends and his foes: Nixon was a man who persevered. In his eulogy at Nixon's graveside, long-time friend and adviser Henry Kissinger brought tears to many eyes when he said, "So let us now say good-bye to our gallant friend. He stood on pinnacles that dissolved in the precipice. He achieved greatly and he suffered deeply. But he never gave up." A great eulogy—and a fitting one for the late president who once said, "A man is not finished when he's defeated. He's finished when he quits."

This story is just one of many. Glance through these other "portraits of perseverance." (You'll find familiar names. What will surprise you is how many times these people failed before their names became so familiar.)

• George Washington lost two-thirds of the major campaigns of the Revolutionary War—but he persevered, he won, and the United States of America exists today because he did.

• When George Frederic Handel wrote his masterpiece, *The Messiah,* he was at the very lowest point in his life—sick, destitute, and so deep in hock that his creditors threatened to send him to debtor's prison. He persevered, and the performance of this masterpiece of sacred music enabled him to pay his bills—and forever enshrined his reputation as one of the world's great composers.

• Louis Pasteur didn't discover his revolutionary process of pasteurization until after he had suffered a paralyzing stroke. "Let me tell you the secret that has led me to my goal," he later said. "My strength lies solely in my tenacity."

• Henry Ford failed and went broke five times before he finally succeeded. Though his successes were great, his failures were frequently embarrassing. The very first Ford car model had a glaring design flaw: Ford forgot to install a reverse gear! But he knew how to achieve his goals: *Just stick to it.* An ambitious young employee once asked Henry Ford the secret of his success. "When you start a thing," Ford replied, *"finish it."*

• Alfred C. Fuller was fired from three jobs and was unable to find work after that. He decided since no one would hire him that he would hire himself. He started making brushes and selling them door-to-door. That was the beginning of the famous door-to-door sales organization, the Fuller Brush Company.

• Bob Hope is an entertainment legend today, but he came close to giving up on show business back in 1928 when he was broke, hungry, and unable to find work. "I was standing in front of the Woods Theater in Chicago," he recalls. "I couldn't get a booking and I was ready to chuck it all and go back home to Cleveland." Just then, a buddy of his from the vaudeville stage walked up and asked how he was doing. "I'm starving," Hope replied, and his friend could see that the funny man was not joking. He put an arm around Hope and walked him over to the office of agent Charlie Hogan. Hope auditioned a bit of his act for Hogan, and the agent liked what he saw. "Son," he said, "I can get you a fill-in booking at the West Englewood Theater. It's only one day, but it'll pay twenty-five bucks. Will that be all right?" Hope—who had only been making ten dollars a show till then—eagerly accepted. "And that," he says today, "was the booking that got me rolling."

• Babe Ruth is known as "the Home Run King" because of his 714 home runs. What is less well known is that he was also "the Strikeout King" of his era, striking out a then-record 1,330 times!

• Theodor Geisel wrote a children's book and submitted it for publication. The first publisher rejected it, and so did the next and the next and the next. In fact, the book was rejected by *twenty-three publishers* in all! However, the twenty-fourth publisher bought it, published it, and sold six million copies! Never heard of Theodor Geisel? Well, maybe you know him better by his pen name: Dr. Seuss! That first book—*And to Think That I Saw It on Mulberry Street* (1937)—was followed by many more million-plus-selling children's classics such as *The Cat in the Hat, Horton Hears a Who,* and *Green Eggs and Ham.*

• General Douglas MacArthur was turned down for admission to West Point—not once, but twice. If he had not persisted and been accepted on the third try, our history books might have told the stories of World War II and Korea quite differently.

• Tom Monahan bought a little hole-in-the-wall pizza shop in 1960, and the business struggled along for eight years until a fire burned up his investment. The insurance company only reimbursed him ten cents on the dollar, but he took that meager sum of money, borrowed some more, invested it all in a new shop, and struggled once again to make a go of it. Two years later, when he fell behind in his loan payments, the bank took over the business. The bank ran his business even further into the ground for the next ten months, then returned the remains of the shop back to Monahan. It was now 1971, he was $1.5 million in debt, and he faced scores of lawsuits from angry creditors. But Monahan refused to accept defeat. Instead, he asked himself, "What can I do to turn this around? How can I make this pizza restaurant stand out from all the rest?" The answer: start the nation's first pizza home-delivery service—an idea that enabled him not only to stay in business and pay off his creditors but to *flourish.* Today, Monahan's company—Domino's Pizza—has more than 3,300 outlets in America and is rated one of this country's top fifty food-service companies.

• Rocky Bleier didn't exactly seem destined for football stardom. He was the very last draft pick in the 1968 NFL college draft. He hardly got his Pittsburgh Steelers uniform on before

Uncle Sam tapped him on the shoulder, dressed him in khaki, and shipped him off to Vietnam. There, his right leg was blown open by shrapnel from a grenade, and his left thigh was pierced by gunfire. His pro football career hadn't even started, and it looked like it was over for good.

But Rocky Bleier wanted to play football. So he forced himself to ignore his limp and his pain. He trained for hours, day after day, to rebuild his strength and agility. He showed up at the Steelers training camp in 1970 and amazed his teammates with his tenacity. When he tore a hamstring, he taped up the leg (against doctor's orders) and kept going. He pumped up his stamina and sharpened his skill on the Steelers' specialty team for three years, then advanced to the Steelers' starting backfield in '74. Within two more years, he helped power Pittsburgh's dominance of the game in the '70s, gaining more than a thousand yards in '76 alone.

A running back's greatest physical assets are his legs—and Rocky Bleier's had been ripped and shattered by steel and lead. But he proved that he had an even greater asset in his soul and his mind: an absolute, unconditional refusal to quit.

• Richard Hooker spent seven years writing his first novel, a comedy based on his experiences in the Korean War. He took his manuscript to publisher after publisher—a punishing gauntlet of rejection. One editor said, "This stuff just isn't funny." Another said, "A comedy about war? That's sick!" In all, he was rejected twenty-one times. But Hooker didn't give up, and finally, on the twenty-second try, an editor at Morrow sent him a contract and an advance check. The book was published, became a hit, spawned several sequels, a movie, and a long-running TV series. The title of the book: M*A*S*H.

• Many people find it hard to believe that Baltimore Colts star quarterback Johnny Unitas was once cut and waived by the Pittsburgh Steelers. In fact, Unitas had come to the conclusion that his fledgling career was already over when he made a desperation call to the Colts, pleading for a tryout. The Colts signed Unitas, and he went on to become a Hall of Famer with some of the most impressive stats in the game: over 40,000 yards of passes, 290 completed touchdown passes, and touchdown passes thrown in 47 consecutive games—an NFL record. Not bad for a Steelers reject!

• When Mary Kay Ash started her cosmetics company in 1963, everyone predicted disaster. Her accountant told her she was paying too much commission to her salespeople. Her attorney gave her a list of all the cosmetics firms that had already gone bankrupt that year. A rival firm smugly offered to buy her out for pennies on a dollar, predicting she would fail. "The odds were against me," she recalls, "but even back in 1963, I did know four things for certain: (1) People will support that which they help to create. (2) In this great country there is no limit to what an individual can accomplish. (3) If given the opportunity, women are capable of superior performance. (4) I was willing to work long, hard hours to implement my convictions." Mary Kay Ash persevered, and today she presides over Mary Kay Cosmetics, one of the largest and most profitable cosmetics companies in America.

• Country music star Randy Travis has been called an "overnight success"—but the people who called him that don't know the whole story. Travis and his wife, Lib Hatcher (who was also his manager), worked and sacrificed for ten long, lean years in order for him to become an "overnight success." During those years, Randy auditioned for—and was turned down by—every record producer in Nashville. Meanwhile, Lib ran a nightclub that billed her husband as the featured attraction. She often had to pawn her jewelry and other valuables in order to pay bills and meet payroll. The nightclub patrons had no idea that when the club's star entertainer, Randy Travis, wasn't onstage, he was washing dishes and frying catfish back in the kitchen. Randy and Lib stayed focused on their dream, and after ten years of struggle, the dream began to come true: Randy recorded a song called "On the Other Hand." The song became a hit, which led to a major album, then a nationwide tour, then videos, more albums, and even a movie deal. "If you work at something long enough," says Travis, "and keep believing, sooner or later it will happen."

Sustainer of Champions

I once saw talk show host Sally Jessie Raphael interviewed on TV. The interviewer asked, "What is the source of your talent?" She tossed her head and laughed, "Talent? Oh, my! Let me tell you something: The only talent is perseverance." I love that statement. You and I may not be the smartest, strongest, or most highly skilled people in the world. We may not be Phi Beta Kappa or All-American or Miss Universe. But in the long run, none of that really matters. The only talent is perseverance. If you have that extra something called stick-to-it-ivity, you have practically everything you need to be a success.

The character quality of stick-to-it-ivity is so important because there are so many obstacles that stand between ourselves and our dreams. There are people who try to discourage us and tear us down. There are well-meaning people who try to get us to set aside our dreams and "be sensible." There are practical barriers: lack of money, indifference, time pressures, stresses, and problems to be solved. There are trials and misfortunes that cloud our focus and rob us of our will to move forward: bankruptcies, illnesses, divorce and other relationship problems, and tragic losses such as the one Brian Shaw suffered. All of these obstacles are out there, trying to keep us from our dreams. Our job is to punch through them, duck under them, leap over them, zigzag around them, and keep pressing toward our goal.

Some of the obstacles we face are actually *within* us—emotional and personality barriers such as laziness, weariness, self-doubt, worry, insecurity, fear, and procrastination. Many of us know what we need to do in order to succeed, but we think that's too difficult, or that we'll get our hands dirty, or that we don't want to lower ourselves to such tasks, or that somebody else ought to make things easy for us. But, as E. M. Gray has said, "The successful person has the habit of doing the things that failures don't like to do. The successful person doesn't like doing them either, but his dislike is subordinated to the strength of his purpose." The strength of our purpose must propel us to our dreams, forcing us to do the things we don't want to do, in order to achieve the things we deeply want to achieve.

I have been invited to share "my Disney speech" at many conventions and corporate gatherings. One of my favorite stories comes from Art Williams, former football coach and now insurance executive. Here's Art's message:

It's so simple that it's "revolutionary." The fact is, this formula, or principle, is misunderstood enough and overlooked enough that it can truly be called "magic" by those who understand it. Ready? Here it is:

- You beat 50 percent of the people in America by working hard.
- You beat another 40 percent by being a person of honesty and integrity and standing for something.
- The last 10 percent is a dogfight in the free enterprise system.

Just take a minute and let it sink in. I don't care if you're building a football team, going into business, or running the country as its president, you beat 50 percent of the people *at any level* just by working hard consistently over a long period of time. I get so mad when I read some of those get-rich-quick books on the market today. They talk about how you need to work smart, not hard, to succeed. Wrong! Nobody wants to tell you about the bone-wearing, backbreaking work it takes to succeed, but I can promise you one thing. You aren't going to get to square one if you aren't willing to work harder than you've ever worked in your life.

This all-important quality of stick-to-it-ivity is the same quality expressed by the apostle Paul when he said,

> We are hard pressed on every side, yet not crushed; we are perplexed, but not in despair; persecuted, but not forsaken; struck down, but not destroyed. . . . Therefore we do not lose heart. Even though our outward man is perishing, yet the inward man is being renewed day by day. For our light affliction, which is but for a moment, is working for us a far more exceeding and eternal weight of glory. . . .
> One thing I do, forgetting those things which are behind and reaching forward to those things which are ahead, I press toward the goal for the prize of the upward call of God in Christ Jesus.[2]

Enduring affliction. Pressing for the goal. Reaching for the prize. This is the character-stuff of which champions are made.

Paul understood the power of stick-to-it-ivity almost two thousand years ago.

Do you know who Ernest Shackleton was? He was the Irish-born explorer who attempted to reach the South Pole. In fact, though he tried several times to achieve his life's objective and conquer the South Pole, he never succeeded. He came within three days' journey of his objective, but he turned back. Why, then, should we care about a man who *failed* in his great goal in life? When you've heard his story, you'll know.

Several previous attempts had been made to reach the Pole. In fact, Shackleton himself had been a member of Robert F. Scott's unsuccessful expedition in 1904. In 1908, Shackleton's own expedition began its march toward the Pole, starting from McMurdo Sound and moving out across the Beardmore Glacier. On January 9, 1909, Shackleton and his men reached a point closer to the Pole than any other expedition had reached—just ninety-seven miles from the Pole, or about a three-day journey. Without question, he could make it to the Pole—and to fame and fortune. But supplies were dwindling. If he pushed on, some of his men would probably not survive the return trip. So Shackleton made the difficult decision to turn back. He pushed himself and his men to return to the coast, where a ship awaited them with orders to depart—with or without the Shackleton party—on March 1. Shackleton and his men arrived at the ship precisely on March 1.

Ernest Shackleton tried again with a voyage that left England in 1914. In January 1915, his ship, the *Endurance,* was trapped in the ice, still hundreds of miles from the Antarctic continent. Shackleton and his men remained aboard, trying to free the ship for the next ten months. In November, the ice won, crushing and sinking the *Endurance,* and stranding the men on the ice with nothing but tents, two lifeboats, and a dwindling store of supplies. Seeing that the expedition was doomed without outside help, Shackleton and two of his men climbed into one of the lifeboats and set sail across 870 miles of ocean, arriving at South Georgia island, east of Tierra del Fuego. They were nearly dead when they came ashore. They climbed a mountain range and made their way to the whaling station on the far side of the island. There they organized a rescue attempt for the men they had left behind.

The relief ship battled two months of stormy weather, wending its way through iceberg-mined seas. Finally, the ship reached the twenty-two men who had been left behind. By the time they returned to England, all of these men had survived eighteen months of subzero weather, living on bare subsistence rations. Despite the perils and hardships that he and his men endured, despite his failure in two attempts to reach the South Pole, Ernest Shackleton brought *every single man* of his party through the ordeal alive. That is success under unbelievably harsh circumstances—and it is owing entirely to Shackleton's intense and tenacious stick-to-it-ivity.

One of the truly great stories of perseverance that I have seen with my own eyes is that of a young man named Donald Royal. He was the number five man on the Magic team—fifth on our starting roster when it comes to publicity and attention as well as jersey number 5. Professionally, Donald has had a tough career. A Notre Dame alum, he played in the late 1980s for Pensacola and Cedar Rapids in the minor Continental Basketball Association, then moved up to the NBA with the Timberwolves, then played a season in Tel Aviv, Israel (where he once narrowly escaped death from a terrorist's bomb), then back to the CBA in Tri-City, Washington, then back up to the NBA with San Antonio, then to Orlando. Reading his resume is like following the dizzying ricocheting of a pinball!

For most pro hoop players, being cut from a CBA team is wake-up call: time to find another career. But Donald had his sights set on the NBA. He persisted. He continually worked on his game. After joining the Magic—a team where a lot of glory and attention goes to the pyrotechnic performances of players like Shaq, Penny Hardaway, Nick Anderson, and Horace Grant— Donald Royal turned in a steady (and steadily improving) performance. Precisely because he's not a razzle-dazzle player, he provided some key strengths to the Magic team. He's a strong defensive player, a tough rebounder for his size, and a strong offensive player in a supporting role. He also provides a beautifully choreographed back-screen for the infamous Shaq Attaq.

"I'm a role player," he once told a reporter for the *Sporting News* with characteristic team-player humility. "It's no big deal for me not to score a lot. I'm a guy who's out there to do the little things."[3] But Donald's a role player with very respectable stats. During the 1994–95 season, he averaged 9.1 points, 4.0 rebounds, and 2.8 assists per game while shooting .475 from the floor. He has patented an explosive move to the hole, and he has improved his outside shot, frequently surprising his opponents with effective sixteen- or eighteen-footers. Whereas a lot of players would have hung up their sneakers after the rigors of a CBA career, Donald Royal stuck to his dream—and he now has a multiyear, multimillion-dollar contract and an NBA starting position to show for it.

Wheaties may be the breakfast of champions, but stick-to-it-ivity is the lunch, dinner, and between-meal snacks of champions! It's what keeps us going when everyone around us is ready to quit. It's what separates the winners from the rest of the herd.

Persistence is the sustainer of champions.

ADVICE FROM THE GREATS

This chapter has been a bit different from the other chapters in this book: fewer tips and principles, more stories, more personal snapshots. And there's a good reason. There is only *one* principle, *one* tip when it comes to stick-to-it-ivity: *Stick to it!* I've found that the most inspiring, instructive lessons I've ever received in the subject of perseverance have come from simply observing the lives of people who have done it. When your back is on the canvas, when you're down for the count, when the crowd is booing you, it helps to see that other people have been where you are . . . and to know that they have battled their way to a knockout victory!

I have always found the arena of sports to be a microcosm and a metaphor for the arena of life. Virtually every lesson that applies to winning in sports applies equally well to achieving success in life. The same essential character qualities that make a person a standout rebounder or quarterback or marathon runner also lay the foundation for a standout executive, entrepreneur, salesman, pastor, entertainer, author, or parent. Stick-to-it-ivity is the key, whether your goal is a corner office, a seat at the Million Dollar Round Table, a best-selling novel, or the end zone in a bowl game. Here are some people who can say it better than I:

- "When I was a third-string quarterback at Georgia Tech, I didn't quit," says Pepper Rodgers. "When I was second-string as a junior, I didn't quit. And when I was a senior, I got hurt and I could have quit. But I didn't. I persevered and ended my career as the Most Valuable Player in the Sugar Bowl. Everybody thought I was a great player, but I wasn't. I was just great at not quitting."

- "It's always interesting to me," says sports psychologist Jim Loehr, "that the great athletes don't feel their greatness is due to great genes. One [factor] that constantly emerges in psychological tests of greatness is the level of drive. That's the single greatest predictor of all. How passionate is the person going after a particular goal? So many people who rise to greatness in sports, like Larry Bird or Wayne Gretzky, don't feel they're genetically gifted. Mental toughness, most athletes will tell you, is the deciding factor. They are able to get the emotional part together better than most of their counterparts. You look at Bird, and you didn't believe he could be that great when he stood next to all those super Ferraris. Obviously he had something beyond genetic superiority." That extra "something" is a quality called *stick-to-it-ivity*.

- "My doctor told me I would never pitch again after I hurt my arm," recalls ex-major-league pitcher Tommy John, "but I said, 'You're a great doctor and I believe in you. But you're wrong about this. I won't quit. I'll come back. You did an excellent job on my arm, and now the rest is up to me. I know how much pain my body can stand—and it's quite a bit. I know how hard I can work, and if it takes eighteen hours a day, I'll do it. I will come back.'" And he did.

- "All athletes," says Olympic silver-medal-winning gymnast Cathy Rigby, "or for that matter anyone with career ambitions, have times when everything seems to go wrong. They're tired; motivation slips—and they can think of a hundred and one reasons not to do whatever they're supposed to do. I found that at those times I would push myself the hardest—do extra routines, a few more exercises, concentrate harder. This was when I would see my biggest improvement—after the slump—maybe in two or three days or two or three months—it would happen."

- My old pal, former Dodgers manager Tommy Lasorda, sees perseverance as a kind of spiritual quest. "When things got tough," he says, "we'd refer to a little piece of paper that Dusty Baker carried in his pocket. I'd like to share it with you—it's from Romans 5:1–5: 'Tribulations bring about perseverance, and perseverance brings about proven character, and proven character brings about hope, and hope does not disappoint.'"

And with the last word on the subject, one of football's legendary coaches, the late George Allen, offered his definition of stick-to-it-ivity when he was chairman of the President's Council on Physical Fitness:

> One of the most difficult things everyone has to learn is that for your entire life you must "keep fighting" and adjusting if you hope to survive. No matter who you are or what your position, you must keep fighting for whatever it is your desire to achieve.
>
> If someone is not aware of this contest and expects otherwise, then constant disappointment occurs. People who fail sometimes do not realize that the simple answer to everyday achievement is to keep fighting. Health, happiness, and success depend upon the fighting spirit of each person. The big thing is not what happens to us in life—but what we *do* about what happens to us.[4]

George Allen didn't just preach those words. He lived them. During his years as a head coach in the NFL, he took two bottom-of-the-barrel teams—first the Los Angeles Rams and then the Washington Redskins—and he transformed them into winning teams. He racked up an incredible sixteen-year run of consecutive winning seasons. He took teams to the Super Bowl. *He kept fighting.*

Finally, in 1990, after twenty-three combative years as a head coach in pro football, George Allen retired. He had just barely begun to settle in and enjoy his retirement when the phone rang. The athletic department at Long Beach State University was on the phone, pleading with Allen to come out of retirement and rescue their ailing football program.

"I'm seventy-two years old," Allen gruffly replied. "I'm retired from pro ball. I don't need the aggravation of coaching a college team."

Long Beach persisted and pleaded with him to consider the job.

"You can get another coach somewhere," said Allen. "You don't need me."

"If you don't take the job," said Long Beach, "we'll have to cancel the entire football program."

"You guys are in that bad shape?"

"Our program is the worst."

"And that's supposed to make me want to come coach there?"

"Well . . ."

"All right. I'll do it."

So Allen—this feisty, over-the-hill NFL coach—was now the coach of a perennially losing college team. Arriving at the campus, Allen found a football squad that was underfunded, low on morale, lacking in facilities, and laughed at by the student body. Looking around at his ragtag, dispirited troops, he said to himself, *This is gonna be the biggest challenge of my life!*

He went to the art department and had signs made up that read:

> ## The difference
> ## between winning and
> ## losing is *this much*.
>
>

He had these signs hung up around the locker room. Then he went to work rebuilding a team. He started by setting an example—running laps and doing sit-ups and push-ups. He wanted to show the team that he didn't demand anything from them that he didn't also demand from himself.

And he demanded *everything!*

After the Long Beach 49ers lost their first few games, he sat them down and lectured them—hard. "I see you guys losing out there," he said, "and then you come in here joking and laughing.

I don't see how you can do that. I don't see how you can live with yourselves when you lose. It's clear what you guys need: a fighting spirit. You need intensity and focus. You need to want to win. So from now on, practice is going to be twice as tough."

The student body continued to laugh rather than support the team. Sportswriters dumped on the Long Beach team and the "old man" who coached them. Allen called his players together and told them, "We aren't quitting just because everyone says we should. We've got to see this thing through." And see it through they did.

In their next game, the 49ers pulled the turf out from under top-ranked University of the Pacific, 28–7. Then came the homecoming game against longtime rival, Fullerton State—and for the first time in years, the Long Beach bleachers were packed with cheering fans! Although Long Beach trailed by a point as the game neared the final gun, Long Beach yanked a turnover from the hands of a bewildered Fullerton quarterback. Seizing the opportunity, Long Beach came through with a breathtaking field goal with six seconds remaining on the clock. Allen's team had hung in there—focusing, hustling, battling, persevering their way to a 37–35 win in the fading moments of the game.

Suddenly, a team that had been repeatedly told they were losers now saw themselves as champions. They went into their final game of the season—against UNLV—with a 5 and 5 record. They were just one victory away from a winning season, their first in years. "How bad do you guys want this game?" asked Coach Allen. The 49ers responded with a roar of defiance and determination. They wanted it, and they went out on the field and got it: a grueling 29–20 victory. As the final gun sounded, a chant went up in the stands, "We love George! We love George!"

That win made seventeen straight winning seasons for George Allen—sixteen in the pros and one as coach of a formerly ragtag crew of college kids at Long Beach State. After the win, Coach Allen turned his coaching efforts toward encouraging his team of champions to become winners in the game of life. He changed the signs in the locker room to:

The difference
between winning
and losing is
staying in class!

He encouraged them to take the same belief in themselves, the same drive, the same stick-to-it-ivity that had made them winners on the gridiron, and to apply it to their studies and their lives.

Then, only a month and a half after the victory over UNLV, Coach Allen's wife returned from an outing and found him on the carpet of their living room, dead of a massive heart attack.

The team rode together to the memorial service in two buses and sat together at the front of the sanctuary. George Allen's son, Bruce, gave a eulogy for his father in which he read from a "Things to Do" list that the late coach had written just days before his death:

1. Win a Championship.
2. Have Every Player I've Recruited Graduate.
3. Build a Stadium.
4. Then Take a Tougher Job.

That is a list written by a man who understands and lives by the principle of stick-to-it-ivity. It is the mark of a champion. It is the code of a winner.

In the next chapter, we confront the final secret behind a magical kingdom, a magical basketball team, and a magical, miraculous way of life: the secret Walt Disney called . . .

Well, just turn the page and see! Magical Secret No. 5: Have Fun!

MAGICAL
SECRET

N U M B E R 5

Have Fun!

CHAPTER 9

Can You Believe They *Pay* Me to Do This?

○ *I always try to look on the light side of things, and I live every day just as if it were New Year's Eve.*
Joe Engle, longtime minor-league baseball owner, Chattanooga, Tennessee

○ *Everybody's got a laughin' place—trouble is, most folks won't take the time to look for it.*
Sign on the wall at the Disneyland attraction, Splash Mountain

○ *I want to be remembered as someone who was fun to live with.*
Billy Graham, at age 75

○ *Most of my life I have done what I wanted to do. I have had fun on the job.*
Walt Disney

had a deadline staring me in the face: Labor Day weekend 1990. I was heading up a group that was trying to bring a major-league baseball team to Orlando—a companion team to the Magic basketball organization that was already up and running. The pressure was on, and we had one big problem: We didn't have an owner!

To start a new sports team, you've *got* to have an owner—but the ownership group we started with had collapsed in July. So we had about six weeks, from mid-July until early September, to get a new ownership group in place. Even though the league would not make a decision until June 1991, we had to have an ownership group firmly in place by Labor Day if we wanted to be in the running. So I scrambled, I worked contact after contact, I made call after call, I beat the bushes—but I still couldn't come up with anybody who had a few spare millions lying around to invest in a baseball club.

As the deadline approached, my mission began to look completely hopeless. I went through each day with a big black storm-cloud raining over my head. Then, just two weeks before the Labor Day deadline, the phone rang. It was my old friend, Billy Zeoli, and he had some good news. "Hey, Patrick," he said, "I think I may have found an owner for your baseball team."

"No kidding!" I whooped. "Who? Where? When can I meet him?" Instantly, the storm-cloud over my head began to evaporate. I felt like throwing out my arms and singing, just like Julie Andrews in *The Sound of Music.*

"His name is Rich DeVos," said Billy. "He's the cofounder of Amway, and he's a dear friend of mine. Rich is up in Grand Rapids, and he says he's willing to talk to you."

On the Friday before Labor Day, I flew to Michigan and had a one-hour meeting with the Amway King himself. I didn't know it then, but that was the beginning of what would become a warm friendship between Rich DeVos and myself. According to *Forbes,* he is one of the richest men in America—but what *Forbes* doesn't tell you is that he is one of the kindest and most big-hearted men in America as well. He is also very astute and decisive. Before our one-hour meeting had ended, Rich had made up his mind to back Orlando's bid to be the next home of a new major-league team.

I returned home so lighthearted and energized by our meeting that I almost got to Orlando ahead of the plane! Within a couple of days, however, I was brought right back down to earth. Somehow, the story of Rich's involvement had leaked, and the media was all over the story. We had planned to keep the deal under wraps until our big press conference. Instead we found ourselves fielding calls from reporters and fending off rumors that were constantly popping up in the press. Many months of pressure on this baseball effort really had me uptight.

The day of the big announcement arrived, and I was very uncomfortable. The media had gathered in the pressroom at the Orlando Arena, and the atmosphere was tense and wary. I was mentally preparing myself for the conference, and I could feel the tension throughout my body. *Sports is supposed to be fun,* I thought. *So why am I not enjoying this?* In the last few minutes before the conference was to begin, I walked through the team offices on my way to the press area on the lower level. Along the way, I passed through an office belonging to one of our basketball scouts, and something caught my eye: a piece of paper tacked to the bulletin board. My eyes were drawn to that paper as if by magnetism, and there I read these words:

> We choose to have fun.
> Fun creates enjoyment.
> Enjoyment invites participation.
> Participation focuses attention.
> Attention expands awareness.
> Awareness promotes insight.
> Insight generates knowledge.
> Knowledge facilitates action.
> Action yields results.

I stood there for about a minute, reading and rereading those words. I was totally riveted. If ever there was a perfect message for me, it was *that* precise message, coming at *that* precise moment: Successful results can be ours—*and it all begins by choosing to have fun.* I needed to hear that, because I hadn't been having any fun up to that moment. I needed to be reminded: *We* make the decision whether we're going to have fun. *We choose it!* And when we have fun at what we do, we are naturally more effective and successful.

As I read those words, I felt a smile break out across my face. *Okay, Williams,* I told myself, *get on out there and have fun!* There was a springlike bounce to my step as I continued on out to the pressroom. I leaped onto the podium and faced the press with a new sense of energy, exuberance, and fun. I announced that Richard DeVos had agreed to be the owner for the new baseball franchise, and then Rich made a statement from Grand Rapids via speaker phone.

All of us who were part of that effort hoped that this would be the beginning of an exciting new chapter in the history of baseball—and the history of central Florida. But the expansion plans never materialized. The National League chose to bypass Orlando in favor of Denver and Miami.

Yet something good still came out of those efforts. Rich DeVos and all the other members of the DeVos family became so caught up in the magic of Orlando, Florida, that when the Magic basketball team became available for sale in the summer of 1991, they moved right in and bought the team. Rich didn't become the baseball mogul he originally planned to be. Instead, he became a major mover in the world of pro *basketball.* Having worked with Rich for some four years now, I can say that it has been a great association—*and it's been a lot of fun!*

IT ALMOST SEEMS ILLEGAL!

As I look back over my life in sports, what can I say? It has been fun! Oh, yes, there have been tough times, difficult people to work with, moments of great fear and knots in the stomach, plenty of stress, difficulties, and problems to solve. But as I think back on that seven-year-old boy named Pat Williams who fell in love with baseball after watching his first major-league game, I think, *How fortunate I've been to have spent my career in the field of sports, doing work I truly love!* My job was fun. I worked with fun people. My job description was "Find new ways to entertain and generate fun!"

For the past twenty-seven years, I've had the fun of working in the National Basketball Association, with forty-plus home games to put on every year, watching the greatest athletes in the world, entertaining families and fans, giving them a memorable and fun evening. Looking back, I realize that every single paycheck I've received since I was twenty-two years old has been from a pro sports team. Every once in a while, I sit back and look at my life and think, *Wow! Can you believe they pay me to do this? It almost seems illegal!*

I probably average thirty letters a month from people across the country, begging for a job opportunity with the Magic. Every time I have to send back a "Thanks-for-your-interest-but-no-thanks" letter because we have no openings, I can't help thinking how fortunate I've been to spend my entire adult life in the sports world. I continually feel charged up about my job because I know that every day will bring me a challenge or project that is unique, special, and *fun* to tackle.

DEAD SERIOUS ABOUT FUN

I like to think of myself as a fun guy. I've written joke books, and I like to break up a crowd with an after-dinner speech. But you know what the biggest complaint about me is? "Pat, you just don't know how to have fun!" The first time I heard that, I thought it was the craziest thing I ever heard of! But it is true. It seems that most men—myself included—are trained early on to put our serious game faces on, like cheerleaders at a funeral to play the role of professional lemon tasters, to charge toward that career goal of success. It's okay to be ambitious, but we need to learn that along the way, as we charge toward our goals, it's okay to have fun. In fact, it's *crucial* to have fun. It's crucial in sports, in business, and in family life.

I got a lesson in fun from one of the greats of baseball even while this book was being written. It happened when I was invited to play in an "old-timers'" baseball game. (Don't ya love it when they call you an "old-timer"?) I played catcher, and the first baseman on our team was none other than the great Pete Rose. I mean, who would have thought I would ever play baseball on the same diamond with Pete Rose? I felt like I should get down on my knees and shout, "I'm not worthy! I'm not worthy!"

I had my three oldest boys—Jimmy, Bobby, and David—in the

dugout during the game. That was a great treat for them, because they got to rub shoulders with a bunch of guys they had only seen before on TV and on trading cards. You will remember that Bobby was a high school baseball player and really loves the game, so afterward I took him over to Pete and said, "Pete, I'd really like you to talk to Bobby about *hustle*. You were synonymous with the word *hustle* when you played the game, and I'd love to have you talk to him about it."

Pete looked from Bobby to me and said, "You know, I really don't like that word, *hustle*. What I like more is the word *enthusiasm*. I went out there and had so much fun doing my job that I just had to do well at it. The way I see it, God gave me certain physical skills. Not great skills, but good skills. By themselves, good skills are not enough to make it in this game. But what God *really* gave me at birth, in addition to good ability, was *great* desire, *great* determination, and *great* enthusiasm. There was not one day in my baseball career that I was not excited to be at the ballpark. I couldn't wait to get there every day. And when I got out on the diamond, I had a ton of fun playing baseball. That's why I had a special career."

I'll tell you someone else who's having a special career: Shaquille O'Neal. Read his book *Shaq Attaq!* and hear him tell about all the things he does—playing basketball, shooting movies, making Reebok and Pepsi commercials, cutting rap CDs. He'll tell you he's not in it primarily for the money (though the money he makes is considerable). He'll tell you, "You gotta make it fun. I went out there every day with the approach that it's got to be fun. . . . The Shaq Attack ain't stopping, bro, it's just getting started. My ball, my court, my game."[1] That's the attitude I see on Shaq's face whenever I watch him in action—whatever action he's into at the moment. He's always having *fun*—and that's a major part of his success!

I've been involved with two other fun-loving characters during my NBA career. One was center Darryl Dawkins whom we drafted right out of Evans High School in Orlando in 1975. Darryl never had the kind of career we expected, but, boy, was he fun.

Right after he moved to Philly as an eighteen-year-old kid, I called his new house. His answering machine blurted out, "This is the Dawk, and I'm ready to talk!" I started laughing so hard that I forgot to reply, "Well, this is Pat, and I'm ready to chat!"

Darryl's big trademark was the funny names he gave his dunks. He was very much into rhyme and hyperbole: "Yo mama, in-your-face-disgrace and no-playin' get-out-of-the-wayin' backboard-swayin' game-delayin' super spike."

Then one night in Kansas City, Darryl tore a backboard down while dunking. The next day the dunk would forevermore be known as "Chocolate Thunder-flyin', Robinzine-cryin', teeth-shakin', glass-breakin', rump-roastin', bun-toastin', wham-bam, glass!" Say that fast ten times.

Darryl claimed two mysterious planets as his residence—Lovetron and Chocolate Paradise. He said he specialized in inter-planetary funkmanship, though it was never made clear what exactly that was. He needed five minutes after each game just to get his jewelry on, gold and diamond doodads, including several strings of necklaces, each emblazoned with several of his person-ally conceived nicknames, among them Sir Slam, Dr. Dunk, Chocolate Thunder, and Master of Disaster.

Darryl fairly oozed charisma, and there was an appealing charm about him. He was not malicious, and he was obviously having so much fun out of living that you could not take offense at his wild braggadocio. I guess it's only natural that Darryl has ended his career playing for the Harlem Globetrotters. Maybe that's where he belonged all the time.

In 1984, we drafted the other fun-loving player, Charles Barkley. Charles was a showman from the start. He'd do anything to stir up a crowd and make them have fun even while he was scoring 35 points and grabbing 20 rebounds. Charles would taunt the other team, ride his own teammates, mock the refs, tease the crowd, clown around with the mascot or dance team, whatever.

Charles seemed to be having so much fun during a game that everyone in the building got caught up in the whole atmosphere. But I think the most fun Charles has is with the media. He's always giving them funny quotes and outlandish stories, always stirring things up. In fact, there's a book out with nothing but funny Charles Barkley quotes. (I'm quoted in there a few times myself.)

Charles has said he wants to enter the political scene in his home state of Alabama when his playing days are over. One day I said, "Charles, why do you want to enter the Alabama gubernatorial race?"

He said, "Because I want to be the gubernor."

My favorite Sir Charles story? Several years ago he wrote his autobiography. (Charles wrote it as soon as he figured out who the main character should be.) He made some outlandish statement in the book that whipped the media into a frenzy. When the sportswriters challenged Charles, he said, "I was misquoted." I love it. Misquoted in your own book!

"Fun?" you ask. "A magical secret of success? Come on!"

But I'm dead serious . . . in a fun sort of way. You've gotta have fun in order to be successful. You've gotta have fun along the way in order to get to your dreams. Remember if it's fun for you, it will be fun for others. If you can't enjoy your job, you're paying too big a price.

In his book *Walt: Backstage Adventures with Walt Disney*, former Disney writer-director Charles Shows recalls, "Life at Disney Studio usually was one continuous round of laughter, jokes, and plain fun."[2] Though Disney himself could often be a tough and demanding boss, there was a playful, fun side to Disney that Charles Shows illuminates for us in the following anecdote:

> It has been said that men are only grown-up little boys, and I'm sure that a lot of men never grow up. Such a man was Walt Disney.
>
> When Disneyland first opened, I took my mother and father for a tour of Walt's Magic Kingdom. Being a railroad man, my father was looking forward to a ride on Disneyland's spectacular scale-model Santa Fe train. We boarded the train and it started forward. As it started to pick up speed, my father said, "Look!" I glanced out the window and saw a man racing alongside the speeding train in a hopped-up jeep. He was trying to catch us! As he narrowed the gap, I recognized the train-chaser as Walt Disney himself! The jeep roared alongside the puffing steam engine, and he waved wildly, beeping the horn, as if challenging the sleek metal monster to a race.
>
> The Santa Fe Flyer's steam whistle answered the jeep's beep with a series of bright, loud toots, and Walt laughed gleefully like a little boy.
>
> We were still talking about the experience later that day when we

took a ride on Disneyland's impressive Mississippi River steamboat. My parents were especially excited about being aboard the paddle-wheel riverboat, because in their younger days they had cruised down the real Mississippi River on a real paddlewheeler.

We climbed up to the captain's bridge. A series of sharp, loud blasts erupted from the steamer's whistle. The next moment, to our surprise, popping out of the captain's quarters and grinning like a youngster with a brand-new toy was—Walt Disney!

Walt was a warm, genial host, and he insisted on personally escorting my mother and father around his new make-believe kingdom. This is the Walt Disney my parents will always remember and I will never forget.[3]

Fun was one of Disney's magical secrets—and it should be yours and mine as well.

STAY LOOSE

There is a powerful message about the power of fun embedded in *The Mighty Ducks,* that hugely successful Disney movie about a youth-league hockey team that rises from the bottom of the barrel to the top of the heap. The film opens with a flashback scene in which a tough, overbearing coach named Jack Riley pressures young Gordon Bombay to make a crucial penalty shot. "If you miss this shot," he says, "you'll let me down and you'll let your team down!" The boy goes out on the ice, shoots, and just *barely* misses the goal. The shame of that loss weighs down on Gordon Bombay for years afterward.

Bombay grows up to be the coach of a struggling team, the District Five Ducks. When he first takes over the team, he coaches in much the same style as his old coach, Jack Riley. He berates, he pressures, he teaches his team to cheat. But gradually he learns the lesson of the sport of hockey that he should have known all along: In order to fly on the ice, you've gotta have *fun!*

In the climactic moments of the movie, Bombay takes his team of Ducks into a championship play-off game against the top-rated Hawks, coached by none other than his old coach, Jack Riley.

Riley has not changed a bit. He berates his players. He sends them onto the ice with shouts of "Pressure! Pressure!"

The Hawks quickly take the lead. But while Riley is piling the pressure on his players, Bombay sends his team onto the ice with a grin and a shout, "Let's have *fun* out there!" The fun pays off: The Ducks begin to score—and with every goal, Bombay gathers his Ducks around him for a chant: "More fun! More fun!"

Meanwhile, Riley has a conniption. He rages at his young Hawks. With verbal abuse and insults, he ratchets the pressure steeply upward. "You blow this game," he snarls, "and *nobody* makes the team next year!"

The Ducks proceed to have fun, using all sorts of impossible gimmicks to score goals—from ballet-style pirouettes to a wedgelike flying vee—and they bring the score to a dead-heat 4–4 when the final gun sounds. But one of the Hawks has fouled a Duck player, giving the Ducks a penalty shot—and a chance at the win. If a young player named Charlie Conway can make the shot, the Ducks will take the championship.

In a scene that parallels the opening flashback, Coach Bombay has a talk with young Charlie. But instead of pressuring Charlie (as Coach Riley once pressured young Gordon Bombay), Coach Bombay tells Charlie, "You may make it, you may not. But that doesn't matter. What matters is that we're here. Look around. Who'd ever have thought we would make it this far? Take your best shot. I believe in you Charlie, win or lose."

And Charlie grins, goes out on the ice, and takes his shot. He has *fun* out there! And the Ducks win the game.

That's fantasy, right? A happily-ever-after ending to a Holly-wood sports fantasy. That doesn't happen in real life, does it?

Yes, it does! The amazing thing is that this scenario from a Hollywood movie is *true!* I've seen it again and again in the world of sports, and in the world of business, and in every aspect of life: *If you want to be a winner, have fun out there!* Former Philadel-phia Flyers coach Fred Shero knew that the message of *The Mighty Ducks* is true, because he taught it to his own team. "Hockey is a children's game played by men," he once said, "and since it is a child's game, they ought to have fun." And NHL center Wayne Gretzky adds, "I love playing the game. It's no different than little kids who go out and play for the fun of it. We're just big kids playing a game."

Fun keeps you loose, keeps you from freezing up in the clutch situations. Pressure is a given in any competitive enterprise, from sports to business to ministry to government, and pressure creates friction. Pressure and friction can keep you from doing your best work and performing at your highest level. Fun lubricates your brain, keeping the pressure and friction from wearing down your body and seizing up your mind.

I find that fun is just as important to the Orlando Magic as it was for the Ducks in that Disney movie. Sure, even the "fun and games" of professional sports is work—often tough, grueling, sweaty work, full of pressures, deadlines, and stress. There's a lot of money riding on the performance of the entire Magic organization—and that's serious business. But over everything we do, like a big Magic-blue canopy, is an aura of joyous, wondrous fun. It *has* to be fun—or it just isn't worth going to work! If you stay in the shower a long time in the morning because you don't look forward to work, find another job.

Baseball player Andy Van Slyke knows the value of fun, of not taking yourself, your opponents, or your critics too seriously. "I try to have fun at whatever I do," he says. "The problem with a lot of players today is that they don't have enough fun. They should be shooting the breeze with people when they're walking through the airport, kidding with the taxi driver or with the fans. Or with the media. A lot of players think dealing with the media is a spinal tap, that it's painful. That's a bad attitude to have, when you can have so much fun with them. I have fun with the media, but I don't take them too seriously. I realize the press is something that's read today and forgotten tomorrow."

Mike Schmidt, the great Philadelphia Phillies Hall of Famer, is a longtime friend of our family. In fact, we named our fourth biological child after Mike. He is a fun guy to talk with and kick back with—but during his years with the Phillies he was totally serious about his game. Today, looking back on his great career in baseball, he has only one big regret: "I wish I'd enjoyed the game more than I did. I really didn't enjoy the game that much. The game was work for me. I was so focused on playing the game at a really high level. It was awfully important for me to lead the league in everything every year. I wish I had done some things differently. I'd have been more fun, been a little looser."

And here are some other fun words of advice from some of the top names in the sports world:

- Jimmy Johnson, former coach of the Dallas Cowboys, said, "When a situation, even a winning situation like the Cowboys, stopped being fun for me, it was time to leave. I won't go back into a situation where fun isn't a factor."

- Jimmy's successor with the Cowboys, Barry Switzer, agrees: "Coaching isn't life or death. It's a wonderful opportunity, and that's the way I'm going to coach it and have fun with it and do the best I can."

- Sportswriter Robert Creamer, author of the book *Babe: The Legend Comes to Life,* said in 1995 on the anniversary of Babe Ruth's one hundredth birthday that the great slugger was "fun— fun to watch, fun to play with, fun to play against, fun to read about, fun to be around. He was loud and boisterous and never dull. He lent a spark and a fire to everything he was near."

- "When you have confidence, you can have a lot of fun," says former NFL quarterback Joe Namath, "and when you have fun, you can do amazing things."

- Former Duke University basketball player Cherokee Parks said, "I want us to go out there and work as hard as we can. The main thing is to have fun with it. You can always put your nose to the floor and work your tail off all the time, but if you're not having that much fun, what's the point?" And Parks' former teammate Grant Hill, now starring with the Detroit Pistons, adds, "Cherokee's a little different. He's the jester on the team. He keeps everybody loose. There were times when you wondered if he took things seriously, but he's fun out there, and that carried over to the rest of us. Practices were intense, but fun."

- "When the game begins," says Hall of Famer Willie Stargell of the Pittsburgh Pirates, "they don't say, 'Work ball!' They say, 'Play ball!' It's supposed to be fun."

- Olympic figure skater Brian Boitano recalls that fun was a key factor in his gold-medal-winning performance. "I wasn't thinking gold or anything," he said. "I was doing what I came to do, which was to have fun."

•   And one of the best female athletes ever, Olympic gold-medal-winning sprinter Florence Griffith Joyner—yes, my daughter's friend Flo-Jo herself!—said, "Most competitors are so focused they don't want to take the time to say hello, but I'm always chatting. It relaxes me. When I run relaxed, I have fun, and no one can beat me."

So take the advice of people who have been there. Stay loose. Enjoy your game. Have *fun* out there.

FUN EQUALS FREEDOM

In every business organization I've watched or been a part of, I've seen that the people who rise to the top tend to be people who have a well-developed sense of humor—and even a sense of the ridiculous. And there is a good, practical reason for this. "Common sense aside," says sports marketing executive Mark McCormack, who lives in Orlando and has become a friend, "the most important asset in business is a sense of humor, and the ability to laugh at yourself or the situation. Laughter is the most potent, constructive force for diffusing business tension, and you want to be the one who controls it. If you can point out what is humorous or absurd about a situation or confrontation, can diffuse the tension by getting the other party to share your feeling, you will be guaranteed the upper hand. There are very few absolutes in business. This is one of them, and I've never seen it fail."

Fun keeps you human. Fun makes working and living worthwhile. Fun makes you the kind of person people want to be around, do business with, work alongside, and listen to. The truly great bosses, executives, and managers are fun people to be around. The truly great political personalities are fun people to know. The truly great teachers and preachers make their lessons and sermons fun to listen to.

Pastor, seminary president, and radio Bible teacher Charles Swindoll knows the value of fun in his own life. Fun, he says, equals freedom. In his little book on holy fun called *Laugh Again,* the president of Dallas Theological Seminary says, "Cynthia and

I are into Harley-Davidson motorcycles. I know, I know . . . it doesn't fit our image. What would ever possess me to start messing around with a motorcycle, cruising some of the picturesque roads down by the ocean? It's about forgetting all the nonsense that every single moment in life is serious. It's about breaking the bondage of tunnel vision. It's about freedom. That's it, plain and simple. It's about being free."

HE WHO LAUGHS, LASTS

Fun energizes the body. The simple pleasures of playing and being silly get your circulation going, recharge your nervous system, and clear the fog of stress and worry from the pathways of your brain. Laughter expands the lungs and charges your cells with oxygen. Fun is the best medicine you can get—and better than any medicine you can buy.

My friend Pam Smith is the team nutritionist for the Magic, and she has also taken on the Williams family as a feeding project (probably her toughest professional challenge yet!). She has appeared on NBC's *Today Show,* Dr. James Dobson's *Focus on the Family,* and many other media outlets, talking about good nutrition. I was recently surprised to learn that, in addition to good food and regular exercise, she recommends a daily dosage of laughter and fun as a requisite for good health. In her book *Food for Life,* she writes,

> Incredibly, only one activity other than exercise produces the stress-busting endorphins: laughter. Zig Ziglar calls laughter "internal jogging," and that's pretty close to the effect it has on the body. It's a mini-workout. Can you believe it? One hundred laughs a day provide a cardiovascular workout equivalent to ten minutes of rowing or biking. And laughing simulates a stress-release in the same way. When you laugh, you're telling your body that your stressful circumstance is no big deal. It can't be that bad if you can still laugh. More words from Solomon: a heart at peace gives life to the body, Proverbs 14:30. Laughter even helps us fight infection by releasing hormones that can cut the immune-dampening effects of stress. Now, that's something to laugh about!

The bottom line is that if we look after ourselves, our bodies will look after us. Taking care of ourselves is a small investment with tremendous return. It does more than add years to our lives. It adds life to our years.[4]

LOVE WHAT YOU DO AND DO WHAT YOU LOVE

In February 1994, I visited the Ted Williams Hall of Fame and Museum, which is located near his retirement home, not far from Ocala, Florida, for the first time; this was the opening celebration. Ted Williams was one of the greatest hitters who ever played the game of baseball. He was also my boyhood idol, as I mentioned earlier. (I'm also partial to his last name.) As I walked into the museum, the first thing I noticed was Ted himself, now in his late seventies, sitting in a chair like a king holding court upon his throne, his big voice booming, his grand personality dominating the room. The next thing I noticed was that Ted was surrounded by greatness: Some of the most legendary figures in the game were in that room, celebrating the occasion along with Ted. Joltin' Joe DiMaggio was there. So were Stan Musial, Bob Feller, and dozens of other sports greats. It was incredible.

I had brought a picture with me—a large black-and-white photo I had picked up years earlier and had kept in a frame on my office wall. The photo was of Ted Williams and Babe Ruth and was the only photo ever taken of these two baseball giants standing side by side. Ted's son ran interference for me so that I could get through the crowd that surrounded Ted Williams. When I got close enough to speak to him, I showed him the photo and asked if he would sign it for me. He grinned broadly as he looked at that photo, no doubt remembering a summer day in 1943 when he struck that pose alongside the great Babe. Then he said, "It'll be a *pleasure* to sign this picture!" I handed him a permanent marker I had brought along for the occasion, and in a big flowing script he inscribed his name across the front of his Red Sox uniform.

Today, that picture is back on my office wall, an even more valuable memento now that it bears his signature. In case you were born too late to remember the greatness of this man, let me tell you a little bit about Ted Williams. In a playing career that ran from 1939 to 1960 (with five years out for service as a pilot in WWII and Korea), he compiled a total of 521 home runs and a lifetime batting average of .344. He was the last .400 hitter in the twentieth century, batting .406 in 1941. He won the American League Triple Crown (best batting average, most home runs, and most runs batted in during a single season) twice in his career. There is a reason for the greatness of Ted Williams: *he was consumed with a passion for baseball.* It was *fun.* Ted Williams loved what he did and he did what he loved.

As a boy, Williams played baseball early before school and again after school. Sometimes he skipped school altogether so he could play baseball. He began playing professionally with the San Diego Padres at age seventeen, and whenever he wasn't playing a game or practicing with the team, he was out on the diamond all by himself with a bat and a bag full of balls, practicing his swing. He took a bat and a bunch of balls with him wherever he went during his military years, and whenever he wasn't in the air as a pilot, you could find him on the ground, hitting baseballs.

At age seventy-six, Ted Williams looked back on his illustrious career and said, "Fun? The most fun in baseball is hitting the ball! My whole life was hitting. Hitting, nobody ever had more fun."

Have fun. Love what you do. Be passionate about your work. You can't be successful doing a job you hate.

Ask anyone who is preparing for a career: "Why did you choose this career path?" The answer that usually comes back: "Money." But money is a miserable reason for choosing a career. If you are paid a million dollars a year to do a job you hate, you are underpaid. But, as business writer Harvey Mackay says, "Find something you love to do and you'll never have to work a day in your life!"

In 1901, industrialist J. P. Morgan found himself with a million-dollar dilemma. His company, United States Steel, had just taken over the steel company founded by Andrew Carnegie. In the process, U.S. Steel acquired a contractual obligation to pay the top Carnegie executive—Charles M. Schwab (whose story I alluded to in Chapter 4)—a salary of a million dollars a year. As incredible as such a salary would seem today, it was even more unheard of at that time. Morgan was beside himself. He felt the salary was completely insupportable. So he called Schwab in for a meeting, showed him the contract and—with a bit of stammering and hesitation—asked what should be done about it.

Schwab took the contract from Morgan's trembling fingers and ripped it into pieces before Morgan's astonished eyes. Schwab would have been within his legal rights to enforce the contract. Instead, he shook hands with Morgan on a salary deal that—though still a sizable amount of money—was a mere fraction of his previous salary.

"I didn't care what they paid me," Schwab later told an interviewer from *Forbes* magazine. "I wasn't moved by monetary motives. I believed in what I was trying to do and I wanted to see it brought about. I cancelled that contract without a moment's hesitation. So why do I work? I work just for the pleasure I find in work, the satisfaction of developing things, of creating, of the associations that business begets. The person who does not work for the love of work, but only for money, is not likely to make money nor to find much fun in life."

"The real successful people among us are those who have carved out a life for themselves doing the things they love," said Rush Limbaugh on his astonishingly successful radio show in March 1994. Rush knows. He has done it. "The key to genuine success," he continues, "is to *be yourself*. Find an opportunity where *you* can be *you,* where you can do the things you love, because there you will be the best you can be. You'll be happy, you'll be motivated, you'll be doing your best because you'll be doing what you *love* best. It's not easy to reach a place where you can do what you love. Not everybody is able to do it. Most people look at a job as doing what you *don't* want to do, putting in your time so you can pay yourself back every so often with a nice vacation or weekend off or whatever. But *real* success—if you can pull it off—is doing what you love."

Now, I know that not everybody gets to have a job like I do. Most people only get to enjoy the action and excitement of professional sports on a weekend basis, and then only as a spectator. But I truly believe that everybody can—if they really want to, and if they really desire to be successful—do work they truly love and enjoy.

For example, I know of one plumber who just enjoys the heck out of his work. He is a fun and funny plumber. He's proud of what he does. When he finishes a toilet repair job, he stands beside his work, beaming proudly. He lifts the lid off the tank and invites you to look at the great new valves, levers, stoppers, and chains he installed. He eagerly invites you to try out his work. "Go ahead," he says, "give it a good, hard flush!"

Give him an opening, and he'll tell you all about the history of plumbing, the advantages of copper or PVC pipe versus lead, the reason that the pipes under sinks have that U-shaped trap in them that's always getting clogged (and no, it's not to make more work for plumbers). He loves to crawl around under houses, because he finds all kinds of interesting things under there, such as forty- and fifty-year-old beer bottles left by the original builders.

This guy also loves to tell plumber jokes. When he hands you his bill, he says, "Time to pay the piper!" And if your basement's flooded, he says, "Hey, it's not so bad—you always wanted an indoor pool!" During times of inflation, he observes, "You know, the price of food is getting so high, even we plumbers are beginning to notice!"

So you don't have to be in professional sports to have fun— you just have to love what you do and do what you love! How do you do that? I would suggest three ways:

1. Figure out what you love doing, then find someone who will pay you to do it.

2. If you're in a job you hate, figure out what you would rather do, what you have fun doing, and then pursue that goal with all you've got! Make sure you have your new job lined up before you quit your old job, but start right now to find that job you can be enthusiastic about every day. Take the fun job, even if the money's not great to start with. If you can be gungho about your job, if you can have fun at what you do, the money and promotions will come.

3. Whatever job you're in right now, adopt a "have fun" attitude! Make a decision that you're going to be enthusiastic

about your work. Even if you don't expect to make a career out of delivering pizzas or stocking shelves, make sure that you are the most cheerful, happy pizza-hauler or shelf-stocker in the company. The tips, promotions, raises, and plaudits go to the person with the ready smile and the eager attitude. They go to the people who are *fun* to be around!

Not everybody can have my job. Not everyone can have a great sports-oriented career like Shaq or John Madden or Ted Williams or Michael Jordan. But I truly believe that all people can find ways to have fun in their professions. And those that do are the likeliest candidates for success.

WHAT DO YOU DO WITH SUCCESS?

Someone once said, "How much we *enjoy* what we have is more important than how *much* we have. It's not *what* we have, but what we *enjoy* that constitutes our abundance." Absolutely true! So many people have more money and fame than they know what to do with. They have not only achieved but vastly exceeded their goals—and still they are not content! They haven't figured out how to enjoy life! "There are two things to aim at in life," said Logan Pearsall Smith. "First, to get what you want; and after that to enjoy it. Only the wisest of people achieve the second."

I've known a lot of people who would be considered successful by the usual standards of the world. They are brilliant. They work hard. They persevere. They have achieved great heights. They are rich. They are famous. *And they are miserable!* To me, that is not the picture of success. That is out-and-out failure. That is blowing your life.

If you are making money by the ton but getting no enjoyment out of life, then something is seriously out of whack. If you are so driven to achieve that you never stop to enjoy your family, friends, and the pleasures of life, then you have a major maladjustment inside you. If you are a joyless, obsessive workaholic, then do something about it. Your life needs fixing—quick! See a shrink! Pray for healing! Join Workaholics Anonymous (yes, there is such an organization, and I'm dead serious about it). My driven, workaholic friend, you need help now!

"When I recall the past," says that living entertainment institution, Bob Hope, "I find it is the simplest things—not the great occasions—that in retrospect give off the greatest glow of happiness. The moments that I remember most vividly are not those about rubbing elbows with the great, or the awards I've received, as much as I enjoy all that. What I remember best are quiet moments with my family, unwinding on the golf course, convivial times with old friends. In short, having fun."

A truly successful person is able to look ahead to future joys, look back on fun memories, and fully enjoy the present moment. What do you do with success? *Enjoy it!*

THE NOBEL PRIZE FOR FUN

The one person in my professional life who, more than anyone else, taught me the value of fun was baseball's Hall of Fame owner-executive-promoter extraordinaire, Bill Veeck. (In case you just got in from Mars and didn't know, Veeck rhymes with "wreck.")

Let me tell you why Bill Veeck is such a legend. First, baseball was in his blood. His father was a Chicago sportswriter, and he himself got started in the game by selling peanuts, popcorn, and scorecards in the stands at Wrigley Field. He worked alongside Chicago Cubs manager Charley Grimm in the late 1930s and early 1940s. Soon he began doing what he eventually became famous for: Buying struggling teams and turning them into crowd-pleasers. He started by buying the Milwaukee Brewers, a Cubs farm team, and he helped move the club from last place in 1941 to first in 1943 through 1945. In 1946, he headed the syndicate that bought the Cleveland Indians—a team that hadn't won a pennant since 1920—and two years later the Indians won not only the pennant but the World Series. He later owned the St. Louis Browns and the Chicago White Sox, which won the American League Pennant in 1959.

Second, Bill Veeck was a promotional wizard. In 1951, as owner of the St. Louis Browns, he came up with a brilliant idea that accomplished two goals: 1) It got a man on base, and 2) it entertained fans at the stadium. His idea was to put three foot six inch Ed Gaedel in to pinch-hit. The opposing pitcher, Bob Cain, found it well-nigh impossible to put a ball into Gaedel's petite-sized strike zone, so Gaedel got a walk to lead off the game. Because of his promotional brilliance, Veeck was often able to take over a major-league team and see its annual attendance double (the Indians' attendance jumped to 2 million fans under his leadership in the 1940s, and his White Sox's attendance topped 1.5 million in the late 1950s and early 1960s).

Third, Bill Veeck was a beautiful human being. In a time when racism was an institutional given in our society, Bill just flat-out didn't care if you were white or black or green. He looked at people as *people,* and he looked at baseball players as *baseball players.* That's why he hired Larry Doby to play for the Cleveland Indians—the first black player in the American League. And that's why he brought Satchel Paige up from the black baseball leagues to play for Cleveland—a couple of gutsy moves for the late 1940s.

Fourth, Bill Veeck's passion was giving people a fun time. He prized entertainment right up there with winning and making money. He was the Walt Disney of baseball, and his passion for creating excitement and making people happy showed in everything he did. As he reflected in his 1962 autobiography, *Veeck as in Wreck,* "My philosophy as a baseball operator could not be more simple. It is to create the greatest enjoyment for the greatest number of people, not by detracting from the ballgame, but by adding a few moments of fairly simple pleasure. My intention was always to draw people to the park and make baseball fans out of them."

I was twenty-two years old when I first met Bill Veeck in 1962. Three years later, I completed my first year as general manager of the Philadelphia Phillies farm club in Spartanburg, South Carolina, under Bill Veeck's mentorship. It had been a long, tough season because, candidly, we didn't have a very good team. Despite the team's lackluster performance, however, the fan response had been good. We drew 114,000 people, which was a huge crowd to attract to that level of baseball. Still, I was very down and discouraged over the fact that the team had finished the season near the bottom of the rankings.

Well, there I was, at the end of a season that had been

something of a mixed bag—a losing season on the diamond but a winning season at the box office. I felt like those lyrics in the Peggy Lee song: "Is that all there is?" I felt let down and empty. I had invested six or seven months of my life, working sixteen-hour days, my first season as a general manager was over, and what had I accomplished? Was it worth it? I just didn't know.

So I called Bill Veeck.

I felt fortunate to call Bill Veeck my friend. He had taken me under his wing when I moved to Spartanburg, and I had learned a lot from him. I idolized his promotional genius, and I had consulted him regularly with questions and problems as I felt my way around the baseball business. So I poured out all my discouragement to Bill over the phone, and he listened very patiently. When I was finished, he said, "Pat, just how many people did you draw to the ballpark this season?"

"A hundred fourteen thousand," I said.

"How many of those people were entertained and had a good time?"

"Well . . . I think *all* of them had a good time."

"Then, tell me one other thing you could have done this summer that would have provided this much fun, enjoyment, and entertainment to that many people?"

I paused a moment, thought it over, then replied, "Well, I'm not sure I could have done anything."

"Let me tell you something," said Veeck. "You never, ever have to apologize for showing people a fun time."

During that phone call, my entire outlook was transformed. I realized that I was doing something important, something valuable, something significant in the lives of thousands of people. That conversation had a profound impact on the rest of my career, right up to this present moment, because that's what I've been doing for the last thirty years. Though I don't claim to be another Bill Veeck—there will *never* be another—I've certainly patterned myself as a manager and entertainment maestro in the Bill Veeck tradition.

The person who knew Bill best also said it best. "He was such fun to be around," said his wife, Mary Frances, in her speech at Cooperstown, New York, when Bill was enshrined in the Hall of

Fame. "He was a pied piper." And Bill's son—minor league general manager Mike Veeck—learned the lesson of his dad's life. "Fun is still legal," he once said. "You don't have to be somber to get things done. You can have fun."

Bill Veeck put a lot of things in perspective for me. I'm glad there are doctors and nurses and police and firefighters in this world, because those people are heroes who literally save lives. I'm also glad there are teachers and preachers, because they fill our heads with knowledge and our hearts with wisdom so we can live our lives profitably and responsibly. I'm glad there are political leaders, because the best of them make the world a better place (and the worst of them are eventually discovered and flushed out). These are all noble callings, and the people who respond to the challenges of these callings are to be commended.

But I think it is no less a noble calling to be a great baseball or basketball player. Or a television actor or film star. Or a musician, singer, songwriter, or music producer. Or a circus clown or acrobat. Or a standup comic or a dancer. These are the people who give us our entertainment. A surgeon may save your life with a scalpel, but entertainers help to make that life he saved worth living and enjoying. Entertainers bring *fun* into the world.

Meadowlark Lemon, the former Harlem Globetrotter, said, "You never lose when you bring joy to people, when you put a smile on a face that lasts forever. When a Globetrotter game is over, folks never remember the final score. People remember the laughter."

Walt Disney and Bill Veeck were great men, but they don't give out many awards for their kind of greatness. I've never heard of anyone winning the Nobel Prize for Fun—although I think it's a great idea. Having fun and giving fun to others is one of the noblest and best things human beings do for one another. It's also one of the most human things we human beings do.

And you know what? We don't have to be professional entertainers to be fun people! I think every dad and every mom should lead the way in making the home a fun place. Every boss and manager should set the tone for making the office a fun place in which to work and be productive. Every teacher should show every student that learning is fun. Every preacher should show his congregation that they worship a God who knows how to laugh and who made funny and fun-loving human beings in His own image.

So sing, dance, laugh! Ride a motorcycle. Strap on your rollerblades and play street hockey with the neighborhood kids. If you score a goal, jump up and down and chant, "More fun! More fun!"

Next time you make spaghetti, take the lids off the pots and clang them like cymbals. You'll feel silly, and you'll get wet—but it's fun!

If you have a mind to, stick some beans up your nose.

Life is grand. Life is a hoot. Get out there and have *fun!*

But hold it! Don't go yet! You've got one more chapter to read, and then you're free to go out and play. So turn the page, because *here comes my big finish* . . .

CHAPTER 10

What *Is* Success, Anyway?

○ *The greatest of all miracles is that we need not be tomorrow what we are today, but we can improve if we make use of the potentials implanted in us by God.*
Rabbi Samuel M. Silver

○ *Purpose in life is not to find your freedom, but your Master.*
G. Campbell Morgan

What is success?
When I was in my teens and early twenties, there was only one definition of success for me: to be a professional baseball catcher. I fell in love with baseball the day my dad took me to Shibe Park in Philadelphia for my very first big-league baseball game. That was in 1947, and I was seven years old at the time. I pursued that dream of success for the next decade and a half, from the neighborhood sandlot and schoolyard, to a baseball scholarship at Wake Forest University, to two years in the minors, catching for the Phillies farm club in Miami in 1962 and 1963. I

breathed baseball, I ate baseball, I slept baseball, I dreamed baseball.

But I didn't realize my dream, as I've mentioned before. After two years playing my heart out in the obscurity of the Florida State League, I had to face it: I was already in the twilight of a mediocre career. One of my teammates back then was pitcher Ferguson Jenkins, who later became a Hall of Fame pitcher in the major leagues. He likes to tell people, "Pat Williams was the toughest man I ever pitched to—and he wasn't a batter, he was my catcher!" (And I'll get you for that yet, Fergie!)

I had my dreams—but I was also a realist. I could see that my baseball career was fading like a meteor in an August sky. It was a frightening realization, like staring into some deep, dark abyss of the soul: I was failing in the number one goal of my life. My sixteen years of struggle were coming to nothing.

It's hard to see a dream die. But I had to survive and adapt, so I found a new goal, a new definition of success. I made up my mind that I was going to find something to succeed in—something so big that my fizzled baseball career would hardly rate a footnote compared to my *real* epoch-making achievements. I had always been gregarious, a doer, a talker, an organizer, a creative dreamer. The Phillies recognized these qualities in me, as well as my love for the game, so they asked me to help out in the front office of the Miami club. I looked on it as a valuable apprenticeship, a chance to learn everything I could about running and promoting a sports club. I worked hard and kept my eyes and ears open.

In 1964, I became assistant general manager, and then in 1965 I was hired for my first general manager post, with the Spartanburg, South Carolina, Phillies. I approached my job with an intense and single-minded passion. I was working and promoting baseball practically every waking hour of every day. I made good money. I got things done, and I was recognized. The Western Carolinas League named me Executive of the Year for three years running, 1965 through 1967. I became president of the ball club my third year, and was honored with this trophy and that award, and in 1967 I was named Minor League Exec of the Year by the *Sporting News*. I was in the driver's seat on the road to success, and I had the accelerator jammed to the floor!

But somewhere in the back of my mind was a gnawing sense of doubt, of disappointment—even a tinge of depression. I figured that my upwardly mobile, thrill-packed, accolade-filled life should bring me happiness and a sense of satisfaction. I understood the rules of the game: You work hard, stay focused, hustle, keep moving forward, and success will come your way. Sure, there's sacrifice involved, but the rewards are worth it, right?

Wrong.

The more praise and success came my way, the less satisfied I felt, the more lonely and isolated I seemed to be. I was getting a lot of glory, a lot of ego rushes, a lot of emotional highs—but they were soon over, and the satisfaction they gave me was gone by the next morning. There was a craving inside me, and I thought I was stuffing all the right things into it—yet the craving refused to be satisfied. I was completely baffled: What was I doing wrong?

THE R. E. LITTLEJOHN RULES FOR SUCCESS

During this period, I was forced to rethink the basic premises of my life. What was I living for? What were my goals? What was success all about? One man who had an enormous influence on me as I was rethinking these premises and questions was one of the owners of the Spartanburg club, Mr. R. E. Littlejohn, a man I mentioned earlier. When I first arrived in Spartanburg in February 1965, Mr. R. E. (yes, that's what everybody called him—Mr. R. E.) was on a trip out of town. His wife, whom everyone calls Sam, was in the office, and she showed me around the place. Then she said something that struck me: "You're going to enjoy working with Mr. R. E. You'll never meet another man like him." And she was right!

Mr. R. E. Littlejohn was a successful man, a "bigshot" in Western Carolinas League baseball—yet he did not conduct himself as you would think a "bigshot" would. He was a generous, courteous, kindly man—yet he was also strong, direct, and decisive. As his wife Sam predicted, he was a man unlike anyone I had ever met before. In fact, he made such a profound impact on my life that Jill and I named our firstborn son after both my own father and Mr. R. E.—James Littlejohn Williams. The man was simply the most *exemplary* human being I had ever known—and I wanted to emulate him.

During the four years I worked with him—four of the most fascinating, growth-filled years of my life—I saw him living daily, consistently by what I call "The R. E. Littlejohn Rules for Success." To this day, I try to live by these same rules—rules such as:

1. *Have faith in God.* Seek His guidance in every decision, no matter how big or small. Mr. R. E. was a firm believer in Colossians 3:23: "And whatever you do, do it heartily, as to the Lord and not to men." That means that work is a sacred duty and that God is our Boss. Seeing God as our Employer motivates us to do our best work.
2. *Sell yourself to others.* Make a good first impression; then work hard to build and maintain trust.
3. *Manage your own life.* If you can't manage your own affairs and your own family, why should anyone trust you with a business or other major responsibility?
4. *Genuinely care about the people who work with you.* Say thank you. Be kind. Find out about their needs and hurts, and try to help them. Caring builds trust, loyalty, and cooperation. And it's the right thing to do.
5. *Pay your dues.* We all have to learn to crawl before we can do the hundred-yard dash. Learn the value of patience and of gaining experience. Don't expect to start at the top. Instead, focus on learning at every level, every rung along the ladder, in order to become an effective executive.

These were some of Mr. R. E.'s rules. Living by these rules, he became a successful businessman, a successful baseball club owner, and a successful husband and father. He was strong and he was gentle. He was steel and velvet all in the same package.

Many great owners, athletes, and coaches live by rules like these, even posting signs to remind themselves and others of such values.

THREE DOORS, THREE VALUES

Shortly after the beautiful America West Arena was completed, Phoenix Suns president Jerry Colangelo gave me a tour of the facility. My favorite part was the Suns' locker area, which consisted of a palatial dressing room, a complete weight center, and a practice facility.

As we were leaving the locker area I noticed three doors leading out of the room. Over one door was a verse of Scripture on a big plastic board. It said: "Where were you when I laid the earth's foundation? Tell me, if you understand.—God (Job 38:4)."

Over the second door I saw this verse: "Whoever loves discipline loves knowledge, but he who hates correction is stupid. (Proverbs 12:1)."

The third door led right onto the playing court. Over this door was another sign: "The game is scheduled, we have to play it—we might as well win.—Bill Russell, Boston Celtics, 11 titles in 13 years."

I was fascinated by these signs, so after I got home I called the Suns' coach, Paul Westphal, to ask why he put them there.

He said, "Well, when these famous and talented players walk out the first door, I want them to be humbled by God's question, which is 'Great as you players are, where were you when I created the world from scratch?'

"When they go through the second door I want them to realize that if they won't willingly accept my discipline and teaching they are stupid. . . .

"And when the players go through that final door I want them to be reminded that the only reason we play this sport is to win games."

Bill Russell later told me, "Back when I was playing, the players would grumble about the long season and how tired they were. I'd say 'Look, I'm playing forty-six minutes a night. You've got to put forth the same effort whether you win or lose, so why not win?'"

I think Paul Westphal has a clear handle on what it takes to be a winner in life. I've also learned a lot since those days in

Spartanburg with R. E. Littlejohn. I realized this the day of my forty-first birthday.

"I'LL TAKE CARE OF THE WINS AND LOSSES"

In Chapter 3, I let former Boston Celtics head coach Red Auerbach tell this story from his perspective; now I want you to hear my side. Paradoxically for a book about success and winning, it's a story about failure and losing. But I think it's fitting for the last chapter of this book. After you read it, I think you'll see why.

My forty-first birthday fell on Sunday, May 3, 1981, and there was no birthday gift I wanted more than to have the 76ers beat the Boston Celtics that afternoon. There was a lot riding on that game. It was the seventh and final game of the conference championship play-off series. If we beat Boston in this game, we would win the Eastern Conference championship. From there, we would go on to play Houston for the NBA crown. If we lost it—the season was over. For five straight years, the Sixers had been favored to take the championship, and for five straight years we had failed. We had taken a lot of heat from fans and sportswriters for those failures, and the heat was on to do it right this time.

We had started the series strong, jumping out ahead of Boston, three games to one, thanks in large part to Julius "Dr. J" Erving, who was playing at the peak of his game. Boston was a tough competitor, of course, but we thought we had it locked. There were three more games to play, and all we had to do was win one more game and the seven-game series was ours. We led game five all the way to the fourth quarter—then in the last minute-and-forty, we blew a six-point lead and lost the game by a point.

Okay, we thought on our way into game six, still two more games to play. We'll do it. Again, we jumped out to a crushing, game-controlling lead—and again the lead evaporated in the fourth quarter. With just seconds on the clock, Boston led by a point, and we had the ball. The ball was inbounded to our hot-shooting guard, Andrew Toney. As he went up for the shot, Boston's Kevin McHale blocked it. We lost again—and suddenly we were no longer a shoo-in for the league championship. It was a dead heat.

And the deciding game would be played in enemy territory, on the parquet floor of the Boston Garden.

You could feel a change in the mood of the Sixers as they approached the final showdown in Beantown. The unconfined optimism that had characterized earlier games had given way to a grim determination. "Gonna win!" had changed to "Gotta win!" Boston Garden is a tough house to play—a real pressure cooker. The fans are loud and raucous. Banners of past conference and league championship titles festoon the walls and hang from the rafters, taunting and haunting you—and the Celts had garnered more titles by far than any other team in NBA history.

The final game—my birthday game—followed the same pattern of games five and six, with Dr. J and the Sixers rocketing to an impressive early lead, followed by a fade in the third quarter and a vicious seesaw, back-and-forth, nailbiter of a fourth quarter. Then, in the middle of that fourth and final quarter, the Sixers started moving ahead, stretching out to a seven-point lead. I was floating, tasting the Eastern title.

I have to tell you something: I can't sit still during a regular season game, much less a play-off or championship game for all the marbles! I get up, I walk, I pace. My heart was in my throat as I watched our team do battle against the Celts. It was a courageous, hard-fought performance. With the gut-thumping noise from the Celtics crowd, you could hardly hear yourself think. I thought, *This is so beautiful, whipping the Celts on their home court after almost blowing the series. Once we get past Boston, it's on to Houston for the big finish! There'll be no stopping us—*

That's when things began to go wrong.

The Sixers missed a few shots on offense, gave up a few points on defense. Right at clutch-time, we had inexplicably gone cold! Couldn't hit a thing! The Celts were tight and tense too, but they were making shots. They hustled and pressed us, hungry for the win. They tied us. Then they surged ahead of us. Then they dropped behind. Then they moved ahead. The lead changed hands a few times until finally, in the final minute, we were tied up.

With the clock nearly gone, Boston roared down the court in a controlled fast break. The ball passed from man to man and finally ended up in the hands of Larry Bird, who spiked the go-ahead basket off the glass for Boston. The Celts were ahead by two.

The Sixers called a time-out.

I was pacing up and down the runway, out into the hallway, behind the stands, tearing my hair out! We had enough time to make one shot, but I had a feeling of dread, a foreboding of doom. We were *that close!* But I feared that the last bucket by Larry Bird had snapped our backbone.

I knew the time-out would be a long one because of television commercials, so I ran out behind the stands and dashed into the hallway. I was not just tense, I was practically in tears. Winning this game meant *everything* to me. I opened the first available door and went inside—and then I realized I had just ducked into a broom closet! It didn't matter. I just wanted to be alone for a few moments to compose myself and to pray.

Five years! I thought. Five years of almost making it, five years of losing the play-offs we were favored to win. Here we were, a shoo-in, a sure bet—and we had blown it. Now the whole season came down to a few seconds on a clock and one shot at the basket.

I burst into tears. I had been building for this championship ever since I became general manager of the Sixers in 1974. Every negotiation, every trade, every acquisition, every meeting, every trip to the office, every phone call had been focused on that title and making the 76ers a championship team. Not only had I dedicated myself to that goal, but every member of our front office staff, our scouts, our coaches, and our players had dedicated themselves to it. Some teams would have felt lucky just to get into the play-offs, but for us, getting into the play-offs was practically a given. We wanted to *win* it, and nothing less than winning would satisfy.

I wanted it so badly that I sobbed out a prayer, right there in that broom closet. "Lord, please let us win! I'll do anything You want! I'll work harder for You. Just let us make this shot! Just let us win this game!"

Through the closed door of that broom closet, I could hear the thundering roar of the rowdy Boston crowd, demanding the sacrifice of Philadelphia blood, demanding the final climax of the

Celtics' miraculous turnaround. It was a sound to make your bones turn to gelatin and your blood turn to ice. It's hard to imagine any place on earth more saturated with emotion than Boston Garden, that afternoon in May 1981—the crowd's emotions, the teams' emotions, and my emotions there in that closet.

Suddenly, in the midst of all that churning emotion, I felt something strange—a sense of quiet, a sense of peace that seemed to wash over me. I felt the voice of God speaking directly to my mind—and that voice had a soothing, gentle effect. "Calm down," I heard Him say. "Get a grip on yourself, Pat. I'll take care of the wins and the losses. You just be available to Me."

I heard the horn signaling the end of the time-out. I flung open the door of the closet and dashed up the runway to see the outcome of the game—and of the play-offs, and of the entire season. The plan was straightforward: We would inbound the ball from half court, lob it to the basket, and attempt a tip-in for the victory.

I didn't feel confident of victory, but I felt calm. I sensed the peace of a God who understood my frailty and who didn't chastise me for making such a big deal out of a ballgame. Sure, in one sense it was a big deal. Winning is the goal of my professional life as a general manager—and it should be. The better a team does, the more support it receives, the more press it gets, the bigger the box office. It's a game, but it's also a business.

But sometimes you lose. You should never enjoy losing, never take it lightly, never shrug it off—but neither should you let a loss, even a loss in the play-offs, destroy your emotional and spiritual equilibrium. You have to keep these things in balance.

The crowd was electrically wired as the ball was inbounded. Thousands of throats were screamed raw as the ball was lobbed from Bobby Jones to Dr. J, who tried to get in close for the shot. Pressured by the clock, he made a valiant effort, but the ball fell away, nothing but air. Our fate was sealed. We had failed. We had lost.

As the Boston stands exploded in triumph, the Sixers turned and trudged off the court, down into the locker room. I went down and joined them. The locker room felt like a morgue. The despair was so thick you could have cut it with a knife, and the misery of that day was just beginning.

The team was very quiet as they showered and got back into their street clothes. We all boarded the bus, which pulled out of the Garden and into a scene that was part traffic jam, part mob riot. A group of Boston fans decided to make our day complete by taunting and jeering, rocking the bus, and throwing stones and bottles at us. It was really scary. Wasn't it enough that the Celts had clobbered us in the arena? I felt bad for the team, for the Philadelphia fans, and for myself. Yet, even during the rioting and jostling of the bus, I still felt the calming, reassuring peace of God.

Finally, the bus driver was able to put some distance between us and the yahoos from the Boston Welcome Wagon. As the bus made its lonely way down the freeway toward Logan International, I couldn't help but think back fifteen years to my days with the Spartanburg Phillies. We had won the league championship. We had run up a string of twenty-five straight victories. We had drawn a record crowd of 173,000 fans in a community of fewer than fifty thousand. In stark contrast to this game, that season had been such a thrill.

And yet I remembered going home to my apartment in Spartanburg the night of the league championship. The cheers were silenced, the excitement was over, and I was all alone with my success. It all seemed so hollow. And the question came to me: "Is that all there is?"

How strange that years later, after a crushing, heartbreaking play-off loss, and after being the target of taunts and beer bottles, I felt peace. There was no voice in my mind asking, "Is that all there is?" I knew that there was more than winning and losing. I was stinging from that defeat, as was every other person in that bus. But I was going to be okay. Even in defeat, I had more to be thankful for, more to live for, than I ever had fifteen years earlier at the end of a championship season.

The following year was almost a replay of 1981. We ended up in a bruising play-off battle with Boston, culminating in another Sunday afternoon final-game nailbiter in Boston Garden. Only in 1982, we won. Near the end of that game, I went back into that same broom closet and I thanked God—not for the win so much as for the lesson that He is truly in charge of the wins and losses. Not long afterward, the Lakers clobbered us in the NBA title matchup. You win some, you lose some, and I know how it feels to do both. I hate to lose—always have, always will. But each time I'm tempted to ask, "Why, God?" I remember the words He gave me in that broom closet in 1981: "I'll take care of the wins and losses. You just be available." And I remember the peace He gave me, a peace that surpasses my understanding.

What is success? It's an old, old question, and the answer is the same today as it was two thousand years ago. "For what will it profit a man," asked Jesus, "if he gains the whole world, and loses his own soul? Or what will a man give in exchange for his soul?"[1] Having tons of money, power, fame, and pleasure is not real success. It's just so much stuff. It's *nice* stuff, but you can't buy your own eternal soul with it. The only real success in life is achieving what matters most to you in every dimension of your life—achieving strong family relationships, achieving career excellence, and most of all, achieving peace with yourself and with God.

That's real success and many men have realized this.

REAL SUCCESS

I have been impacted by many great lives in the years since I knew Mr. R. E. Littlejohn. One of the most influential in recent years is a man I referred to in the previous chapter, the man to whom this book is dedicated, my friend Richard DeVos. As I mentioned before, Rich is the cofounder of Amway and one of the owners of the Orlando Magic. *Forbes* magazine has estimated his wealth at $4.5 billion—and that fact alone would make him a success in anybody's book. But I believe that true success is something much deeper than net worth or the power to run major corporations—and Rich is successful by that standard too.

Richard DeVos came from modest beginnings in Grand Rapids, Michigan. As a boy, Rich didn't earn great grades, but he was always a person of great enthusiasm and great determination. He went into business with his boyhood buddy, Jay Van Andel, right after World War II. Their first business was a flying school and charter service, Wolverine Air Service. They added on a restaurant business, and in 1948, they sold everything and went on a sailing trip around the Caribbean and South America together. During that trip they talked and dreamed about new business ventures, new ways of developing and marketing products, and new ways to be successful. The trip was an adventure: These two young men set out knowing next to nothing about sailing and navigation, and they got lost, ran aground, and eventually had to be rescued by some American merchant marines. This adventure further cemented their friendship and gave them the idea for their next business: an import company specializing in Haitian wood-carved products. That business failed—bigtime!—but Rich and Jay persevered and bounced back.

In 1959, borrowing and modifying some of the early multilevel marketing concepts of a vitamin and food-supplement company called Nutralite, Rich and Jay founded a new direct sales company they called Amway—short for "the American Way." They started the company in their basements with the help of their wives, Helen DeVos and Betty Van Andel. They formulated and packaged their own first product—an all-purpose liquid organic cleaner. From that one basement-produced product, the company has grown into a 400-product megacorporation with annual sales of $4.5 billion in seventy countries. The phenomenal growth of the company comes from the fact that the products are distributed through people who are their own boss, whose earning capacity is limited only by their capacity for hard work. The American work ethic— "the American Way"—is the key. Using the Amway principles, many distributors are able to earn six-figure incomes.

In 1991, Rich and other members of his family bought the Orlando Magic for a cool $85 million. Part of his reason for wanting to be involved in the ownership of an NBA team is that team ownership gives him a wider platform to preach his gospel of success through perseverance and hard work. Rich loves young people, and he wants junior-high, high-school, and college-age youth to learn his principles for becoming successful in America. "You can own a huge corporation and most young people aren't impressed," he says. "But when you own the Magic and get your picture taken with Shaquille O'Neal, kids listen!"

What drives Rich DeVos? He has money, power, fame, and pleasure. He has several pleasure yachts, several beautiful homes, and the freedom to live his life pretty much the way he chooses. I can tell you, however, that none of these things drive Rich DeVos. I know him, and I can tell you there is a deeper kind of success at work in his life. He is driven to be successful and to produce excellence because he wants his efforts to reflect credit on God and to improve the lives of people everywhere. He is a generous man who donates money and valuable time to many worthy organizations, including several churches, charitable organizations, and hospitals.

As I've gotten to know Rich, I've become increasingly impressed with a number of areas in his life. First, he's the best communicator I've ever heard, whether in a one-on-one setting or at an NBA All-Star chapel or at an Amway rally before a crowd of forty thousand people. He's a riveting speaker, and he commands the respect and rapt attention of everyone in his presence.

Second, Rich has a brilliant business mind. God has given him a sixth sense to discern which businesses will work and which won't. It's exciting for me to sit in meetings and hear him share his business philosophy and acumen.

Third, the man has wisdom. Certain people are blessed with an ability to understand problems and arrive at practical, fair solutions, and Rich is one of those people. He can sit in a meeting, sort through all the flying verbiage, and wisely move a group to a course of action. That is a great talent.

Fourth, Rich is a great delegator. He believes in hiring good people, giving them responsibility, backing them up to the hilt, supporting them in every way, and then letting them do the job themselves.

Fifth, he has a true love for people. He enjoys being around people, and he treats everyone with attention and respect, from the president of the United States (and he is personally acquainted with several presidents, past and present) to the company janitor. He cares, he listens, he relates, he gets along, he communicates. God has given Rich the ability to love people and ask for nothing in return. He demonstrates this every time he writes a letter. He always signs his letters: Love 'ya, Rich.

Sixth, he has a wonderful sense of humor. He loves a good joke and loves to laugh. Rich's face is always highlighted by an impish grin when he sees a humorous situation developing.

Seventh, he is an encourager. When Rich spoke at the NBA All-Star chapel service in Orlando, 1992, he told about a meeting he once had with Walt Disney, and he quoted Disney as saying in that meeting, "There are three kinds of people in the world today. There are 'well-poisoners,' who discourage you and stomp on your creativity and tell you what you can't do. There are 'lawn-mowers,' people who are well-intentioned but self-absorbed; they tend to their own needs, mow their own lawns, and never leave their yards to help another person. Finally, there are 'life-enhancers,' people who reach out to enrich the lives of others, to lift them up and inspire them. We need to be life-enhancers, and we need to surround ourselves with life-enhancers."

Well, that's exactly the kind of person Rich DeVos is—a life-enhancer. Ask him what his role is with Amway or the Orlando Magic or any other organization he's a part of, and he'll tell you, "I'm the head cheerleader!" He has a wonderful ability to praise, encourage, inspire, and motivate. When he comes to visit the Orlando Magic, he'll pop into my office, spend a few minutes asking about me, my work, my family, and then he'll close with an uplifting word. I always feel motivated, inspired, and energized after even a few minutes with Rich DeVos. He makes you feel so good about yourself that you actually feel you could plow through a wall for him, and accomplish anything in the world.

Rich worries about a generation that is being taught that success is something that happens by chance or through some sort of conspiracy on the part of "the Establishment." He wants young people to know that success is an option for everyone who is willing to work hard and learn the ropes. "When people get stuck in poverty," he says, "it's usually their own choice. They don't realize it, but by complaining about their poverty instead of doing something about it, they are choosing their own failed future. If you hang out with failures and adopt the attitudes of failures, you will also be a failure. If you look to successful people as your model, if you listen to what they say, if you work hard and persevere the way successful people do, you'll make it."

Richard DeVos is a bold, unapologetic capitalist. He lives capitalism, and he preaches it. He loves America and sells his belief in the American Way wherever he goes. But he also believes that capitalism should be compassionate, and he practices compassion and generosity in his own life. Rich is sometimes criticized as a "fundamentalist" and a "right-winger," but to me he is just a guy who has always done his best, always tried to serve his God, always honored his country, always respected the people around him, always been compassionate toward people with needs, always been a powerful motivator and an energizer of others. He's a *true* success story—and I'm proud to call him my friend, so much so, that in 1993 when Jill and I adopted an 11-year-old Brazilian boy, we changed his name to Richard as a tribute to Rich DeVos.

Since those days in Spartanburg I've tried to live for this kind of success. And it's made a great difference in my life and in the life of those I love.

MAGIC ALL AROUND YOU!

In the fall of 1993, I got a call from the office of Dave Thomas—yep, *that* Dave Thomas, the guy in the Wendy's commercials, the founder of that great square-patty burger chain, and now the author of a book about success called *Well Done*. Dave Thomas's secretary was on the phone, and she said he was in the process of writing a book and was going to include stories of a number of people he knew of or had heard of. "Mr. Thomas would like to include the story of your family in his book," she said. "He was adopted as a child, and he really appreciates what you have done in adopting fourteen children."

I didn't know him, had never even met him, and I was honored that he wanted to include my family in his book. So a few weeks later, a writer came down and spent a day with us, gathering information for the book. When the writer left, we thought that was the end of the process, and we wouldn't hear any more until the book came out. But a few more weeks passed, and we got another call from Dave Thomas's office in Columbus, Ohio. "Mr. Thomas would like to visit you in your home in Winter Park and take some pictures with your family to use in the book. Would that be all right with you?"

"Send him over!" I said.

So, one afternoon in April 1994, a big old bus pulled up in

front of our house. Out piled a bunch of photographers and publicity types—and, of course, Dave Thomas, looking exactly as he does in his Wendy's commercials. Needless to say, our kids went bug-eyed. Dave walked in and started shooting hoops in the backyard with the kids while the photographers set up. Dave is amazingly like he appears in the commercials—a high-powered entrepreneur with a face as genuine, warm, and benign as Captain Kangaroo's and a genuine love for people and for kids. We all posed for pictures with Dave, just like he was the kids' own long-lost grandfather. He gave them all Wendy's T-shirts with his picture on them, and within thirty or forty minutes, he was on his way.

As Dave was leaving our house, our kids' swimming coach, Kevin Meisel, pulled up to take the kids to swimming practice. You should have seen his jaw drop when a living, flesh-and-blood Wendy's commercial walked out of our front door and right toward the curb where Kevin was standing. Dave shook hands with Kevin and said, "Hi, I'm Dave Thomas." And Kevin said, "I know!"

Again, we thought that was about the end of it until the book would appear—but there was more to come! In October 1994, we got *another* call from Dave Thomas's office. "In conjunction with the release of the book," said his secretary, "Mr. Thomas wants to honor a number of individuals with the first of his Well Done Awards. He would be pleased if you would be his guest at Carnegie Hall in New York in November." I wouldn't have missed it for the world. I flew to LaGuardia, jumped into a cab, and asked the cabby, "How do I get to Carnegie Hall?"

His answer: "Practice, practice, practice." (Everybody's a comedian!)

The cabby took me to Carnegie Hall, where I was ushered in. There I was, in that hallowed place where the world's most famous performing artists had stood. The ceremony began with Dave Thomas as master of ceremonies. He introduced each person to be honored that night—some I knew, some I didn't. I immediately recognized Pat Robertson, Mrs. Norman Vincent Peale, and actor Lee Majors. When it was my turn to get up and speak, I breathed a silent prayer, "Lord, thank You for bringing me this far. Thank

You for this incredible opportunity. Thank You for showering me with more blessings than I deserve. Please give me the right words to say."

Then I briefly told the story of my fourteen adoptions, of my initial unwillingness to do this, and of how God broke through to my heart. I told how, in 1983, I adopted two little South Korean girls. Then I briefly traced the arrival of each of the children from different parts of the world, which makes a total of nineteen children. I closed by saying, "Many people have asked us why we have done this. The only thing I can say is that God has really spoken very directly to our hearts and given us an intense desire to do this. Perhaps the desire which He has given us is best expressed by an anonymous poem that hangs in the entryway of our home. Our friend Bobby Malkmus did the poem in needlepoint, and here is what it says:

> Some would gather money
> Along the path of life;
> Some would gather roses
> And rest from worldly strife;
>
> But we would gather children
> From among the thorns of sin.
> We would seek dark almond eyes
> And a carefree toothless grin.
>
> For money cannot enter
> In the land of endless day,
> And the roses that are gathered
> Soon will wilt and fade away
>
> But oh, the laughing children
> As we cross the sunset sea,
> And the gates swing wide to heaven,
> We can take them in, you see.

I finished reading that poem, and the people in that hall just went berserk, applauding, cheering, and some even crying. I don't think they were applauding Pat Williams so much as they were saying, "Yes! That's what life is really all about! That's what real success is: changing lives, and making one tiny piece of the world a little bit better! Yes! Yes! Yes!"

Chasing money isn't success. Chasing fame isn't success. Sitting in a hammock and sipping lemonade isn't success. To me, the real success in my life comes from being a good dad to my nineteen kids, passing on my faith and values to them, watching them grow up strong and confident, and offering them up to God and to the world as a gift, to make this world a better place. It is for the sake of those nineteen kids, and for God's sake, that I make sure, day by day, to:

- Think "tomorrow,"
- Free my own imagination,
- Strive for lasting quality,
- Have "stick-to-it-ivity," and
- Have fun!

My friend, don't miss the magic that life has in store for you. Latch on to these five magical secrets. Make them your own. Dream your dreams, then hammer those dreams into reality. Build your castles, your railroads, your starships, your cities, your mountains. Reach for the blue sky—and grab a big handful of it! The magic of life is going on all around you! So what are you waiting for, my friend?

Go for the magic!

NOTES

Chapter 1: Hammering Dreams into Reality
1. Quoted by Randy Bright in *Disneyland: Inside Story* (New York: Abrams, 1987), 103.

Chapter 2: Yesterday, or, The Past Is a Canceled Check
1. See 1 John 1:9.

Chapter 3: Today, or, What to Do Until Tomorrow Gets Here
1. Psalm 118:24.
2. Matthew 6:34.
3. Dru Scott, *Stress That Motivates: Self-Talk Secrets for Success* (Los Altos, Calif.: Crisp, 1992), 67.
4. Dru Scott, *How to Put More Time in Your Life* (New York: New American Library, 1980), 28–41.

Chapter 4: Tomorrow, or, How to Build the Rest of Your Life
1. Charles Shows, *Walt: Backstage Adventures with Walt Disney* (La Jolla, Calif.: Communication Creativity, 1980), 147.
2. Bob Thomas, *Walt Disney: An American Original* (New York: Simon and Schuster, 1976), 11–14.
3. Stephen R. Covey, *The Seven Habits of Highly Effective People* (New York: Simon and Schuster, 1989), 98.
4. Benjamin J. Stein, "Mistakes Winners Don't Make," *Reader's Digest,* November 1994, 205.
5. Charles R. Swindoll, *Come Before Winter and Share My Hope* (Wheaton, Ill.: Tyndale House, 1985), 26.

Chapter 5: Blue-Sky Thinking

1. Bob Thomas, *Walt Disney: An American Original* (New York: Simon and Schuster, 1976), 16.

Chapter 6: You Can Do *Anything!*

1. Frank Thomas and Ollie Johnston, *Disney Animation: The Illusion of Life* (New York: Abbeville, 1981), 23.
2. Charles Shows, *Walt: Backstage Adventures with Walt Disney* (La Jolla, Calif.: Communication Creativity, 1980), 154.
3. Proverbs 23:7.
4. Donald Robinson, "Mind Over Disease: Your Attitude Can Make You Well," *Reader's Digest,* April 1987, 73–75.
5. Proverbs 22:6.

Chapter 7: "Good Enough" Never Is

1. Charles Shows, *Walt: Backstage Adventures with Walt Disney* (La Jolla, Calif.: Communication Creativity, 1980), 140, 142.

Chapter 8: Stubbornness with a Purpose

1. Frank Thomas and Ollie Johnston, *Disney Animation: The Illusion of Life* (New York: Abbeville, 1981), 23.
2. 2 Corinthians 4:8–9, 16–17; Philippians 3:13–14.
3. Quoted by Bill Heller in "The Fifth Man," *Sporting News,* January 23, 1995, 33.
4. Quoted in *Reader's Digest,* December 1991, 123.

Chapter 9: Can You Believe They *Pay* Me to Do This?

1. Shaquille O'Neal with Jack McCallum, *Shaq Attaq!* (New York: Hyperion, 1993), 197, 202.
2. Charles Shows, *Walt: Backstage Adventures with Walt Disney* (La Jolla, Calif.: Communication Creativity, 1980), 56.
3. Ibid., 151–52.
4. Pam Smith, *Food for Life* (Orlando: Creation House, 1994), 134.

Chapter 10: What *Is* Success, Anyway?

1. Mark 8:36–37.

ABOUT THE AUTHOR

Pat Williams is senior executive vice president of the Orlando Magic. He helped found the Orlando Magic basketball team in 1989. As part of the Magic management team, Pat has helped guide the team from a losing expansion club to one of the top teams in the NBA in just a few short years. Before taking the helm at the Magic, Williams was the general manager of the Philadelphia 76ers for twelve years, including their 1983 championship season. Pat was also general manager of the Atlanta Hawks and the Chicago Bulls, a post he took at the age of twenty-nine. Pat and his wife, Ruth, reside in Winter Park, Florida. They are now the parents of *nineteen* children, including fourteen who have been adopted from four foreign countries.